INDIA'S GREENFIELD URBAN FUTURE

AF664217

INDIA'S GREENFIELD URBAN FUTURE

The Politics of Land, Planning and Infrastructure

Edited by

Ashima Sood

Loraine Kennedy

Orient BlackSwan

All rights reserved. No part of this book may be (i) modified, reproduced or utilised in any form, or by any means, electronic or mechanical, including photocopying, recording or by any information storage and retrieval system, in any form of binding or cover other than in which it is published, without permission in writing from the publisher; or (ii) used or reproduced in any manner for the purpose of training, development or operation of artificial intelligence (AI) technologies and systems, including generative AI technologies, without permission in writing from the copyright holder.

INDIA'S GREENFIELD URBAN FUTURE: THE POLITICS OF LAND, PLANNING AND INFRASTRUCTURE

ORIENT BLACKSWAN PRIVATE LIMITED

Registered Office
3-6-752 Himayatnagar, Hyderabad 500 029, Telangana, India
e-mail: centraloffice@orientblackswan.com

Other Offices
Bengaluru, Chennai, Guwahati, Hyderabad,
Kolkata, Mumbai, New Delhi, Noida, Patna

© Orient Blackswan Private Limited 2022
First published by Orient Blackswan Private Limited 2022

ISBN 978-93-5442-361-1

042770

Typeset in
Gentium Plus 10.5/12.5
by Manmohan Kumar, Delhi

Printed in India at
Kensington Printing & Packaging, Noida 201 301

Published by
Orient Blackswan Private Limited
3-6-752, Himayatnagar, Hyderabad 500 029, Telangana, India
e-mail: info@orientblackswan.com

For sale only in India, Pakistan, Bangladesh, Bhutan, Nepal, Sri Lanka and the Maldives

Contents

Figures and Tables

FIGURES

TABLES

Abbreviations

ADDA	Asansol Durgapur Development Authority
BAPL	Bengal Aerotropolis Project Limited
BBMP	Bruhat Bengaluru Mahanagara Palike
BDA	Bangalore Development Authority
BETPL	Bangalore Elevated Tollway Private Limited
BJP	Bharatiya Janata Party
BMRDA	Bangalore Metropolitan Regional Development Authority
BRADA	Bhangar-Rajarhat Area Development Authority
BWSSB	Bangalore Water Supply and Sewerage Board
CAG	Comptroller and Auditor General
CBD	central business district
CDA	Cyberabad Development Authority
CDP	Comprehensive Development Plan
CEO	chief executive officer
CIDCO	City and Industrial Development Corporation
CITB	City Improvement Trust Board
CMWSSB	Chennai Metropolitan Water Supply and Sewerage Board
DC	district collector
DFC	Dedicated Freight Corridor
DICDL	Dholera Industrial City Development Limited
DIPP	Department of Industrial Policy and Promotion
DMIC	Delhi–Mumbai Industrial Corridor
DMICDC	Delhi-Mumbai Industrial Corridor Development Corporation
DSIR	Dholera Special Investment Region
DSTPS	Durgapur Steel Thermal Power Station
ELCIA	Electronics City Industries' Association
ELCITA	Electronics City Industrial Township Authority
EWRC	East West Road Corridor
GHMC	Greater Hyderabad Municipal Corporation
GICC	Gujarat Industrial Corridor Corporation
GTPUDA	Gujarat Town Planning and Urban Development Act

HGCL	Hyderabad Growth Corridor Limited
HMDA	Hyderabad Metropolitan Development Authority
HUDA	Hyderabad Urban Development Authority
IT	information technology
ITES	IT-enabled services
JICA	Japan International Cooperation Agency
JNNURM	Jawaharlal Nehru National Urban Renewal Mission
KBNIR	Khushkhera–Bhiwadi–Neemrana
KEIPL	Khed Economic Infrastructure Private Limited
KEONICS	Karnataka State Electronics Development Corporation Limited
KIADB	Karnataka Industrial Areas Development Board
KNI Airport	Kazi Nazrul Islam Airport
LAA	Land Acquisition Act
LVC	land value capture
MBSIR	Mandal-Becharaji Special Investment Region
MIDC	Maharashtra Industrial Development Corporation
MLA	member of the Legislative Assembly
MoU	memorandum of understanding
NDA	National Democratic Alliance
NGO	non-governmental organisation
NHAI	National Highways Authority of India
NICE	Nandi Infrastructure Corridor Enterprises
NIMZ	National Investment and Manufacturing Zone
OMR	Old Mahabalipuram Road
ORR	Outer Ring Road
PPP	public–private partnership
RCS	Regional Connectivity Scheme
RDA	Regional Development Authority
SEZ	Special Economic Zone
SIPCOT	State Industries Promotion Corporation of Tamil Nadu Limited
SIR	Special Investment Region
TNRDC	Tamil Nadu Road Development Company
TPS	town planning scheme
UDAN	*Ude Desh ka Aam Naagrik*
UIMs	Urban Integrated Megaprojects

UPA	United Progressive Alliance
WBHIDCO	West Bengal Housing Infrastructure Development Corporation
WBIDC	West Bengal Industrial Development Corporation Limited

Preface

The impetus for this collection came from observations of the emerging frontlines of Indian urbanisation. Evident as much in the visual vocabulary of India's booming metropolitan peripheries as in the policy pronouncements on the smart city agenda was the fantasy of the blank slate, of starting India's urbanisation project afresh.

While a nascent scholarship was beginning to investigate both the rhetoric and reality of these utopian imaginaries in various settings, the case studies in this literature rarely, if ever, spoke to each other. Yet, there was no denying the sheer ambition, and even hubris, that linked the Lavasas and Rajarhats to the soaring span of the Delhi–Mumbai Industrial Corridor (DMIC).

Starting in the mid-2010s, our discussions about these new landscapes crystallised in a special issue in the *Economic & Political Weekly Review of Urban Affairs* on the theme of greenfield urban development. We went back and forth over what to call the phenomenon we were attempting to describe. Key to our understanding were two dimensions: first, the unmistakable nexus between spatially targeted investments in urban development in these settings and economic growth agendas in the policyscape. Second, and equally important, we wanted to highlight the continuities that connected the new millennium's city-building enterprise to its forebears in Chandigarh, Bhilai and Navi Mumbai.

Conceptualisations such as integrated megaprojects captured several important features of these sites—the reification of privatised planning and the commodification of land. However, our framework led us to question whether the phenomenon was in fact 'new'. What departures, if any, did it represent with older state-led models of 'new town development'? In the end, we settled for the descriptor of 'greenfield', which provided a large enough frame for analysing the diversity of the cases in our collection.

The themes in the collection ranged from struggles over land acquisition and real estate dynamics to emerging forms of governance and place-making in sites of new township development in India. The geographies of the articles in the special issue were equally varied: from Rajarhat New Town Kolkata to Bangalore's Electronics City, Andhra's Amaravati development and Gujarat's Dholera. In bringing together new work by emerging as well as established scholars, we aimed to spark a conversation on the greenfield endeavour and the pointers it provided to India's urban future. It was equally important to connect the Indian experience to Asia and the Global South through an engagement with the wider literature. Articles went through double-blind peer review by leading international scholars, providing a depth of context to the framing.

This volume is an expanded collection based on that special issue. The very newness of the trend whose contours the original collection had traced demanded a revisit to assess how those early prognostications had fared. We also wanted to bring in a broader array of scholars into the fold, to make possible sharper insights into the landscapes that were becoming visible.

The effort of assembling this volume has yielded surprising rewards. On the one hand, essays by Sai Balakrishnan and Sudeshna Mitra have expanded and deepened our understanding of the political economy of 'highway urbanisation' or 'corridor urbanisation', first described by Shriya Anand and Neha Sami in their work on the DMIC. Gopa Samanta and Akash Banerjee's report on the Andal Aerotropolis, offering a portrait of progress in stasis, resonates with Preeti Sampat's analysis of the 'rentier economy' in Dholera. And not least, Anna Dewaele's comparative case approach to new towns provides an important historical anchor for understanding the backdrop against which contemporary India's greenfield agenda is playing out.

In the time since the original collection appeared, Lavasa was declared a 'billionaire's folly' by news major Bloomberg.com while the Aamby Valley had languished for a long while on the auctioneer's block. The chief hazard of choosing as our subject the stuff of pink paper headlines was the risk of it becoming dated by the next news cycle.

Nonetheless, the essays in this volume succeed in gesturing towards the underlying institutional and political economy processes that determine the destiny of the urban project. We hope that this volume will provide grounding for future explorations beyond the ephemeral.

We extend our thanks to Roopa Sharma and Nilanjana Majumdar of Orient BlackSwan for shepherding this volume from its earliest beginning and to Anjali Aggarwal Gupta and Suchetana Ghosh Dostidar for their careful edits. We are grateful to our contributors for their patience through this long journey and to the unnamed reviewers of the special issue and this volume. We are also extremely thankful to the *Economic & Political Weekly* editorial team and especially to then editor Rammanohar Reddy, whose encouragement was instrumental to our bringing together the collection. We would also like to acknowledge the members of the *Review of Urban Affairs* editorial advisory group—Amita Baviskar, Karen Coelho, Vinay Gidwani, Anant Maringanti and Partha Mukhopadhyay.

This book honours the migrant construction workers building the greenfield frontier that is the topic of these chapters.

Ashima Sood, Ahmedabad
Loraine Kennedy, Paris

Publisher's Acknowledgement

For granting permission to reproduce copyrighted material in this volume, the publishers would like to thank the following organisations and individuals:

Economic and Political Weekly for 'Scaling Up, Scaling Down: State Rescaling along the Delhi–Mumbai Industrial Corridor' by Shriya Anand and Neha Sami; 'Making Sense of Place in Rajarhat New Town: The Village in the Urban and the Urban in the Village' by Ratoola Kundu; 'Dholera: The Emperor's New City' by Preeti Sampat; 'The Rise of Private Governance in Bengaluru's Electronic City' by Mathew Idiculla (originally published as 'New Regimes of Private Governance: The Case of Electronics City in Peri-urban Bengaluru'); and 'The Politics of Urban Mega-projects in India: Income and Employment Linkages in Chennai's IT Corridor' by M. Vijayabaskar and M. Suresh Babu, which were previously published in the Review of Urban Affairs, *Economic and Political Weekly* Vol. 51, Issue No. 17, 23 April 2016. We thank *EPW* also for 'Roads to New Urban Futures: Flexible Territorialisation in Peri-urban Kolkata and Hyderabad' by Sudeshna Mitra, previously published in the Review of Urban Affairs, *Economic and Political Weekly* Vol. 53, Issue No. 49, 15 December 2018: 56–64.

Armand Colin, Dunod, for 'New Town Building in the Postcolonial Era' by Anna Dewaele, originally published in French as 'Une expérience de planification urbaine postcoloniale: le cas des villes nouvelles indiennes (1947–1991)' in *Annales de Géographie* Vol. 720, Issue No. 2, 2018: 145–168.

Pacific Affairs, The University of British Columbia, for 'Highway Urbanisation and Land Conflicts: The Challenges to Decentralisation in India' by Sai Balakrishnan published in *Pacific Affairs* Vol. 86, Issue No. 4, 1 December 2013: 785–811.

1

Rescaling, Speculation and Governance on India's Urban Frontier

Greenfield Development as Tabula Rasa

LORAINE KENNEDY AND ASHIMA SOOD[1]

Perhaps the most emblematic image of urban transformation in contemporary India is that of the high-rise gated community, mounted aloft a thousand billboards across the gleaming expressways and bypasses of new India's metropolitan centres. Promising high quality infrastructure and amenities, aspirational lifestyles and sanitised vistas of work and leisure, the high-rise gated community appears to be premised on a decisive break from older ways of living in the Indian city. Indeed, this discontinuity is embodied in the geographic location of the gated community itself; with exceptions such as the reconfiguration of Mumbai's mill lands, such high-rises are largely a feature of the peri-urban and greenfield frontier—the Gurgaons and Greater Noidas, Navi Mumbais, Rajarhats, Whitefields and Cyberabads.

Unpacking the symbolism of the high-rise gated community in the Indian city makes clear a second feature: the gated community often appears as a visible motif for underlying economic and structural transformations, led by new real estate dynamics produced by the 'unlocking' of land markets as much as by policy-promoted growth of information technology and high-end service sectors. It is at the intersection of these phenomena, where policy and private agendas come together, that the genesis of this volume lies.

NAMING THE PHENOMENON

Our interest in the spatiality and governance of this new 'urban frontier' and the constellations of public–private interests underpinning it derives from two observations: first, a renewed interest in building new cities, variously labelled 'smart', 'green' or 'integrated'; second, a growing tendency to instrumentalise the urban in pursuit of economic growth. A brief discussion of both will help situate the essays in this volume and explain why we have chosen to bring together two usually distinct policy and research areas, planned urban development (Wang et al. 2010; Sood 2021) and strategic planning for economic growth (Kennedy and Zérah 2008; Goldman 2011; Kennedy 2014), as well as perspectives from various strands of critical urban studies.

India is not unused to building new cities, with state initiative from pre-colonial to colonial and postcolonial times responsible for establishing iconic capital cities such as Jaipur, Kolkata or Chandigarh. In recent times, the formation of new states has initiated proposals for new capital cities like Naya Raipur and Amaravati. Linking past and present, city building can thus be seen as an enduring idiom of politics in India. Political leaders strive to leave their mark in space, a legacy carved in stone; meanwhile, in current permutations, new city building creates opportunities for substantial pecuniary gain for ruling parties through real estate development and speculation. Notwithstanding these lineages, greenfield urbanisation takes diverse forms and responds to different imperatives. Bold policies announcing '100 new cities' or '100 smart cities' purport to offer planned solutions to rapid urban growth and to the presumed demands of the global economy.

Altogether, as Kalia (2006) reminds us, this policyscape continues a long-standing ambition of building no less than 300 new cities by 2000. The most distinguished of these lineages are the pre- and postcolonial steel towns documented by Sivaramakrishnan (1978) (see also Sood and Rath 2017). Nor is the new town a uniquely Indian prototype (Gotsch 2009; Moser et al. 2015).

The second phenomenon, urban development in relation to strategic planning for growth, also manifests itself in various ways. On the one hand, there is an increasing tendency for policymakers to position the city as a 'growth engine', giving rise to urban restructuring projects (Kennedy and Zérah 2008; Dupont 2011; Goldman 2011). On the other, industrial policies increasingly emphasise development of new urban hubs to attract investment (Kennedy 2007, 2014; Sood 2015). Since the 1990s, many states have begun to rescale economic development policies in favour of those regions most equipped to engage with global flows, starting with the largest city regions. As competition to attract mobile capital became stronger, state governments began to leverage their fixed assets, namely, land resources, most abundant in peri-urban areas (Kennedy and Sood 2019) or in riverbanks previously considered off-limits (Follmann 2015). The constitution of land banks, through eminent domain and enclosure processes, is central to the pursuit of these policies. Common patterns of greenfield urban development include industrial parks and townships built through public–private partnerships on the urban peripheries, for example, Sri City near Chennai, Manesar Integrated Model Township near Delhi, HITEC City/Cyberabad on Hyderabad's western edge. In the case of interstate industrial corridors, strategic urban 'nodes' constitute critical components of the overall policy design.

Both types of state strategies, planned urban development and strategic planning for growth, have in common their tendency to put in place special regulatory frameworks, ad hoc rules and regulations, to facilitate or expedite policy goals and to insulate the newly created spaces, such as new towns, industrial enclaves, corridors, special development areas, from 'interference' from social and political realities. Whether the motivation for such frameworks is to bypass laws and regulations perceived as too restrictive (Roy 2009) or rather to put in place 'privatised' forms of urban governance and planning, assumed to be more efficient, such efforts amount to a disavowal of existing forms of regulation (Kennedy and Sood 2019). They can be seen to arise from a common fantasy, which is to start from a clean slate or tabula rasa.[2]

The tabula rasa fantasy links the various manifestations of greenfield urbanisation, whether the building of new satellite cities and suburban nodes (Dholera, Gurgaon, Navi Mumbai, Rajarhat New Town or Bengaluru's Electronics City) or emerging landscapes of corridor and 'highway urbanisation', as Balakrishnan describes them in this volume. Other examples include the Chennai IT Corridor, Delhi–Mumbai Industrial Corridor [DMIC], the Bengaluru–Mysore Infrastructure Corridor or Hyderabad's Outer Ring Road. Beyond the essays of this volume, studies have looked at newer sites such as Lavasa and Magarpatta (Sami 2013; Balakrishnan 2019a), among others. Attempts at estimating the size and scale of the phenomenon are still in an incipient stage, but one recent database compilation undertaken by Sood and her co-author suggests over

7,000 residential or commercial constructions above Rs 10 million in investment over the period 1995–2019 (Sood and Jain 2021).[3]

A few caveats are in order before proceeding further. The first is conceptual: to speak of a 'terra nullius' is a claim of considerable hubris against the backdrop of the long-standing and variegated forms of human habitation in the Indian subcontinent. It is worth considering, for instance, that the span of the DMIC, one of the most ambitious projects of greenfield urbanisation in contemporary India, could well encompass the terrain of the Indus Valley civilisation.[4] Moreover, the book's focus on greenfield development on the urban edge does not in any way suggest that it is the only dynamic site of urbanisation. A body of literature documents endogenous growth processes occurring in diverse types of settlements across the length and breadth of the country, often unrelated to metropolitan processes, in what has been coined 'subaltern urbanisation' (see Denis and Zérah 2017). That these complex histories of occupation and tenure should engender protracted and irreconcilable patterns of contestations over land is no surprise.

The second is methodological: all of the essays in this volume are based on primary data collection, which allows the authors to enrich their analyses and engagement with larger theoretical and policy issues with first-hand observations. It gives voice to the actors in the processes under study. Fieldwork-based research, however, also throws up methodological challenges. In some instances, the essays published here provide the very first preliminary analyses of their specific cases and, in the absence of published official data, it has not always been possible to cross-check all the information. Nonetheless, the situated research presented is grounded in lived experience, and provides an opportunity for informing critical public debate on processes unfolding on the urban frontier.

CONFRONTING THEORY AND EMPIRICAL RESEARCH

The essays in this volume address a wide range of urban themes including, for instance, the process of assembling land for the establishment of new cities, the modes of governance that are emerging in integrated townships, and the social and economic impacts of various greenfield projects. Several essays focus on the actors of the urban frontier, including both those in charge of implementing greenfield agendas, state agencies or private real estate firms seizing opportunities opened up by policy and those resisting those policies by refusing to part with their land or give up their livelihoods. Other essays undertake to analyse the spatial and social fragmentation produced through privatised governance, bypass techniques and differential service delivery. Lending weight to the importance of greenfield urbanisation on the national scale, the evidence brought to bear in this set of essays has broad geographical scope, ranging from Hyderabad, Kolkata, Chennai, Navi Mumbai, Chandigarh, Gurgaon to corridors including Bengaluru–Mysore, Pune–Nashik and the DMIC which traverses six states.

The essays in the volume here align along three broad axes. The rise of 'corridor' or 'highway' urbanisation is the first of these. This alignment puts into dialogue essays by Sai Balakrishnan on the Bengaluru–Mysore and Pune–Nashik highways, Sudeshna Mitra on New Town Kolkata's East West Road Corridor Project (EWRC) and Hyderabad's Outer Ring Road (ORR) Project, and Shriya Anand and Neha Sami's investigation of the DMIC. Together these chapters foreground important themes of governance and especially state rescaling processes (also see Balakrishnan 2019b).

The next axis focuses on the politics of land and the real estate dynamics that have come to shape much of the debate around the greenfield project in India. However, these themes play out in very different ways in the two settings of Dholera (Preeti Sampat's chapter) and Andal (Gopa Samanta and Akash Banerjee's contribution). Whereas the rise of the rentier economy around Dholera has faced significant resistance from the agrarian economy, the struggle around land acquisition has been more muted around Andal. Juxtaposing these two greenfield cases thus yields a more nuanced read into how similar speculative economies find different expression in different sites.

The final axis focuses on the aftermaths of the greenfield project. Dewaele's essay in this volume traces the genealogy of city building and proposes a typology of such projects for the decades following Independence, a period that witnessed the development of more than 100 new towns (Sivaramakrishnan 1978; Shaw 2009).

The chapters by Mathew Idiculla, M. Vijayabaskar and M. Suresh Babu, and Ratoola Kundu draw attention variously to the governance, economy and social transformations that have attended processes of urban development across sites such as Bengaluru's Electronics City, Chennai's IT Corridor and Kolkata's Rajarhat New Town. Themes of spatial inequality, variously understood through the lenses of bypass, splintering or clubs, are especially salient in these settings.

Our aim in putting together this volume was to spark a conversation between literatures that do not always speak to each other across geographic and disciplinary boundaries. Nonetheless, it is possible to glean common ground in the concerns of debates ranging from rescaling and decentralisation to speculative urbanism to theorisations of bypass as they come to be empirically 'fleshed out' in our essays. In analysing the fantasy of the tabula rasa as it plays out in the Indian context, the chapters in this volume engage with these interrelated bodies of theory.

State Spatial Rescaling and the Entrepreneurial State

The first important body of literature relevant to the essays in this volume proceeds from an essentially macro-structuralist perspective that links the evolution of global capitalism to current patterns of urban governance and territorial reorganisation. In a now classical text, David Harvey (1989) posits the shift in European cities from managerial to entrepreneurial urbanism as a response to the crisis of the Fordist–Keynesian accumulation regime and the rise of international finance capital. As national welfare states came under economic (and ideological) pressure and urban spaces emerged as preferred sites for 'flexible accumulation', economic development functions were more or less explicitly delegated to city governments.

The theory of state rescaling then emerged as an attempt to interpret this shift (Swyngedouw 1996; Brenner 1998; Jessop 2002). Referring to a state's efforts to adapt its internal scalar architecture to the changing institutional conditions that undergird the global economy, state rescaling is used to refer to a whole range of state policies and regulations which seek to reshape geographies of economic activities or reorganise social and economic relations (Brenner et al. 2003). Various strands of this literature converge to assert the strategic role of cities in the contemporary processes of remaking of political-economic spaces across geographical scales (Brenner and Theodore 2002).

Despite India's distinct political economic history and relatively limited engagement with global capitalism until the 1990s, state rescaling theory offers useful insights for interpreting institutional and scalar changes in state action (Banerjee-Guha 2009). In India, rescaling is associated with the restructuring of a state-led model of economic development and, of critical importance, with a period of stronger growth, in contrast with the European context where it is largely conceived as a defensive strategy in response to the economic slowdown (Kennedy 2014). Occurring at both national and sub-national scales in India, state restructuring processes are reconfiguring the 'intermediary architectures' between local and supra-local economic processes, including investment procedures, infrastructure supply and local regulatory frameworks. State governments have become more significant than in the past in shaping the conditions for capital accumulation and circulation, for instance, by leveraging their constitutional control over land (Gupta and Sivaramakrishnan 2011; Ren and Weinstein 2013; Kennedy 2014; Sud 2014).

However, in a significant departure from rescaling theory, India's municipal governments have not experienced a significant enhancement of their mandates, which remain restricted to managing basic services (Ruet and Tawa Lama-Rewal 2009).[5] State governments have effectively resisted initiatives to empower the local scale, especially the 74th Constitutional Amendment, and various judicial decisions have upheld their discretionary power on this issue (Sivaramakrishnan 2011: 96–99). This helps explain why state governments are the dominant urban actors in India's largest cities, adopting entrepreneurial postures, for instance, by promoting large-scale infrastructure and mixed use projects in their large cities (Kennedy 2007; Kennedy and Zérah 2008; Ren and Weinstein 2013). Such projects require land, and many state governments have been racing to identify and acquire 'available' land, which includes various categories of 'government land' and village commons, as well as privately owned land, located in strategic areas. Equally important have been efforts to 'normalise' land and real estate markets in urban India, thereby facilitating the entry of foreign firms and capital (Joshi 2009; Denis 2011; Halbert and Rouanet 2013; Searle 2014).

It is important to recall that rescaling is not a zero-sum game; greater scalar significance of India's states does not imply a lesser role for the national state. Scale-making is always an unfinished, contested process (Brenner 2004). As both the United Progressive Alliance (UPA) and the current National Democratic Alliance (NDA) regimes have demonstrated, the national state is equally entrepreneurial, continually asserting its will to drive industrial policy and to pressure states to comply, as we see in the cases of, for example, Special Economic Zones (SEZs), National Investment and Manufacturing Zones (NIMZs), Make in India, etc.

The greenfield projects discussed in this volume are compelling illustrations of rescaling strategies.

The next chapter in our collection by Sai Balakrishnan engages with the issue of scale through the lens of 'highway urbanisation', a contested process that involves consolidating land and converting it to urban uses. Taking as cases two inter-urban highways, the Bangalore–Mysore and the Pune–Nashik, the chapter examines how the realisation of such large-scale projects, which span existing territorial jurisdictions, gives rise to new and hybrid institutions. The analysis shows how these formations emerge from unique socio-historical contexts and how they mediate among various state scales involved in negotiations with actors on the ground.

Intra-urban highways in Kolkata and Hyderabad are the topic of Sudeshna Mitra's chapter, where they are analysed as inter-scalar spatial strategies. Here too, new modalities are imagined for managing and delivering land for large-scale road infrastructure, but in the urban context these instruments also aim to provide an implicit state guarantee to private investments in peri-urban real estate markets.

Both Anand and Sami's and Sampat's contributions deal with the DMIC, a colossal project that aims to promote both industrial and urban development in the form of 24 manufacturing cities, several logistics hubs and residential townships. The DMIC expresses the intention of the central state to influence the geographies of socio-economic activities within the country, to regulate and reorganise social and economic relations within this massive area spanning six states, and also to redefine geographies of statehood within the federal framework. The manner in which it is being implemented effectively rescales 'state space' by creating ad hoc institutions at various levels (special purpose vehicles, state-level corporations) and outsourcing project planning and management to private consultants, who work within specific frameworks. It also shapes state space by curtailing the constitution of democratically elected local bodies through the notorious 'industrial township' 'loophole clause' (Article 243Q of the 74th Constitutional Amendment Act) (Sivaramakrishnan 2011: 169; also Sood 2015). In this way, the DMIC project gives expression to the logic of 'exception', in Aihwa Ong's (2006: 5) sense, an 'extraordinary departure in policy that can be deployed to include as well as exclude' and to the fantasy of tabula rasa. Yet, as the SEZ policy has shown, any attempt to impose a uniform framework is bound to be contested by other actors—state governments or mobilised social groups—who can make claims to control local space (Jenkins et al. 2014). The slate is never clean; existing patterns of socio-political relations and legacies of mobilisation shape the reception of top–down directives.

An illustration of contested scale-making within the DMIC is the assertion by the Gujarat government of its prerogative over the territory within its state borders, and its success in negotiating with the Central government to replace the initially planned nodes (Bharuch–Dahej and Vadodara–Ankleshwar) with one of its own choice, Dholera. Sampat's chapter in this volume explicitly focuses on this greenfield city-making project, designed in its current avatar as a 'smart' city. It is being developed as a 'Special Investment Region' (SIR) under the Gujarat SIR Act 2009, and will be managed by Regional Development Authorities appointed by and responsible to the state government, instruments that embody state space. As Anand and Sami state in this volume:

> Dholera is setting an important precedent for the establishment of new cities under the DMIC framework, creating spaces of

> exception in governance terms that will exist and function outside the purview of current urban government frameworks.

When it comes to understanding the entrepreneurial state, the case of the DMIC alerts us to the complex intercourse between private and state actors as well as state actors at different scales that characterises projects of greenfield urbanisation in contemporary India. Sampat's study of village communities in Dholera relates in vivid detail how such rescaling strategies, as they seek to reshape India's economic geography, reconfigure social and economic relations at the local scale through 'rent-driven urbanisation'.

Governance and Exception

Among the cases focused on contemporary processes, another key theme is the increasing tendency for state actors to rely on 'extraordinary departures from policy' (Ong 2006) to expedite policy goals and insulate newly created spaces from 'interference', or in other words, to bypass social and political realities. As we have argued above, these strategies of 'bypass' and 'exception' have been central to realising the policymakers' vision of the tabula rasa. Indeed, the bypass of street politics, in Bhattacharya and Sanyal's (2011) sense, depends critically on creating exceptions to the democratic forces unleashed at the local scale by the 73rd and 74th Constitutional Amendments. In this volume, Anand and Sami highlight the deployment of the Regional Development Authority in the DMIC as a way to bypass municipal governance. Yet, we can also see the central land ordinance and its use in facilitating land pooling Dholera as part of the same phenomenon (Sampat's chapter in this volume) as much as the use of 'exemption' as a tool of flexible planning in the making of Gurgaon (Gururani 2013). In their contribution, Gopa Samanta and Akash Banerjee alert us to the invocation of the exception in West Bengal's Andal Aerotropolis. As they note:

> ...the Andal Aerotropolis has been adopted under the state's 'Smart City' initiatives with the appellation 'Golden City', to

> be administered by an autonomous urban local body namely 'Golden City Industrial Township Authority' (GCITA), which will autonomously take up all municipal approvals and clearances, thus ensuring prompt sanction of projects through a single-window clearance system.

Thus, the studies in this volume cast useful light on the deployment of exception as a feature of the workings of the entrepreneurial state, as much as they highlight the speculative urbanism that characterises the assembly of land for sites of greenfield urbanisation, whether in Sriperumbudur–Oragadam on Chennai's outskirts, in Andhra Pradesh's planned capital Amaravati or along the DMIC.

Megaprojects and Speculative Urbanisms

This volume engages with another significant body of literature that examines urban megaprojects, a category that includes, for instance, riverfront redevelopment projects, industrial parks or corridors, and integrated townships, which combine in one large-scale layout economic, residential and commercial functions. Although on a larger scale, even greenfield cities like Dholera in Gujarat or the Andal Aerotropolis, discussed in this volume, are conceived by policymakers as integrated townships with planning and management design contracted to private firms. In many instances, these projects aim to create new urban landscapes and lifestyles, imagined through iconic buildings and mixed-use entertainment/leisure centres.

Although not a recent phenomenon, urban megaprojects are currently receiving renewed attention in academic circles as manifestations of city marketing in the context of neoliberal concerns with competitiveness (Fainstein 2008) or as 'worlding projects' (Ong 2011).[6] Megaprojects are promoted by entrepreneurial states to position their large cities nationally or on a global scale. In that respect, they represent a quintessential rescaling strategy, the aim of which is to restructure the urban economy, compete for investment and also generate returns to both state agencies and private property owners/developers. Examining megaproject development in Asia, Shatkin points out that a key aspect is 'their explicitly profit-oriented and commodified nature, and the powerful role of the corporate sector in their conceptualization, planning, development, and governance' (2011: 80). Figuring prominently in many Indian states' growth strategies in the post-reform period (Benjamin 2000; Kennedy 2007), megaprojects reflect the changing role of infrastructure 'from being a simple precondition for production and consumption to being at the very core of these activities' (Flyvbjerg et al. 2003: 2). In rapidly growing cities, megaprojects are also a means to scale-up urban infrastructure to meet basic needs such as housing and transport infrastructure, to enhance economic 'viability', as was the rationale behind the Jawaharlal Nehru National Urban Renewal Mission (JNNURM). Yet they are also associated across the world with increasing social and environmental risks by feeding land speculation, exacerbating urban sprawl, displacing local populations and livelihoods, through gentrification processes (Gellert and Lynch 2003; Barthel 2010).

Although a 'new paradigm' of megaproject development has been postulated, mainly on the basis of North American and European examples (Diaz Orueta and Fainstein 2008), research has questioned its relevance for cities in India, and in the developing world more generally, highlighting rather continuity in many aspects of the politics and governance (Flores Dewey and Davis 2013; Kennedy 2015). Indian cases have underscored continued reliance on top-down expert-driven knowledge in planning and implementation (Bon 2015; Follmann 2015) and large-scale evictions, for instance in the Sabarmati Riverfront Development project (Desai 2012), undertaken, as Mathur argues, in pursuit of the fantasy of a clean slate (2012: 74).

Of particular interest, compared to both Western and East and South-east Asian cases (Shatkin 2008; Moser 2015), new city and megaproject development in India still tends to be largely state-initiated and state-funded,[7] although private planners and management consultants play an increasingly important role in state-led initiatives (Sami and Anand 2021). Private developers have been much more prominent in real estate development post-2000 (Sood 2021). Even so, as many authors have pointed out, state actors increasingly operate on behalf of private interests, or in ways that benefit capital (Benjamin 2000; Goldman 2011). An analysis of the income and employment linkage effects of the IT corridor in Chennai, a megaproject largely created through public infrastructure investments,[8] shows indirect gains accruing not only to software companies but to local property owners also, for instance, through the provision of housing to IT employees (see the chapter by Vijayabaskar and Suresh Babu in this volume).

Yet, situations vary significantly across the country as studies show, making it necessary to situate each megaproject in its distinct setting, historically grounded configurations of state power and contingencies of citizen resistance and mobilisation. Failed projects too offer hints for understanding local power dynamics and patterns of influence, like the Dharavi Redevelopment Plan (Ren and Weinstein 2013), and are reminders of the open-ended nature of urban politics (Shatkin 2011).[9] Although often schematically framed as a contest between 'occupancy urbanism' (Benjamin 2008) and an elite-driven agenda for urban transformation, the issues are often more complex as the articles on Dholera and Andal in this volume show. Echoing Shatkin's 'landscape of anticipation' (2011: 88), Sampat describes how existing agrarian relations in Dholera are destroyed as landowners, property developers and state agencies all wait for rents generated by the future smart city. In Andal, complexities arise from the double challenge of establishing a 'greenfield' project in an already densely populated area and creating a thriving hub dedicated to IT-based services amidst traditional regional specialisation in manufacturing and mining. These accounts help advance the literature on the real estate dynamics and forces of rent-seeking and financial speculation that shape the metropolitan Indian landscape (Searle 2010; Rouanet and Halbert 2016; Goldman 2011).[10]

Highlighting the role of local actors on the ground, outside the circuits of global capital flows and state agencies, they deepen and complicate Goldman's (2011: 247) prediction that local actors 'must become speculators of one sort or another, taking extreme risks, and must gamble on when government agents or land brokers will tag their possessions next for acquisition, and act before it is too late'.

Spatial Inequalities: Bypass, Splintering or Urban Club?

Much of the urban frontier along the DMIC and at sites such as Dholera and Amaravati remains under construction or on the planning board. It is no surprise then that studies of these sites have focused on the struggles around land and the public–private nexuses that have shaped their rise.

Yet what, if any, evidence can we marshal to plan for or anticipate how these sites will unfold from social, economic, political and spatial points of view? It is arguable that the long and rich history of greenfield urbanisation in India—planned state capitals, satellite cities and others—offers enough empirical grounding to allow scholars, planners and policymakers to make several informed prognoses.

One of these empirical regularities deserves special mention because it seems to recur with such frequency that it can even be called a law of master-planned development in India: the emergence of the unplanned housing and informal economies alongside the planned city. To take but one example, in her magisterial study of Navi Mumbai, Shaw (2003) noted that, in 2000, 'unauthorised settlements' evidently comprised well over a third of the population of the satellite town. This informal economy included a variety of population segments from temporary migrants in the construction industry, living in hastily put together shanties, to domestic and service workers, self-employed or employed in service and industry establishments, as well as villagers displaced by the making of Navi Mumbai.

Bhattacharya and Sanyal (2011: 45) theorise the resilience and growth of this 'need economy', consisting of the subsistence-oriented self-employed and a 'survival circuit' of low-wage service workers in Marxian terms, as an 'eviction, bypass and encroachment' loop that characterises the capitalist 'accumulation economy' of new town developments.

Three of the chapters in this volume—Kundu on Rajarhat New Town, Idiculla on the Electronics City in Bengaluru, and Vijayabaskar and Suresh Babu on Chennai's IT Corridor—engage substantively with the aftermath of large-scale urban development. Deploying very different conceptual/theoretical and methodological tools, they all suggest that patterns of urban dualism are the sine qua non of urban development in this mode. In Vijayabaskar and Suresh Babu's analysis of employment creation in Chennai's IT Corridor, for example, segmented labour markets with highly polarised wage levels and work conditions are 'spatially manifested' through segmented housing markets, with high-end apartment complexes and gated communities alongside slums. These authors' findings also connect with other studies in the same geographical space that have highlighted the informal service economy linkages between Chennai's new economy and workers in the slum resettlement colony of Kannagi Nagar (Coelho et al. 2012; Dupont and Dhanalakshmi 2016).

Positioned in a different disciplinary framing and literature, Kundu's exploration of place-making in Rajarhat New Town near Kolkata is particularly striking for the portrait it draws of the complex relationship between the urban village and gated community, as both sets of residents are 'unsettled by processes of urbanisation'. In this portrait, 'villages and gated communities are not bounded spatial entities', but 'fluid and dynamic places, imbued with heterogeneity and inherent conflicts' over claims to housing and infrastructure as well as 'incremental...investments in a collective associational life'. Concerned with the co-production of spaces, Kundu's work can be situated in an incipient literature on the spatial practices and politics that constitute the new peri-urban landscape of gated communities and private townships.[11] Much of this literature—Goldstein (2016), Cowan (2015) and Srivastava (2014)—is located around Gurgaon in particular, highlighting once again the ways in which specific settings have become emblematic of specific thematics, much as Chennai's IT economy has been the site of studies focused on formal/informal linkages. Transposing themes and analytical lenses emerging in particular settings into new study locales, as Kundu does in Rajarhat, is part of the agenda for this volume.

The salience of splintering in access to 'basic infrastructure such as transport, water, electricity and garbage collection' is the underlying motif that links peri-urban place-making in Rajarhat with the new privatised forms of governance being applied in places like Bengaluru's Electronics City, the subject of Idiculla's essay in this volume. The residential settings in Rajarhat would appear to have little in common with the avowedly non-residential jurisdiction of the Electronics City Industrial Township Authority (ELCITA), but the fragmentation in basic services and infrastructures is an unmistakable feature of these and other greenfield sites in India. Idiculla invokes Graham and Marvin's (2001) influential conceptualisation of splintering urbanism, first formulated against the backdrop of newly built fibre optic telecommunications infrastructures in the West. Idiculla shows that these processes are especially evident with respect to infrastructures such as piped water networks—connected to ELCITA but not surrounding areas—as well as an elevated expressway that joins ELCITA to Bengaluru city.

As other authors have argued in the context of other IT-led transformations of the peri-urban frontier in Hyderabad's HITEC City and Cyberabad developments (Das 2010; Kennedy 2007, 2014), ELCITA appears to represent a 'premium networked space', an island of global connectivity that sought to bypass a sea of 'non-valued' users in 'network ghettoes' (Graham 1999, 2002). Mechanisms of bypass in the domain of infrastructure networks (Graham and Marvin 2001) and settlement patterns (Bhattacharya and Sanyal 2011) would thus appear to be a uniting feature of the new urban frontier.

As much as identifying patterns of bypass and spatial inequality, it is also important to interrogate the theoretical and empirical paradigms that have been used to understand greenfield urban development in India. Thus, Vijayabaskar and Suresh Babu's analysis of linkages in the local economy of Chennai's IT Corridor must be read against a growing literature in economics that seeks to assess the impacts of 'big push' policies that favour concentrated investments in chosen spatial locations, especially through instruments such as industrial clusters and SEZs (Moretti 2014; Wang 2013; Chaurey 2013; Sridhar 2006). While much of this literature, in India and elsewhere, has focused on macroeconomic aggregates such as employment and output, Vijayabaskar and Suresh Babu's intervention highlights the relevance of locally mediated cross-sectoral linkages in any reckoning of the impacts of such space-based policies.

Similarly, Kundu's examination of place-making in Rajarhat is informed by and can be juxtaposed against Dey et al.'s (2013) extended and richly detailed Marxian analysis of the same transforming terrain. In the case of ELCITA, Idiculla appeals to the 'urban clubs' framework to characterise the nature of the privatised regimes of urban governance it represents. It is worth comparing the literature of urban clubs, which emerges from a long-standing lineage in public economics, to the 'premium networked spaces' and splintering urbanism frame because although they originate at very different starting points, both paradigms reach similar predictions about the future course of spatially differentiated provisioning of public goods and infrastructures around emergent centres of urbanism in India.

In particular, while the theory of local public goods, that is, public goods that are prone to congestion, and club goods dates back to the work of Tiebout (1956) and Buchanan (1965), its application to gated communities owes much to the work of Webster (2001) and Glasze (2005) (also see Webster and Glasze 2004). In applying this framework to the Indian case in policy innovations such as the SEZ and the NIMZs as well as industrial townships more broadly, Sood (2015: 1361) has argued that urban clubs transfer key functions of local government such as executive and representative functions, infrastructure and services provision, urban planning, and security to 'private governments'. It is the range of such public goods and amenities assigned to such private governments—from open and recreational spaces to roads, power supply, solid waste management and water supply sources, and social infrastructures—that raises concerns about their spatial effects. For instance, in Hyderabad, the governance of both old and new industrial areas has been outsourced to 'service societies' and to state government bureaucrats, who act as substitutes for the urban local body (Kennedy and Sood 2019).

Whereas the splintering urbanism framework offers a largely deterministic framework for diagnosing patterns of spatial inequality, the urban clubs model provides a more open-ended analytical frame for tracing the impacts of a particular constellation of (policy/governance) conditions. In other words, in this framework, the effects of spatially targeted public services are an empirical proposition rather than a defining feature, without a predetermined direction for change. Thus, the model makes no presumptions regarding pre-existing forms of network infrastructure provision—'monopolistic, integrated and standardized' (Coutard 2008); nor does it assume a 'modern infrastructure ideal' (Coutard 2008; Zérah 2008) with near-universal access to basic services. All of these assumptions have come under critique in the Indian context (Kennedy 2007; Zérah 2008), underscoring the need to distinguish between policy effects, in terms of differentiation/segregation, and 'deeper' causes, located in social norms and practices as well as the political institutions that give expression to them (Lorrain 2005).

Second, this model links back to the broader debate around governance and exception, alluded to above. It foregrounds the role of governance regimes in mediating the effects of spatially differentiated infrastructure provision, as Sood (2015) has argued in the context of contestations around municipal status for Jamshedpur (see also Sood and Rath 2017).

UNITING AND UNDEREXPLORED THEMES

The essays in this volume cover a large terrain, historically, geographically, methodologically and thematically, even as they highlight the disparate imperatives that drive new city-making and greenfield projects in India. Thus, one might ask: what unites the experience of the IT Corridor in Chennai, conceived to strengthen the regional economy, with the ostensibly administrative rationales driving the building of Chandigarh or Navi Mumbai?

Our aim in this volume is to ask: can cases speak to each other? What themes recur across these case studies? And what directions do they suggest for future research?

Dewaele's comparative essay serves to pull together the themes of the volume. Her chapter underscores the political and symbolic significance of city-building in the postcolonial period across diverse cases and spanning various scales, from Chandigarh, the emblem of postcolonial urban planning, to satellite towns initiated by state governments in the 1960s: Gurgaon, Navi Mumbai and Salt Lake City. The latter reveal three different forms of public urban planning, marking the emergence of more autonomous state units responsive to the socio-political realities of their respective jurisdictions.

In putting together this volume, our aim was also to look beyond current struggles over land that animate debates over these new greenfield sites to the urban futures they presage. Although planners and policymakers sometimes contend that the future lives of these new cities-in-the-making cannot be predicted, it is arguable that India's long-standing history with greenfield urbanisation, whether at sites such as Jamshedpur or Chandigarh or Navi Mumbai, offers a rich empirical base to test broader generalisations about patterns of urban growth in India. Indeed, the evidence indicates that the rise of the unplanned city is a reliable correlate of the building of the planned city. Thus, the 'dynamics of dualisation' seen in the growth of the informal economy as well as *bastis* and informal settlements deserve more attention. There is a growing body of evidence to show that spatially targeted provision of infrastructure, which is at the heart of competitive cities policies (Kennedy 2014; Goldman 2011), creates patterns of fragmentation and splintering by fostering an urban club approach to public goods provision.

In looking to directions for future research, several underexplored themes stand out. First, a large literature around and beyond the speculative urbanism thesis has flagged patterns of policy mobility and inter-referencing that characterise urban policy and planning processes in Asia (Roy and Ong 2011; Hogan et al. 2012). What are the nexuses and agendas—for instance, the rise of multinational consulting agencies—that have shaped private sector involvement in the urban policy arena, particularly with reference to the development of greenfield cities and new urban nodes? While the role played by global finance capital (Halbert and Rouanet 2013) and private real estate actors is receiving increasing attention (Goldman 2011; Searle 2010, 2014; Rouanet and Halbert 2016), the construction of a 'global architecture of expertise' (Goldman 2011: 232) and the public–private nexuses that define the mandates handed over to experts need more extensive exploration (Bunnell and Das 2010; Sami and Anand 2021).

Second, although the motif of city as growth engine underlies policy frameworks such as SEZs and NMIZs as well as state-level policies (Sood 2015), it has received relatively little empirical vetting, especially when it comes to local economy linkages. Research is starting to question which types of infrastructure really matter for growth (Misra 2015). Motivated by paradigms of investment-led growth and structural transformation, the policy models facilitating privatised forms of urban development often overlook the spatial growth patterns they engender. For instance, work around Chennai's IT Corridor (Coelho et al. 2012) and small-town Ambur (Coelho and Vijayabaskar 2014), suggests that development and employment growth around 'formal', globally connected sectors tends to remain 'disconnected' and fragmented. Vijayabaskar and Suresh Babu in this volume partially address this gap, but a conceptually richer framework drawing on a diversity of sites and geographic settings can go a long way to informing policymakers. Likewise, the social impacts of space-based policies, highlighting which social groups find employment in which types of jobs need to be more explicitly addressed in policy design.

Third, the privatised forms of governance in the urban clubs have been likened in the literature to 'private...governments' and 'shareholder democracies' (Glasze 2005) that do not grant representation and voice to all residents. On similar lines, SEZs and industrial township authorities largely comprise nominated members from bureaucracy and management, leaving residents without elected representation (Sood 2015). Under these conditions, what kinds of institutional mechanisms exist to mediate between the competing interests of residents/non-residents, workers/management, public/private bodies and others? Where do these mechanisms fall short?

Fourth, ranging from cantonments to campuses to public sector housing colonies, India has witnessed a diverse lineage of enclaves (Dupont 2016). What can we learn from this experience? How do the patterns of exclusion and segregation built into new forms of private urban development, whether gated communities or industrial townships, mould the experience of the urban for residents and non-residents? What kinds of disruptions, fragmentations and unexpected encounters do they produce? Kundu's richly textured ethnography suggests some of the ways this agenda can be advanced.

A significant literature has traced the trajectories of the older 'new cities', whether they be planned capitals or satellite towns and industrial townships (Sivaramakrishnan 1978; Kalia 1994, 1999, 2004; Shaw 2004; Parry and Struempell 2008; Dossal 2010; P. Datta 2012; Dey et al. 2013; Sood 2015; Sood and Rath 2017). Likewise, important insights can be gained from situating India's experience of private and enclave urbanisms within Asia more broadly (Paling 2012; Percival and Waley 2012; Hogan et al. 2012; Roy and Ong 2011).

The task of connecting the lessons from this historical experience to the contemporary policy emphasis on greenfield urbanisation in India remains urgent. In India, the policy slogan of hundreds of new cities, first floated in the first decade of the millennium (*Economic & Political Weekly* 2010), has shown surprising resilience, appearing in the incarnation of the smart city (Datta 2015; Mukhopadhyay 2015). Even as this fantasy of the tabula rasa continues to compel policymakers, its implications for the struggle for equality and the practice of democracy in India remain unclear. It is to this agenda of examining how the right to the city comes to be (un)realised on India's urban frontier that this volume is dedicated.

NOTES

1. The authors are grateful to Marie-Hélène Zérah for her comments on a draft of this essay.

2. This representation is inspired from Jonathan Bach's work on the economic zone as a modernist urban fantasy (2011). Moser (2010) also uses the term in connection with Malaysia's Putrajaya.

3. Sood and Jain (2021) applied three definitional criteria for 'township' to residential, commercial and infrastructural projects from a proprietary database. These criteria encompass policy-defined size thresholds, whether the project title calls itself 'town', 'city' or 'township', and whether it combines commercial and residential products. Over 422 such projects meeting any of the three criteria had been completed, and some 1,060 were in various stages of implementation. For projects announced between 1995 and 2018, a vast majority had private promoters.

4. We are grateful to George Jose for this observation.

5. Even there, basic services like water supply often come under the purview of state government agencies. This is the case in Hyderabad, for instance, with the Metro Water Supply and Sewerage Board.

6. We use a loose definition of the term megaproject, following Susan Fainstein: '(e)ssentially it involves a costly scheme for development of a contiguous area, requiring new construction and/or substantial rehabilitation. Implementation may take a number of years and may be the responsibility of a single or multiple developers. Megaprojects always include a transformation of land uses' (2008: 768).

7. Notable exceptions are the private-led development of 'new Gurgaon' (Gururani 2013; Cowan 2015) and Lavasa (A. Datta 2012; Balakrishnan 2018).

8. On the IT corridor in Chennai, also see Kennedy et al. (2014).

9. This corroborates Altshuler and Luberoff's assertion that 'efforts to realise large-scale investment projects often provide an unusually revealing window on patterns of influence in urban development politics. Such projects involve huge commitments of public resources and often entail significant threats to some interests and values even as they promise great benefits to others' (2003: 4).

10. Goldman (2011: 230) characterises speculative urbanism as a set of worlding practices—the 'imperative to speculate' as part of a 'globalised' and entrepreneurial project of world-city making.

11. An older literature, partially included in a special issue of *Cities* journal, took a broader view of the contestations that characterise urban peripheries in Indian cities. See Dupont (2007).

REFERENCES

Altshuler, A. A., and D. Luberoff. 2003. *Mega-projects: The Changing Politics of Urban Public Investment*. Washington DC: Brookings Institution Press.

Bach, J. 2011. 'Modernity and the Urban Imagination in Economic Zones'. *Theory, Culture & Society* 28(5): 98–122.

Balakrishnan, S. 2018. 'Seeing Mumbai Through Its Hinterland: Entangled Agrarian-Urban Land Markets in Regional Mumbai'. *Economic & Political Weekly* 53(12): 55–60.

———. 2019a. 'Recombinant Urbanization: Agrarian–Urban Landed Property and Uneven Development in India'. *International Journal of Urban and Regional Research* 43(4): 617–32.

———. 2019b. *Shareholder Cities: Land Transformations along Urban Corridors in India*. Philadelphia: University of Pennsylvania Press.

Banerjee-Guha, S. 2009. 'Neoliberalising the "Urban": New Geographies of Power and Injustice in Indian Cities'. *Economic & Political Weekly* 44(22): 95–107.

Barthel, P-A. 2010. 'Arab Mega-Projects'. *Built Environment* 36(2), special issue.

Benjamin, S. 2000. 'Governance, Economic Settings and Poverty in Bangalore'. *Environment and Urbanization* 12(1): 35–56.

———. 2008. 'Occupancy Urbanism: Radicalizing Politics and Economy Beyond Policy and Programs'. *International Journal of Urban and Regional Research* 32(3): 719–29.

Bhattacharya, R., and K. Sanyal. 2011. 'Bypassing the Squalor: New Towns, Immaterial Labour and Exclusion in Post-colonial Urbanisation'. *Economic & Political Weekly* 46(31): 41–48.

Bon, B. 2015. 'A New Mega-project Model and a New Funding Model: Travelling Concepts and Local Adaptations Around the Delhi Metro'. *Habitat International* 45(3): 223–30.

Brenner, N. 1998. 'Global Cities, Global States: Global City Formation and State Territorial Restructuring in Contemporary Europe'. *Review of International Political Economy* 5(1): 1–37.

———. 2004. *New State Spaces: Urban Governance and the Rescaling of Statehood.* Oxford and New York: Oxford University Press.

Brenner, N., and N. Theodore. 2002. 'Cities and the Geographies of Actually Existing Neoliberalism'. *Antipode* 34(3): 349–79.

Brenner, N., B. Jessop, M. Jones and G. MacLeod, eds. 2003. *State/Space: A Reader.* Malden, MA and Oxford: Blackwell Publishers.

Buchanan, J. M. 1965. 'An Economic Theory of Clubs'. *Economica* 32(125): 1–14.

Bunnell, T. And D. K. Das. 2010. 'A Geography of Serial Seduction: Urban Policy Transfer from Kuala Lumpur to Hyderabad'. *Urban Geography* 31(3): 1–7.

Chaurey, R. 2013. 'Location Based Tax Incentives: Evidence from India'. Department of Economics Discussion Papers, Columbia University, New York.

Coelho, K., T. Venkat and R. Chandrika. 2012. 'The Spatial Reproduction of Urban Poverty'. *Economic & Political Weekly* 47(48): 55–63.

Coelho, K., and M. Vijayabaskar. 2014. 'On the Charts, Off the Tracks'. *Economic & Political Weekly* 49(22): 101–10.

Coutard, O. 2008. 'Placing Splintering Urbanism: Introduction'. *Geoforum* 39(6): 1815–20.

Cowan, T. 2015. 'Fragmented Citizenships in Gurgaon'. *Economic & Political Weekly* 50(26–27): 63–73.

Das, D. K. 2010. 'Splintering Urbanism in High-tech Hyderabad'. Ph.D. diss., National University of Singapore.

Datta, A. 2012. 'India's Ecocity? Environment, Urbanisation, and Mobility in the Making of Lavasa'. *Environment and Planning C: Government and Policy* 30(6): 982–96.

——. 2015. 'New Urban Utopias of Postcolonial India: "Entrepreneurial Urbanization" in Dholera Smart City, Gujarat'. *Dialogues in Human Geography* 5(1): 3–22.

Datta, P. 2012. *Planning the City: Urbanization and Reform in Calcutta, c1800–c1940*. Delhi: Tulika Books.

Denis, E. 2011. 'Financing Land in Egyptian and Indian Megacities. The Frontiers of Urban Liberalization'. *Revue Tiers Monde* 2011/2(206): 139–58.

Denis, Eric, and Marie-Hélène Zérah, eds. 2017. *Subaltern Urbanisation in India. An Introduction to the Dynamics of Ordinary Towns*. Springer India.

Desai, R. 2012. 'Governing the Urban Poor: River-front Development, Slum Resettlement and the Politics of Inclusion in Ahmedabad'. *Economic & Political Weekly* 47(2): 49–56.

Dey, I., R. Samaddar and S. Sen. 2013. *Beyond Kolkata: Rajarhat and the Dystopia of Urban Imagination*. New Delhi: Routledge.

Diaz Orueta, F., and S. S. Fainstein. 2008. 'The New Mega-Projects: Genesis and Impacts'. *International Journal of Urban and Regional Research* 32(4): 759–67.

Dossal, M. 2010. *Theatre of Conflict, City of Hope: Mumbai 1660 to Present Times*. New Delhi: Oxford University Press.

Dupont, V. 2007. 'Conflicting Stakes and Governance in the Peripheries of Large Indian Metropolises—An Introduction'. *Cities* 24(2): 89–94.

——. 2011. 'The Dream of Delhi as a Global City'. *International Journal of Urban and Regional Research* 35(3): 533–54.

——. 2016. 'Secured Residential Enclaves in the Delhi Region: Impact of Indigenous and Transnational Models'. *City, Culture and Society* 7(4): 227–36.

Dupont, V., and R. Dhanalakshmi. 2016. 'Settlement Story 6.6 Evictions in the Chennai IT Corridor and New Threats: Low Resistance in Squatter Settlements along the Buckingham Canal'. In *The Politics of Slums in the Global South*, eds V. Dupont, D. Jordhus-Lier, C. Sutherland and E. Braathen, 174–80. Oxon: Routledge.

Economic & Political Weekly. 2010. 'Private Cities'. *Economic & Political Weekly* 45(12): 7–8.

Fainstein, S. S. 2008. 'Mega-projects in New York, London and Amsterdam'. *International Journal of Urban and Regional Research* 32(4): 768–85.

Flores Dewey, O., and D. E. Davis. 2013. 'Planning, Politics, and Urban Mega-Projects in Developmental Context: Lessons from Mexico City's Airport Controversy'. *Journal of Urban Affairs* 35(5): 531–51.

Flyvbjerg, B., N. Bruzelius and W. Rothengatter. 2003. *Megaprojects and Risk: An Anatomy of Ambition*. United Kingdom and New York: Cambridge University Press.

Follmann, A. 2015. 'Urban Mega-Projects for a "World-Class" Riverfront—The Interplay of Informality, Flexibility and Exceptionality along the Yamuna in Delhi, India'. *Habitat International* 45(3): 213–22.

Gellert, P. K., and B. D. Lynch. 2003. 'Mega-projects as Displacements'. *International Social Science Journal* 175(March): 15–25.

Glasze, G. 2005. 'Some Reflections on the Economic and Political Organisation of Private Neighbourhoods'. *Housing Studies* 20(2): 221–33.

Goldman, M. 2011. 'Speculating on the Next World City.' In *Worlding Cities: Asian Experiments and the Art of Being Global*, eds A. Roy and A. Ong, 229–58. Oxford: Wiley Blackwell.

Goldstein, S. 2016. 'Planning the Millennium City: The Politics of Place-making in Gurgaon, India'. *International Area Studies Review* 19(1): 12–27.

Gotsch, P. 2009. 'Neotowns: Prototypes of Corporate Urbanism'. Ph.D. diss., Karlsruhe Institute of Technology, Germany.

Graham, S. 1999. 'Global Grids of Glass: On Global Cities, Telecommunications and Planetary Urban Networks'. *Urban Studies* 36(5/6): 929.

———. 2002. 'On Technology, Infrastructure and the Contemporary Urban Condition: A Response to Coutard'. *International Journal of Urban and Regional Research* 26(1): 175–82.

Graham, S., and S. Marvin. 2001. *Splintering Urbanism: Networked Infrastructures, Technological Mobilities and the Urban Condition*. New York and London: Routledge.

Gupta, A., and K. Sivaramakrishnan, eds. 2011.*The State in India After Liberalization*. London and New York: Routledge.

Gururani, S. 2013. 'Flexible Planning: The Making of India's "Millennial City" Gurgaon'. In *Ecologies of Urbanism in Asia*, eds Anne M. Rademacher and K. Sivaramakrishnan, 119–43. Hong Kong: Hong Kong University Press.

Halbert, L., and H. Rouanet. 2013. 'Filtering Risk Away: Global Finance Capital, Transcalar Territorial Networks and the (Un)Making of City-Regions: An Analysis of Business Property Development in Bangalore, India'. *Regional Studies* 48(3): 471–84.

Harvey, D. 1989. 'From Managerialism to Entrepreneurialism: The Transformation in Urban Governance in Late Capitalism'. *Geografiska Annaler*, Series B, 71(1): 3–17.

Hogan, T., T. Bunnell, C. P. Pow, E. Permanasari and S. Morshidi. 2012. 'Asian Urbanisms and the Privatization of Cities'. *Cities* 29(1): 59–63.

Jenkins, R., L. Kennedy and P. Mukhopadhyay, eds. 2014. *Power, Policy, and Protest: The Politics of India's Special Economic Zones*. New Delhi: Oxford University Press.

Jessop, B. 2002. 'Liberalism, Neoliberalism, and Urban Governance: A State-Theoretical Perspective'. *Antipode* 34(3): 452–72.

Joshi, R. 2009. 'Integrated Townships as a Policy Response to Changing Supply and Demand Dynamics of Urban Growth'. In *India Infrastructure Report 2009*, ed. 3iE Network, Infrastructure Development Finance Company, 167–75. New Delhi: Oxford University Press.

Kalia, R. 1994. *Bhubaneswar: From a Temple Town to a Capital City*. Carbondale and Edwardsville: Southern Illinois University Press.

———. 1999. *Chandigarh: The Making of An Indian City*. New Delhi: Oxford University Press.

———. 2004. *Gandhinagar: Building National Identity in Postcolonial India*. Columbia, SC: University of South Carolina Press.

———. 2006. 'Modernism, Modernization and Post-colonial India: A Reflective Essay'. *Planning Perspectives* 21(2): 133–56.

Kennedy, L. 2007. 'Regional Industrial Policies Driving Peri-Urban Dynamics in Hyderabad, India'. *Cities* 24(2): 95–109.

———. 2014. *The Politics of Economic Restructuring in India: Economic Governance and State Spatial Rescaling*. London and New York: Routledge (South Asian edn).

———. 2015. 'The Politics and Changing Paradigm of Mega-project Development in Metropolitan Cities'. *Habitat International* 45(3): 163–68.

Kennedy, L., and M.-H. Zérah. 2008. 'The Shift to City-Centric Growth Strategies: Perspectives from Hyderabad and Mumbai'. *Economic & Political Weekly* 43(39): 110–17.

Kennedy, L., and A. Sood. 2019. 'Outsourced Urban Governance as a State Rescaling Strategy in Hyderabad, India'. *Cities* 85: 130–39.

Kennedy, L., A. Varrel, E. Denis, V. Dupont, R. Dhanalakshmi, et al. 2014. *Engaging with Sustainability Issues in Metropolitan Chennai*. Chance2Sustain City Report Series. Bonn: European Association of Development Research and Training Institutes (EADI). Available at http://chance2sustain.eu/66.0.html (accessed on 21 May 2022).

Lorrain, D. 2005. 'Gig@city: The Rise of Techno-logical Networks in Daily Life'. In *Sustaining Urban Networks: The Social Diffusion of Large Technical Systems*, eds O. Coutard, R. Hanley and R. Zimmermann, 15–31. London and New York: Routledge.

Mathur, N. 2012. 'On the Sabarmati Riverfront: Urban Planning as Totalitarian Governance in Ahmedabad'. *Economic & Political Weekly* 47(47&48): 64–75.

Misra, B. S. 2015. 'Which Infrastructure Matters More for Growth: Economic or Social? Evidence from Indian States during 2001–2010'. *Review of Urban & Regional Development Studies* 27(3): 177–96.

Moretti, E. 2014. 'Cities and Growth'. Evidence Paper, International Growth Centre, London.

Moser, S. 2010. 'Putrajaya: Malaysia's New Federal Administrative Capital'. *Cities* 27(4): 285–97.

——. 2015. 'New Cities: Old Wine in New Bottles?' *Dialogues in Human Geography* 5(1): 31–35.

Moser, S., M. Swain and M. H. Alkhabbaz. 2015. 'King Abdullah Economic City: Engineering Saudi Arabia's Post-oil Future'. *Cities* 45: 71–80.

Mukhopadhyay, P. 2015. 'The Un-smart City'. *Seminar* 665 (January): 75–79.

Ong, A. 2006. *Neoliberalism as Exception: Mutations in Citizenship and Sovereignty*. Durham, NC: Duke University Press.

——. 2011. 'Introduction: Worlding Cities, or the Art of Being Global'. In *Worlding Cities: Asian Experiments and the Art of Being Global*, eds A. Roy and A. Ong, 1–26. Chichester, W. Sussex; Malden, MA: Wiley-Blackwell.

Paling, W. 2012. 'Planning a Future for Phnom Penh: Mega-Projects, Aid Dependence and Disjointed Governance'. *Urban Studies* 49(13): 1–24.

Parry, J., and C. Struempell. 2008. 'On the Desecration of Nehru's "Temples": Bhilai and Rourkela Compared'. *Economic & Political Weekly* 43(19): 47–57.

Percival, T. D., and P. Waley. 2012. 'Articulating Intra-Asian Urbanism: The Production of Satellite Cities in Phnom Penh'. *Urban Studies* 49(13): 2871–88.

Ren, X., and L. Weinstein. 2013. 'Urban Governance, Mega-Projects and Scalar Transformations in China and India'. In *Locating Right to the City in the Global South*, eds T. R. Samara, S. He and G. Chen, 107–26. London and New York: Routledge.

Rouanet, H., and L. Halbert. 2016. 'Leveraging Finance Capital: Urban Change and Self-Empowerment of Real Estate Developers in India'. *Urban Studies* 53(7): 1401–23.

Roy, A. 2009. 'Why India Cannot Plan Its Cities: Informality, Insurgence and the Idiom of Urbanization'. *Planning Theory* 8(1): 76–87.

Roy, A., and A. Ong, eds. 2011. *Worlding Cities: Asian Experiments and the Art of Being Global*. Chichester, West Sussex; Malden, MA: Wiley-Blackwell.

Ruet, J., and S. Tawa Lama-Rewal, eds. 2009. *Governing India's Metropolises*. New Delhi: Routledge.

Sami, N. 2013. 'From Farming to Development: Urban Coalitions in Pune, India'. *International Journal of Urban and Regional Research* 37(1): 151–64.

Sami, N. and S. Anand. 2021. 'Expert Advice? Assessing the Role of the State'. In *Professional Service Firms and Politics in a Global Era*, eds C. Hurl and A. Vogelpohl, 272–292. Cham, Switzerland: Palgrave Macmillan.

Searle, L. G. 2010. 'Making Space for Capital: The Production of Global Landscapes in Contemporary India'. Ph.D. diss., Department of Anthropology, University of Pennsylvania.

——. 2014. 'Conflict and Commensuration: Contested Market Making in India's Private Real Estate Development Sector'. *International Journal of Urban and Regional Research* 38(1): 60–78.

Shatkin, G. 2008. 'The City and the Bottom Line: Urban Mega-projects and the Privatization of Planning in Southeast Asia'. *Environment and Planning A* 40(2): 383–401.

——. 2011. 'Planning Privatopolis: Representation and Contestation in the Development of Urban Integrated Mega-Projects'. In *Worlding Cities: Asian Experiments and the Art of Being Global*, eds A. Roy and A. Ong, 77–97. Chichester, West Sussex; Malden, MA: Wiley-Blackwell.

Shaw, A. 2003. 'Planning and Local Economies in Navi Mumbai: Processes of Growth and Governance'. *Urban Geography* 24(1): 2–15.

——. 2004. *The Making of Navi Mumbai*. New Delhi: Orient BlackSwan.

——. 2009. 'Town Planning in Postcolonial India, 1947–1965: Chandigarh Re-Examined'. *Urban Geography* 30(8): 857–78.

Sivaramakrishnan, K. C. 1978. *New Towns in India: A Report on a Study of Selected New Towns in Eastern Region*. Calcutta: Indian Institute of Management.

——. 2011. *Re-Visioning Indian Cities: The Urban Renewal Mission*. New Delhi: Sage.

Sood, A. 2015. 'Industrial Townships and the Policy Facilitation of Corporate Urbanisation in India'. *Urban Studies* 52(8): 1359–78.

——. 2021. 'The Speculative Frontier: Real Estate, Governance and Occupancy on the Metropolitan Periphery'. *South Asia Multidisciplinary Academic Journal* 26. Available at https://doi.org/10.4000/samaj.7204 (accessed on 28 June 2022).

Sood, A., and S. Rath. 2017. 'The Planned and the Unplanned: Company Towns in India'. *India International Centre Quarterly* 43(3&4): 91–103.

Sood, A., and T. Jain. 2021. 'City as Infrastructure? Private and Greenfield Urban Development in India'. Grant report, Azim Premji University, Bengaluru.

Sridhar, K. S. 2006. 'Local Employment Impact of Growth Centres: Evidence from India'. *Urban Studies* 43(12): 2205–35.

Srivastava, S. 2014. *Entangled Urbanism: Slum, Gated Community and Shopping Mall in Delhi and Gurgaon*. Oxford: Oxford University Press.

Sud, N. 2014. 'The State in the Era of India's Sub-national Regions: Liberalization and Land in Gujarat'. *Geoforum* 51: 233–42.

Swyngedouw, E. 1996. 'Reconstructing Citizenship, the Re-Scaling of the State and the New Authoritarianism: Closing the Belgian Mines'. *Urban Studies* 33(8): 1499–521.

Tiebout, C. M. 1956. 'A Pure Theory of Local Expenditures'. *Journal of Political Economy* 64(5): 416–24.

Wang, J. 2013. 'The Economic Impact of Special Economic Zones: Evidence from Chinese Municipalities'. *Journal of Development Economics* 101: 133–47.

Wang, L., R. Kundu and X. Chen. 2010. 'Building for What and Whom? New Town Development as Planned Suburbanization in China and India'. *Research in Urban Sociology* 10(3): 319–45.

Webster, C. 2001. 'Gated Cities of Tomorrow'. *Town Planning Review* 72(2): 149–70.

Webster, C., and G. Glasze. 2004. 'Dynamic Urban Order and the Rise of Residential Clubs'. In *Private Cities: Global and Local Perspectives*, eds Georg Glasze, Chris Webster and Klaus Frantz, 217–31. London and New York: Routledge.

Zérah, M-H. 2008. 'Splintering Urbanism in Mumbai: Contrasting Trends in a Multilayered Society'. *Geoforum* 39(6): 1922–32.

PART I

IMPERATIVES

CORRIDORS AND INFRASTRUCTURES

2

Highway Urbanisation and Land Conflicts

The Challenges to Decentralisation in India

SAI BALAKRISHNAN

The 160 villages along the Bangalore–Mysore highway in India, connecting the cities of Bangalore and Mysore, are schizophrenic patchworks of agricultural fields, industrial parks, gated communities and informal settlements. Property developers and industrialists are attracted to these highway villages with their cheaper lands and adjacencies to the well-connected highway. Agrarian landowners in these villages are threatened that these new developments will deprive them of their lands and livelihoods. These villages are fraught with contestations between real estate developers, industrialists and agrarian landowners over land acquisitions and, more broadly, the distribution of costs and benefits of the new highway developments. The Bangalore–Mysore highway represents an emerging pattern of urbanisation in developing countries: the urbanisation along inter-urban corridors. Since traditional institutions, like village governments for villages and municipalities for cities, collapse in these contested territories of overlapping cities and villages, what are the new regional institutions that can efficiently and equitably allocate land amongst competing interests and uses at a regional, that is, corridor, scale? To answer this question, I use a comparative case study method of two highways in India: the Bangalore–Mysore highway in south India, regulated by parastatals, and the Pune–Nashik highway in west India, regulated by farmer-owned land cooperatives. Both parastatals and cooperatives are regional institutions so their jurisdiction is trans-local. Both of them are hybrid institutions, that is, parastatals are public institutions that incorporate market values, and cooperatives are market institutions that incorporate social values. Parastatals, unlike 'general-purpose governments' like municipalities, have more of a market orientation in their financial discretion, internal organisational flexibility, and lower levels of citizen participation and accountability (Burns 1994; Foster 1997).

The cooperatives are institutions that have emerged to remedy the institutional flaws of the pure market, and have more of a social orientation through democratic worker control of the production process and profit making under non-exploitative, more humane conditions (Whyte and Whyte 1991). This chapter highlights the challenges of democratic decentralisation, that is, devolving decision-making authority to local village and city governments, in responding to the challenges of urbanisation at a regional, highway scale. Using the models of parastatals and cooperatives, it takes a first step in articulating the major elements of the new hybrid regional institutions that are emerging as solutions to the new patterns of highway urbanisation.

This chapter is based on nine months of fieldwork focusing on the megaprojects that have been developed along the two case study corridors. For my qualitative research, I selected a cluster of 28 villages, located 30 km from Bangalore city along the Bangalore–Mysore corridor, and 26 villages, located 42 km from Pune city along the Pune–Nashik corridor. These sample villages are representative of the urbanisation changes along the two case study highways. Through open-ended interviews with agrarian landowners who gave up their lands for the new highway developments, elected representatives of the villages, parastatal bureaucrats at the policy and implementation levels, and members of the land cooperatives, I mapped out the main institutional actors in the land consolidation process for these developments. The first part of this chapter sets the context with an introduction to the inter-urban corridors as an emergent pattern of urbanisation, and the challenges it poses to decentralisation. The second part is a narrative of the land consolidation processes surrounding the megaprojects along the Bangalore–Mysore and Pune–Nashik highways. The third part highlights the main findings of this study. It points to the institutional history of parastatals and cooperatives in India, the reasons for their emergence at the turn of the twentieth century, the ways in which they are being reworked to cope with contemporary highway land conflicts and the performance of these regional institutions in allocating land equitably and democratically at the highway scale.

HIGHWAY URBANISATION AND THE CHALLENGES TO DECENTRALISATION

The territorial transformations along Bangalore and Pune's highways are not an aberrant form of urbanisation unique to these cities. They represent a new and developing pattern of urbanisation in India: research forecasts that by 2021, 70–90 per cent of India's urban population will live and work along highways (Sivaramakrishnan and Singh 2001; Sivaramakrishnan 2006), as well as in other developing countries. The UN-HABITAT has identified 'urban corridors' as the 'shape of things to come' (UN-HABITAT 2010). In their 2008 report on the state of African Cities, HABITAT focused on Africa's urban corridors, including the Cairo–Suez, Cairo–Alexandria and Cairo–Said highways in North Africa; the transnational Greater Ibadan–Lagos–Accra highway that cuts across Nigeria, Benin, Togo and Ghana in West Africa; the Nairobi–Mombasa and Kampala–Entebbe highways in East Africa; and the Johannesburg–Pretoria and Maputo–Johannesburg highways in South Africa (UN-HABITAT 2008). A central challenge to this type of highway urbanisation is the absence of regional governance structures that can regulate their growth, leading to 'institutional fragmentation', 'continued spatial segregation of the urban poor', 'private real estate interests shaping most new development' and 'environmental challenges [due to urban sprawl]' (UN-HABITAT 2008: 69). The transnational highways like the 600-km Greater Ibadan–Lagos–Accra one and the 1500-km Beijing–Tokyo corridors complicate the institutional question as they cut across national boundaries, posing problems of fragmentation and poor coordination among sovereign states (Ibid.: 98–99). Highway urbanisation is emerging as a dominant narrative of urbanisation not only in developing countries, but also in the 'advanced industrial' ones (Lang and Dhavale 2005; Dewar and Epstein 2007). By 2050, the inter-state highways in the US are expected to accommodate 70 per cent of the country's population growth and 80 per cent of its employment growth (Lang and Dhavale 2005; Dewar and Epstein 2007).

This research is set within the context of India's 1991 decentralisation policies: the 73rd Constitutional Amendment Act for village governments and the 74th Constitutional Amendment for urban/city governments, aimed at the devolution of decision-making authority to rural and urban local governments, respectively. The evaluation of India's decentralisation policies has attracted much scholarly and policy attention (Chattopadhyay and Duflo 2004; Besley et al. 2007). These studies have focused almost exclusively on the allocation of public services, with little or no attention to the effects of decentralisation on the allocation of land. The emerging trend of highway urbanisation has major implications for decentralisation theories and practices. First, as cities in developing countries expand into massive conurbations that have earned them the epithet of 'endless cities' (Vidal 2010), there is a reverse trend in politics with the decentralisation of decision-making to city and village governments. Second, the urbanisation along highways defies the binary classification of human settlements into urban and rural. Yet, decentralisation reifies the urban–rural dichotomy through devolving decision-making to urban and rural local governments. Third, as pointed out by regional planning scholars, '[t]oday, *regional planning* tends to refer almost entirely to metropolitan planning' (Dewar and Epstein 2007: 109; emphasis in original). But, metropolitan institutions remain centred on the city as their unit of analysis and action, and are unable to respond to political geographies like the inter-urban highways. In the few cases where the regional discourse expands to the scale of the highways, the analyses tend to be normative. For instance, the UN-HABITAT recommended establishing the Greater Ibadan–Lagos–Accra Authority as a 'supra-national' institution to manage the Greater Ibadan–Lagos–Accra corridor in West Africa (UN-HABITAT 2010: 99). But, these normative prescriptions remain pipe dreams, partly because there are other existing institutions that are already engaged in these planning tasks, and partly because there is no political incentive for states to form these institutions.[1] This chapter steps away from normative abstractions towards empirical realities, and investigates the performance of regional institutions that are emerging on the ground to deal with the highway land conflicts.

India is in the midst of a contested political debate on the question of how agricultural land should/can be acquired democratically to accommodate industrial and urban expansions.

After more than a century, the 1898 Land Acquisition Act (LAA)—framed by the colonial government for land acquisitions and which continues to legislate compulsory land acquisition in the twenty-first century—is finally being debated for amendments in Parliament. The political class has been forced to revisit the LAA because of the violent land conflicts the country has been facing over the past decade: the Singur protests that forced an automobile factory out of West Bengal, the clashes over land acquisition for the Yamuna Expressway connecting Agra and Delhi, the human wall formed by protesting tribals against the land acquisition for a steel plant in Orissa. Though an amendment to an antiquated colonial law is long overdue, this alone will do little to solve India's land problems. A point that is missed in contemporary Indian debates on land acquisitions is that none of these conflictual land cases uses the LAA for their coercive compulsory acquisitions. Instead, all of them used parastatals for land acquisition: the Singur lands, for example, were acquired not through the use of the LAA, but by the industrial parastatal, the West Bengal Industrial Development Corporation. The LAA authorises the state to compulsorily acquire land only for 'public purposes'. In India, as elsewhere, the question as to whether the compulsory acquisition of land for private companies for economic development constitutes a public purpose is a hotly debated and unresolved one (Alternative Law Forum 2003). The parastatals, on the other hand, have special legislation to acquire land explicitly for the purpose of industrial and urban development (Ibid.). It is these parastatals that are implicated in land controversies and they are the focus of this chapter.

Urban lands in most Indian states are managed by parastatals. Agricultural lands are managed by district-level revenue departments. Revenue departments were initially set up in the late nineteenth century during colonial rule to extract taxes from agricultural lands, which were a significant source of colonial revenue. Agricultural lands continued to be vested with the revenue departments after Independence. The revenue department's district collector (DC) mediates the negotiations between parastatals and agrarian landowners. Figures 2.1 and 2.2 map out the institutional actors and the steps involved in the consolidation and conversion of agricultural lands to (1) residential uses and (2) industrial uses.

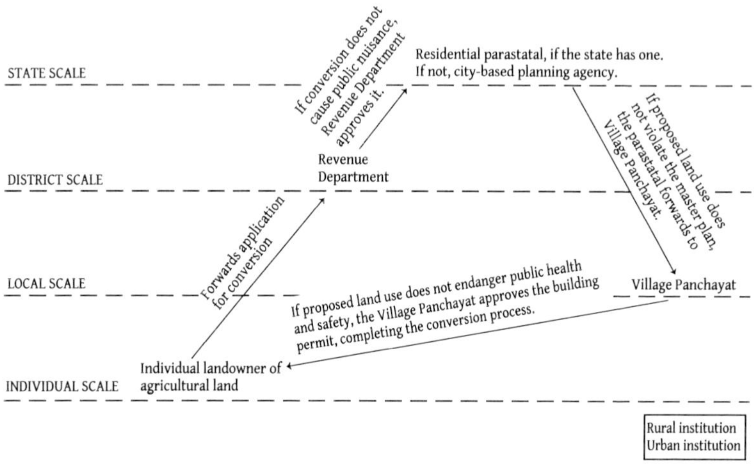

Figure 2.1 Land conversion from agricultural to residential uses

Source: Diagram prepared by author.

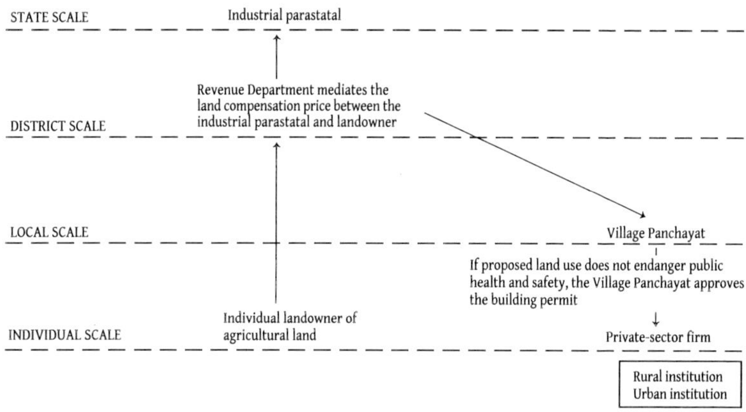

Figure 2.2 Land conversion from agricultural to industrial uses

Source: Diagram prepared by author.

The institutional actors in residential land consolidation and conversion are the agrarian landowners, the revenue department, the residential parastatal, if the state has one—the Bangalore region has residential parastatals like the Bangalore Development Authority, the Pune region does not—and the village panchayat. The actors are the same for industrial land consolidations, except that the industrial parastatal is involved instead of the residential parastatal.

A note on caste: The experiences of the agrarian landowners in land consolidation can be broadly stratified into caste-based experiences, with the opportunities, risks and uncertainties faced by the 'dominant castes'[2] being very different from those faced by the low-caste Dalits and tribals. The dominant caste exercises control over other social groups as landowners, as main sources of credit and as elected representatives of the local democratic institutions. The dominant-caste landowners along the Bangalore–Mysore highway are the Vokkaligas, and along the Pune–Nashik highway are the Maratha-Kunbis. The analytic of caste is a central part of this narrative, and I return to it in more detail later in the chapter.

CASE STUDIES: THE BANGALORE—MYSORE AND PUNE—NASHIK CORRIDORS

Bangalore–Mysore Corridor

The sample cluster of 28 villages along the Bangalore–Mysore highway is located in an area called Bidadi. The Bidadi area has seen dramatic changes since the 1980s, with large industrial and residential developments coming up amidst its otherwise agrarian landscape of millet and mango fields. This chapter focuses on three large developments in the Bidadi area: the Bidadi Industrial Area project, the Nandi Infrastructure Corridor Enterprises (NICE) township and the Bangalore Metropolitan Regional Development Authority (BMRDA) township.

The largest industrial development along the Bangalore–Mysore corridor (Figure 2.3) is the 750-acre Bidadi Industrial Area. Large multinational companies have set up manufacturing plants here. C.M.L. is one of the most powerful politicians in Ramnagara district. His family is the largest sugarcane landowner in the area. Due to the agricultural labour shortage in the area, C.M.L. has now diversified his economic activities to education. He owns an engineering college in Bidadi and spends most of his time as administrator of his educational institution. C.M.L. was the member of the Legislative

Assembly (MLA) of Bidadi constituency in the mid-1990s, when the industrial parastatal, the Karnataka Industrial Areas Development Board (KIADB), approached him on behalf of a Japanese company. Since economic liberalisation in 1991, India had shifted from a Central government-led model of balanced economic development to a more state-led model of territorial competitiveness. This shift meant that the state of Karnataka, in which the Bangalore–Mysore highway is located, had to compete with other Indian states to attract large-scale mobile capital. C.M.L. played a crucial mediating role between the industrial parastatal and his Bidadi constituents in consolidating land for the new industrial development.

> In 1996, a Japanese team had come to this area. They wanted a factory. They had four to five options—one was at Noida, another Pune, third was Chennai, fourth was this one, fifth was Hyderabad. D. C. Thimmiah was the chief development officer at KIADB. We were close. He met me and told me the team is coming: 'I will bring them here, whatever support you can give, give it.' I attended the meeting, farmers on one side, [Japanese company] officers and state government officers on the other. I, as MLA, was in *dhoti* [a traditional garment worn by Indian males] and ordinary shirt, as though I was also one of the farmers. In the meeting, I assured them not to worry...That evening, when we were waiting with the Japanese [company] representatives, without informing, unofficially, Mr. Chandrababu Naidu [then chief minister of Andhra Pradesh, the state in which Hyderabad is located] arrived here at the [hotel] to meet the [Japanese] team. Any convenience they wanted, he was willing to give: please come to Hyderabad. There was an invitation from the chief minister of Maharashtra to go to Pune.[3]

C.M.L. was at the crossfire of multiple, competing interests—the KIADB was applying pressure to find land for the Japanese company; at the same time, he could not afford to alienate his agrarian constituents through forcible land acquisition. Faced with these pressures, the best way to acquire large tracts of land for industry without agitating voters is to appropriate common lands for industrial development. The district-level revenue

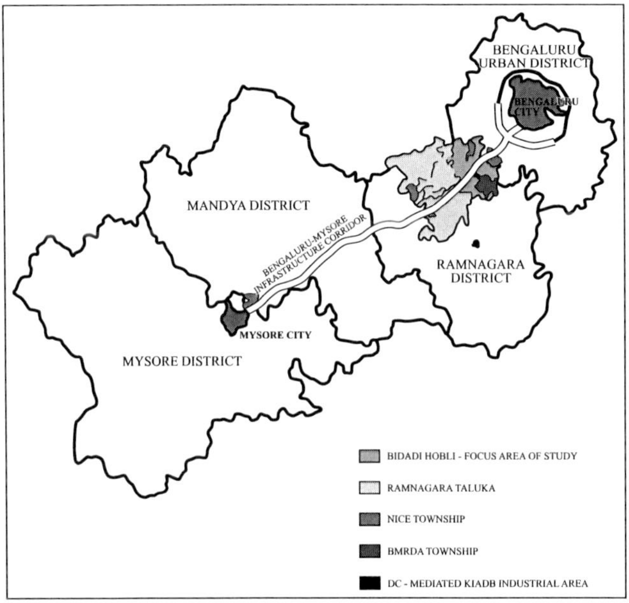

Figure 2.3 Parastatal regulated developments along the Bangalore–Mysore Highway

Source: Township locations obtained from BMRDA by author. Map prepared by author.

department owns all common lands within villages. To minimise political unrest, the MLA and the DC identified the Bidadi area with its large tracts of common land as the site for the industrial area. The revenue department handed over the 144 acres of *gomala* land—common lands used as grazing grounds for cattle—to the KIADB. The DC then proceeded to negotiate with the 500-odd farmers of the plots adjacent to the grazing lands. Most of these farmers were peasant agriculturalists, with small landholdings of less than 4 acres. The DC, as the price-fixing authority, negotiated a land compensation rate with the farmers, and the negotiations were completed without any protests. The KIADB sold the acquired lands to 20 large industrial firms. C.M.L.'s family continues to be active in Bidadi politics: his son is now an elected representative of the village panchayat.

Landowners who gave up their lands for the industrial development have now transitioned to the industrial economy. Local residents aspire to permanent jobs in these industries, but many of them, even those with the requisite skills, are employed as unskilled daily-wage and contract labourers. The factories are reluctant to employ local labour for fear of unionisation, but to avoid social unrest they permanently employ residents who are recommended by the village panchayat. The Bidadi Industrial Area is located within three village panchayats: Ittamadu, Manchanayakahalli and Bidadi. Sitamma is a Dalit-elected representative of Ittamadu village panchayat, and she outlined the procedure for a village resident to get a job in the factory:

> You [the person looking for a factory job] go to the *adhyaksh* [head of the elected representatives] and give him a form. The factory will only accept you if the *panchayat* recommends you. The factory does not take local labour because they will do *galatta* [stir trouble]. But *adhyaksh phone madthare* [the adhyaksh will call], then they will agree. You cannot go directly to the factory for a job, it is only through recommendation. You need good marks in the exams. It works on recommendation and education. These recommendations are for permanent jobs, and sometimes even for *coolie* [daily wage] jobs.[4]

Sitamma echoed the phrase 'adhyaksh phone madthare' multiple times during our conversation, reiterating the critical role of the village panchayat head as the gatekeeper of these factory jobs. To fulfil Sitamma's urban aspirations for her son she is educating him in engineering and is confident that he will get a permanent factory job on graduating:

> My son is in diploma college in Jnanabharati [a college in Bangalore]...I cannot give him too much, the least I can do is give him an *olle jeevana* [good life]. After that [his diploma], he will get work in the factory.

Village residents with close connections to the elected representatives have brighter prospects of landing the coveted permanent factory jobs. Others work as informal labourers, finding jobs through contractors who supply the factories with daily-wage labourers. Though Bangalore–Mysore had a highway connection, in 1988, the government of Karnataka decided to construct a new six-lane corridor parallel to the existing one. The rationale for the corridor was to decongest Bangalore's development by spurring regional development along the new corridor, and to reduce travel speeds between Bangalore and Mysore. In 1994, the state government selected the NICE: a consortium of three companies based in Pune, Pennsylvania and Boston. According to the build-own-operate-transfer contract, the industrial parastatal—the KIADB—would take on the responsibility of land acquisition for the 7,000-acre toll-based corridor and an additional 21,000 acres for five new townships that will be developed along it. The infrastructure corridor will be transferred to the government after 30 years, but the townships along the corridor will be sold to the private consortium. The NICE corridor and its five townships have been mired in litigation since 1994, with non-governmental organisations (NGOs) challenging the acquisition of agricultural lands for private township development. Karnataka has three competing political parties: the Congress, the Bharatiya Janata Party (BJP), and the Janata Dal (Secular) [JD(S)]. Though the initial 1994 contract was signed by the JD(S) chief minister, Deve Gowda, he is now at the forefront of the protests against the NICE project. When the BJP came to power in 2008, the NICE consortium aligned itself with the BJP, and BJP politicians accused Gowda of instigating the farmers for his own political advantage (*The Hindu* 2010).

In 2006, H. D. Kumaraswamy, then the chief minister of Karnataka, announced his intention of setting up the 9,000-acre 'knowledge city' project, called the Bidadi Integrated Township Project. The BMRDA advertised the project as 'offer[ing] the same or more comforts/facilities as available in Bangalore city minus the congestion, traffic bottlenecks in a serene and environmentally rejuvenating atmosphere'.[5] The township is located within the boundaries of nine village panchayats. The project was to be implemented as a public–private partnership between the BMRDA and the private developer. The BMRDA has the authority to plan the metropolitan region, but it does not have the authority to acquire lands. The BMRDA requisitioned the industrial parastatal for the state, the KIADB, to acquire land for the project. In October 2007, the BMRDA selected a Delhi-based builder and a Dubai-based company, in a 50:50 joint venture partnership, as the project developers.

As the BMRDA was going through the process of selecting the developer, the agrarian landowners whose lands were to be acquired for the Bidadi township project staged a protest in the district headquarters and they filed a writ petition in the Karnataka High Court against the BMRDA for proposing to acquire cultivable agricultural lands. This landowners' association, called Ranganatha Rytha Hitarakashan Samiti, consisted of around 200 aggrieved farmers, and it was led by four of the largest landowners in these villages. The majority of landholdings in these villages varied from 1 to 5 acres in size; the four leaders of the farmers' association owned around 60 to 80 acres of fertile, irrigated lands. One of these large landowners, Shivanna, was a Congress politician, and his opposition to the project stemmed from personal loss and political rivalry. When I met Shivanna in December 2010, it was clear that he had moved from township protestor to partner:

> In January 2006, we did a *doddagalatta* [big protest]. The project did not have any benefits for farmers. Then the CM [Chief Minister, Kumaraswamy] called us. CM asked us, 'This is a good project, why are you protesting?' I said, 'Your project is good, but what is the benefit for farmers, for the losers?' He said the losers will get 60:40 deal—for every acre of land that we give up, 40% of the developed land will be returned to us. Now, we will not stop the project, but we need something that will benefit us. Through the 60:40 deal, farmers also get a valuable property...Here, the farmers are finding it difficult to practice agriculture.[6]

Due to agricultural labour shortages, larger landowners are agreeable to giving up their lands if the land consolidation deal is perceived to be fair. These landowners have learned from the Bidadi Industrial Area experience, and are willing to give up their land if they can also benefit from the land value increment of their re zoned lands:

> In 1994, the government gave farmers a good rate, INR 600,000 [USD$12,000] per acre, but the farmers did not know how to use the money, and the lands are now more than ten times in value. We do not want to be in that situation. That is why we do not want the money. Through the 60-40 deal, we will get valuable property.[7]

Apart from this financial arrangement, Shivanna and the other local leaders were offered targeted incentives to lure them to cooperate with Kumaraswamy on the project. Though Shivanna was a Congress politician at the village panchayat level in 2006, he is now an elected representative at the district level on a JD(S) ticket.

With the bust in Dubai's property market following the 2008 global financial crisis, the Delhi builder's Dubai-based partner withdrew from the partnership and the former too pulled out of the Bidadi township project. In 2010, the BMRDA resumed the project and invited requests for proposals (RFPs). The property market had changed since its earlier RFP, and one of the BMRDA decision-making bureaucrats said that a lesson learnt was against such megaprojects.[8] Township projects, like the 9000-acre Bidadi one, should be parcelled into a number of smaller projects and tendered to different developers, both for quicker implementation and to make more developers eligible for the development process. But the project inched along at a slow pace. The JD(S) lost the state elections in 2008 and the BJP came to power. A JD(S) local politician in Bidadi was positive that 'the Bidadi township will start in full force once Kumaranna [referring to H. D. Kumaraswamy as "big brother Kumar"] comes to power'.[9]

Pune–Nashik Corridor

The land cooperatives along the Pune–Nashik corridor (Figure 2.4) provide an instructive contrast to the Bangalore–Mysore parastatals. The first of these cooperatives is the Magarpatta township, formed in 2001. Though it is not located along the Pune–Nashik highway, I studied Magarpatta because it is the precedent

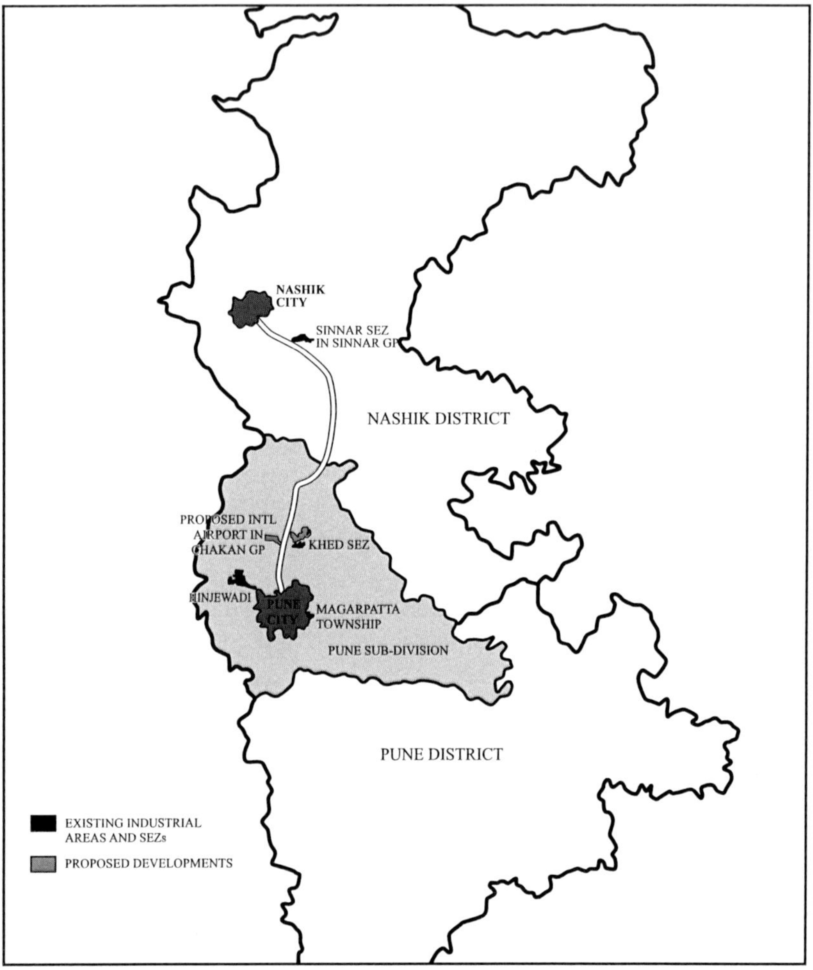

Figure 2.4 Cooperative regulated developments along the Pune–Nashik Highway

Source: Location of proposed developments obtained from MIDC by author. Map prepared by author.

for the other land cooperative cases. While the Magarpatta township is a voluntarily formed cooperative, in 2006, the first parastatal-mediated cooperative was formed in the Khed area, around 42 km from Pune along the Pune–Nashik corridor. Inspired by the successes of the Magarpatta and Khed cooperatives, other land cooperatives started proliferating in the Pune region. Soon after the formation of the Khed cooperative, the villagers of Avsari Khurd—a village adjacent to the Khed villages—pooled 3,500 acres of lands and approached the Maharashtra Industrial Development Corporation (MIDC) to lease their consolidated lands for industrial development. The villagers of the neighbouring villages of Chakan agreed to part with their lands for the proposed Pune International Airport if they could get a deal similar to the Khed farmers. The revenue department bureaucrats, instrumental in forming the Khed cooperative, negotiated a similar package of leasing 5,000 acres of land owned by farmers' cooperatives for industrial development in Sinnar, an area located 50 km from Nashik along the Pune–Nashik corridor. In this article, I focus on the voluntarily formed Magarpatta township and the parastatal-mediated Khed case.

The Magarpatta township is a 400-acre functional, middle-class enclave of apartments, bungalows, information-technology firms and schools. The landowning farmers who gave up their lands for the township own shares in the Magarpatta shareholding company in proportion to the land contributed. Before the 1990s, the Magarpatta area was the site of fertile sugarcane fields. The largest landowning family in Hadapsar was the joint family of the Magars, a politically influential network whose most prominent member, Annasaheb Magar, had been a Member of Parliament for the Congress Party in the 1970s. During his political tenure, Annasaheb Magar channelled many development projects to his home constituency of Hadapsar, including the setting up of a cooperative sugar factory to benefit the local sugarcane farmers.

The 1980s saw a wave of urbanisation-related changes sweep over the Hadapsar area: the rising demand for the Hadapsar lands to accommodate Pune's explosive urbanisation, and acute labour shortages with the Dalit labourers who lived and worked on the sugarcane fields now finding alternative employment in Pune's informal economy. In the midst of these changes, the Magars saw an opportunity in land development. Annasaheb's nephew, Satish Magar, took the lead in convincing the other Magar landowners not to sell their lands individually to developers, and to instead pool their fragmented landholdings to form a township in collective ownership. The erstwhile sugarcane farmers are now developers-shareholders of the Magarpatta shareholding company.

The Magars' long political history in the area, and their strong political connections, was a key factor in bringing the other farmers together in a collective land development experiment. The Magars' close political connections with top-level state government politicians of the ruling party, including the chief minister at the time, helped them navigate the land regulatory process. The state government granted the Magarpatta township two exemptions: an exemption from the Maharashtra Land Revenue Act condition, which stipulated that only agriculturalists can apply for a conversion of their agricultural lands to non-agricultural uses, and an exemption from the Urban Land Ceiling and Regulation Act, which enabled the state government to acquire urban lands beyond a certain threshold for redistribution for public purposes. Besides the state-level political connections, Satish Magar benefited from the trust relations that his family had cultivated with the area's sugarcane farmers over the past 60 years. A 70-year-old farmer, who gave up 4 acres of his land for the Magarpatta township, spoke of the landowners' trust in the Magar family:

> I have been farming here since 1965... In 1993, our Magar family had a meeting, and all of us were convinced of the [Magarpatta] project. We gave a signature, we did not ask anything, we just gave our signature. We trusted Satish Magar. Annasaheb Magar became an MP [Member of Parliament] from here. He started a sugar factory here for the farmers—20 km from here. All our sugarcane went to this factory. Like Annasaheb Magar helped us, Satish Magar is also helping the farmers with the township.[10]

Stories of Magarpatta's success spread to other regions around Pune. When the bureaucrats of a neighbouring group of villages in

Khed faced resistance against the consolidation of agricultural land for a new industrial development, they adapted the Magarpatta solution to reconcile their land conflict.

In 2006, an Indian company that manufactures automobile components identified 16,800 acres of land in 17 villages in Khed *taluk*. The Khed agrarian landowners opposed the proposed development, and eminent activists and politicians of oppositional political parties congregated in Khed to join the landowners' agitation. The industrial parastatal—the MIDC—approached the DC of Pune district to mediate the land consolidation process. The DC had worked in the MIDC for five years before his transfer to the revenue department, and he had a close working relationship with MIDC bureaucrats. He delegated the power to acquire lands to his revenue department bureaucrat at the sub-district level, Shyam Patil. As a street-level bureaucrat of the revenue department, Patil was familiar with the local leaders of these villages. Most of the villages along the Pune–Nashik corridor, and more broadly in western Maharashtra, where this highway is located, are characterised by peasant agriculture. However, the villages have a few influential families that own larger tracts of land and are politically powerful. Negotiations between the local leaders and Patil resulted in an agreement whereby 15 per cent of the acquired lands would be developed and returned to the farmers to form a land cooperative. Like the Hadapsar area in the Magarpatta case, the Khed villages also faced acute agricultural labour shortage because many of the agricultural labourers—mainly tribals—found alternative informal work in the factories coming up along the Pune–Nashik highway. Though the Kelkars and the other local leaders were eager to transition from an agricultural economy that is fraught with challenges—like labour shortage—to an industrial economy, they initially resisted the Khed development because they felt cheated by the cash compensation offered for their land. Patil was keen enough to recognise their urban aspirations and negotiated a more attractive deal of the land cooperatives with them.

Phase 1 of Khed city is located within four village panchayats: Kanersar, Nimgaon, Dhawadi and Shirur. Mohanseth Kelkar, the *police patil* of Kanersar (the village panchayat-elected representative in charge of law enforcement), and Ramarao Kelkar, the village panchayat *sarpanch* leader at the time of the negotiations, explained the Khed land consolidation process:

> Earlier, even we had protested against the industry. *Sarpanch*es of the 17 villages got together, formed an organisation and in that protest, we went to the district collector's office. We went there asking them to close it [the industry]. With Patil *saab* [Shyam Patil], we discussed what will happen if the industry comes here. Because of this discussion, four villages immediately agreed to the industry. Kanersar was the first village to agree.... Patil *saab* told us, 'you prepare your people, we will arrange whatever you need.' We went around all the farmlands in the village, what to keep and what to remove, we underlined that. We had a *gram sabha* [village assembly] and convinced the people.[11]

The local leaders of the four consenting villages were promised construction and other jobs as additional incentives to convince their villagers to join the project. When construction started in the Khed area, one of the projects was for the construction of homes for those villagers whose homes had been located on lands given up for industry. Mohanseth Kelkar, Ramarao Kelkar and two other friends got together to form a construction company to take over the construction contract for these homes. The employee of the automobile components company supervising the construction said the farmers' construction company was slow in its work, and quality was not up-to-the-mark, but these concessions had to be made as 'confidence-building measures'.[12]

Khed city is now owned by the Khed Economic Infrastructure Private Limited (KEIPL), a joint venture company between a private-sector firm, the industrial parastatal MIDC and the farmers' cooperative Khed Developers Limited. The residents of the four villages will elect one representative each at the gram sabhas, the village deliberative assemblies, and these representatives will participate in KEIPL decision-making. The chief executive officer of the KEIPL is a bureaucrat from the Maharashtra Industries Secretariat, with experience in industrial development. As of May 2012, houses for rehabilitating the displaced residents had been completed, and construction work had started on the boundary walls for the development.

INDIA'S HYBRID INSTITUTIONS: PARASTATALS AND COOPERATIVES

Emergence of Parastatals, Then and Now

Parastatals, as politically insulated institutions, have been accused of bypassing local elected representatives and advancing pro-growth developer and business interests (Burns 1994; Benjamin 2000). Bangalore's parastatals—the Bangalore Development Authority (BDA) and the KIADB—have been mired in litigation since the 1990s over their coercive land acquisition practices, and they have been branded as 'land brokers' (Heitzman 2004: 55) and the 'new decision makers' to whom decision-making has been 'outsourced' (Chamaraj 2009). These criticisms, though justified in light of the coercive land acquisition practices of parastatals, elide the long institutional history of parastatals in India and the changes in the functioning of parastatals since their emergence in the late nineteenth century up to now.

India's parastatals trace their emergence to the City Improvement Trust Boards (CITBs) set up in the late nineteenth century by the colonial government. The CITBs acquired agricultural lands outside the city boundaries and built India's first planned suburbs (Nair 2005). The CITB activities were partly a move to relocate the native poor from slums to these 'model hygienic suburbs' in response to the plague epidemics sweeping through colonial cities (Nair 2005: 51; Kidambi 2007; Legg 2007), and partly a legitimisation of colonial rule through demonstrating the civilising effects of these rationally planned suburbs over the unsanitary and chaotic native settlements (Nair 2005: 51; Kidambi 2007; Legg 2007). The colonial government framed the Land Acquisition Act—the subject of much controversy and debate in India—in 1898 to enable the conversion of agricultural lands in the peripheries into CITB planned suburbs. After Independence in 1947, the demand for urban land continued with the expansion of Indian cities under Nehru's policies of state-led industrialisation. It is at this point that the institutional histories of the Bangalore and Pune regions start to diverge. The planning of new suburbs, and the extension of infrastructural services (mainly water supply and sanitation) to them, is a capital-intensive activity. Cities like Mumbai in Maharashtra, with a flourishing industry and large tax bases, had the financial capabilities to manage these capital-intensive expansions of serviced land (National Institute of Urban Affairs 2004). Cash-strapped cities like Bangalore, on the other hand, turned to international financial institutions like the World Bank, which recommended the setting up of parastatals for more efficient land and service delivery (Sivaramakrishnan and Green 1986). In response to fiscal pressures, the Bangalore Water Supply and Sewerage Board (BWSSB) was established in 1964, followed by the BDA in 1976 as a successor to the CITB. Pune and Mumbai do not have land and water parastatals, and their land, water supply and sanitation responsibilities continue to be managed by the local government. The local governments in Mumbai and Pune in Maharashtra have experimented with innovative models of land consolidation, like the Town Planning Scheme (TPS)—commonly called land pooling or land readjustment, where the local government brings together disparate agrarian landowners within a certain boundary and reassembles their fragmented, agricultural landholdings into serviced plots of regular dimensions; and Transfer of Development Rights, where landowners give up their lands for public purposes in exchange for a transfer of their 'floor space index' (or floor area ratio [FAR] as it is called in the US) to another location. Though the Karnataka Town and Country Planning Act has enabling legislation for land pooling schemes like the TPS, the reliance on urban parastatals like the BDA and the KIADB to acquire land through eminent domain precluded the need for local governments to get involved in land consolidation responsibilities (Ravindra et al. 1997: 129). Not surprisingly, local governments in the Bangalore region lack the institutional capacity to implement land consolidation projects.

Conflicts and litigations over the compensation for compulsorily acquired land have been going on since the start of CITB activities in the late nineteenth century (Kidambi 2007). But, the land conflicts have escalated to an unprecedented level of political urgency, and the 1898 Land Acquisition Act is finally being debated and amended in Parliament. The reason for this belated debate of a century-old act is that, for the first time, the dominant-caste agrarian landowners are challenging the coercive acquisition of their agricultural lands for urban/industrial expansion. The rising environmental awareness on the need to protect grazing lands, lakes and other 'urban commons' is making it more difficult for bureaucrats and politicians to acquire these lands for industrial and urban expansions.[13] However, parastatals and politicians cannot coercively acquire lands from agrarian landowners as the dominant-caste agrarian landowners have been an important political constituency since Independence (Vanaik 1990; Varshney 1998). Dominant-caste agrarian landowners, like Shivanna along the Bangalore–Mysore highway, and the Kelkars along the Pune–Nashik highway, have aspirations to be a part of the 'India Shining' growth story and to transition to an industrial economy and an urban lifestyle. Coupled with these aspirations are the challenges facing an agrarian lifestyle: the dismal prospects of an agricultural future given the vagaries in weather conditions and the shortage of agricultural labour due to labour migration to the informal industrial economy. Though eager to transition to an urban/industrial economy, dominant-caste agrarian landowners will do so only under conditions that are perceived to be fair to them. They are learning from the past experiences of those who gave up their agricultural land for industrial/urban projects in the 1990s and early 2000s, and the raw deal they got in accepting then-prevalent market rates as compensation for land that is now almost 10 to 20 times in value. Local politicians and bureaucrats are innovating with new arrangements—like returning 40 per cent of the developed land to landowners in the BMRDA case and the formation of land cooperatives in the Khed case—that are more inclusive of this agrarian constituency in the benefits of urbanisation. Of the five highway cases studied, it is only the NICE project along the Bangalore–Mysore highway that continues to acquire land in a coercive, top-down manner. This could be because the NICE project is supported by the political party, the BJP, which has not developed a local, cadre-based presence in southern Karnataka.

The Bangalore–Mysore and Pune–Nashik cases alert us to the emergence of three types of agrarian landowning leaders, whose demands for more inclusive development are leading to reconciliatory arrangements like land cooperatives:

First, leaders like Satish Magar blur the distinctions between industrial/urban capitalists and agrarian landed elites. Such leaders have the political, social and cultural capital to '[blunt] the customary contradiction between industrialization on the one hand and the existence of the peasantry on the other' (Varshney 1998: 26), but they are few and far between.

Second, more common are leaders like Shivanna in the BMRDA case and the Kelkars in the Khed case. These agrarian landed elites have the urban aspirations to transition to an industrial/urban economy, but they lack the political and economic resources of the Magars to make this transition themselves. However, they are powerful enough as local leaders to effectively block any urban developments that are not beneficial to them, and the industrial/urban capitalists and the bureaucracy/politicians cannot ignore them.

Third, with decentralisation reforms like quotas for Dalits and women, a new political class of decision-makers is emerging at the village panchayat level. Some researchers point to the positive outcomes of these decentralisation reforms, like the changes in the allocation of public resources to benefit previously excluded groups like women and Dalits (Chattopadhyay and Duflo 2004; Besley et al. 2007). Others are more sceptical of these reforms, arguing that decentralisation has not led to a diffusion of power to citizens, but has consolidated power at the level of village panchayats (Peter Ronald de Souza 2000; Alsop et al. 2000). Though the verdict is still out, it is clear that the decentralisation reforms are changing the composition of local democratic institutions and unsettling entrenched constituencies like the dominant-caste agrarian landowners. The influence of this new class of local decision-makers on highway urbanisation remains to be seen.

The point to underscore is that, in emergent settlement transitions like the inter-urban highways, urban parastatals cannot continue with their old coercive practices of land acquisition. The local bureaucrats along the Pune–Nashik highway have played a central role in mediating land consolidation processes between the parastatals and agrarian landowners. The better performance of the Pune bureaucrats is partly because they are experienced in dealing with TPS and other land assembly methods, unlike the Bangalore bureaucrats, who delegated this responsibility to the urban parastatals, and partly because the Pune region has a long history of sugar cooperatives that is now being reworked into land cooperatives to benefit dominant-caste agrarian landowners. The next section focuses on the emergence and evolution of cooperatives in the Pune region vis-à-vis the Bangalore region.

Emergence of Cooperatives, Then and Now

The new institutional experiments around the Pune region have been praised by the Indian media and policymakers alike as 'inclusive capitalism' (India Knowledge 2008) and 'an equitable model for land acquisition' (Ganguly 2008). The first of these cooperative experiments is the voluntarily formed Magarpatta township. Magarpatta traces its institutional origins to the Pune region's thriving sugar cooperatives, first set up in the 1940s. This section asks why certain regions of the country, like the western Maharashtra region, where the Pune–Nashik highway is located, have a rich cooperative history, and others, like the southern Karnataka region, site of the Bangalore–Mysore highway, do not. Why did cooperative formation in a particular commodity (sugar) burgeon from the 1940s to the 1980s, and why are cooperatives in a different commodity (land) emerging in the same region? Within the Pune region, why are cooperatives emerging in different forms: as voluntarily formed cooperatives in the Magarpatta case and as parastatal-mediated cooperatives in the Khed case? The answers to these questions can shed light on the transferability of the idea of cooperatives to regions like Bangalore that lack a cooperative history, and on the conditions under which different forms of cooperatives can be formed in different regions.

The emergence of sugar cooperatives in some regions of the country, and not others, is linked to dominant-caste agrarian politics and the implementation of land reforms. Soon after Independence in the late 1940s, the democratically elected Congress Party implemented its first phase of land reforms for the abolition of intermediaries—like the *zamindars*, *inams*, *jagirs*—the non-cultivating propertied class inserted between the cultivators and the colonial state as part of indirect rule. With the overthrow of these intermediaries, a new class of beneficiaries—the cultivators who had worked on the lands of the intermediaries—emerged, who became the backbone of Indian democracy in the first few decades after Independence (Hardiman 1981; Dhanagare 1983). Some of India's most successful commodity cooperatives, such as the sugar cooperatives in western Maharashtra and the milk cooperatives in Gujarat, took root in regions where the beneficiaries from the first phase of land reforms—like the Maratha-Kunbis in the former case and the Patidars in the latter—demanded state support to successfully participate in the market economy (Pandey 1994). On the other hand, in the southern Karnataka region, the Mysore princely rulers wanted direct control over their subjects, and they leased out their lands to, and collected revenue from, their tenants without any intermediaries (Pani 1983). After India attained Independence, these tenants who went on to become agrarian landowners (the Vokkaligas in the case of southern Karnataka) had the agricultural expertise to successfully compete in a market economy, and did not need cooperatives. Western Maharashtra's sugar cooperatives got a fillip during the second phase of land reforms in the 1960s and 1970s, the focus of which was the Land Ceiling Act, dealing with the redistribution of surplus lands to the landless. The dominant-caste agrarian landowners who had pushed for the abolition of agrarian intermediaries in the first phase of land reforms resisted the second phase because it threatened their power base. The Maratha-Kunbis in western Maharashtra circumvented the land ceiling reforms by reallocating their lands to different family members (Pani 1983; Chandra et al. 2008), and forming sugar cooperatives with their extended family as members. In contrast, the regional elites in southern Karnataka—the Vokkaligas—exercised control over the marginal landowners not through tenancy, but through indebtedness (Pani 1983). The Vokkaligas are the main source of credit to marginal landowners, and the credit-based form of control precluded the need for forming cooperatives or other institutions to circumvent land redistribution (Ibid.).

The Magars are Maratha-Kunbis. The agrarian landowners in the Magarpatta area have been sugarcane growers and were members of the sugar cooperative factory set up in 1969 by Satish Magar's uncle, Annasaheb Magar. It is this long sugar cooperative history that enabled the Magars to transition from the sugar cooperatives to land cooperatives. But, the transition from one commodity cooperative to another is not as easy as it sounds. For instance, it is easier to convince sugarcane cultivators to join a cooperative because sugarcane is a highly perishable commodity: sugar cannot be extracted from it unless it is processed within 24 hours of harvesting (Sastry 2012). This is a strong incentive for sugarcane cultivators to send their crops to the sugar cooperative. Landowners, on the other hand, have the option of holding on to their land in anticipation of higher market prices, and it takes more effort to convince them to join a land cooperative. Sugarcane cultivators also face lower risks in joining a sugar cooperative because, at a time, they give up a semi-annual, or at the worst, an annual harvest of sugarcane production to the cooperative. Members of a land cooperative, on the other hand, face higher sunk costs and higher opportunity costs in giving up all of their land towards their cooperatives. It takes more convincing and stronger degrees of trust for landowners to come together in a collective land enterprise than it does to join a sugar cooperative. The long history of trust between Satish Magar's family and the agrarian landowners of the Magarpatta area was crucial to the formation of the land cooperative.

The Magars were successful in voluntarily forming a land cooperative because of their past cooperative history, albeit in a different commodity (sugar), more concentrated patterns of land ownership, and an agrarian landowner class that doubles up as the industrial/urban capitalists. On the other hand, the less-educated Khed agrarian landowners, with their fragmented land holdings, lacked the technical expertise and political will to replicate the Magarpatta success. The Khed land consolidation process would not have been possible without the mediation of the revenue department bureaucrats: the DC and his sub-divisional officer Shyam Patil. Both of these bureaucrats had worked in the industrial parastatal, the MIDC, before being transferred to the revenue department. As MIDC bureaucrats, they had been involved in 2003 in the land acquisition for phases 1 and 2 of an information-technology (IT) park, called Hinjewadi, on the outskirts of Pune. The agrarian landowners had received cash compensation from the MIDC for their acquired lands. By 2007, when the MIDC and the revenue department approached the villages around Hinjewadi for acquiring more land for phases 3 and 4, they were met with stiff opposition. Agrarian landowners had witnessed the rollercoaster journey of earlier landowners from 'farmers to millionaires to unemployed' (Ghoge 2009) and refused to give up their lands for future industrial expansion. In areas that lacked past experiences of collective action, the revenue department/MIDC bureaucrats realised that including agrarian landowners as equity members of a land cooperative can cultivate relations of trust among these landowners and the bureaucracy, thus increasing chances of collaboration for future industrial/urban expansions. As pointed out earlier, local bureaucrats in the Pune region had the institutional capacity to implement land assembly projects, through their past experience of working on the TPS. Interactions with Satish Magar following the resounding success of Magarpatta led to the idea of parastatal-mediated cooperatives for Khed.

In contrast to the Pune region, the reliance of the Bangalore region on the urban parastatals for land acquisition, the lack of institutional capacity to envision and implement land consolidation through non-coercive methods, and the lack of a cooperative history are some of the reasons Bangalore's local politicians and bureaucrats have not come up with institutional solutions like their Pune counterparts.

Parastatal-mediated Cooperatives as Emergent Regional Institutions

Pune's land cooperative experiments—Magarpatta township and Khed city—occupy an ambiguous institutional space between the state and the market. They overcome local agrarian landowners' resistances to industrial/urban land consolidations through the land cooperative dimension, but their registration as private companies allows them to structure capital like market institutions. The Magars were clear in their intention to set up 'a private limited company knowing well that the initiative involved so many people and therefore a strong leadership was required, which we found in Satish Magar' (Ganguly 2008). Regional institutions like the KEIPL are a complex assemblage of a land cooperative, an industrial parastatal and private-sector firm, with the intention of leveraging the comparative advantages of these different institutions. The land cooperative is essential in gaining the trust and consent of agrarian landowners. The endemic problem of poor land records, unclear land titles and property disputes in India makes direct land transactions between private-sector firms and agrarian landowners risky for the private sector. However, when land is acquired by the state and transferred to the private-sector firm, the transferred land is declared free of encumbrances. The parastatal plays a crucial role in negotiating with a large number of fragmented landowners, and conveying encumbered land to the private sector. The private-sector firm has the technical and financial expertise to deal with such large-scale industrial/property developments. Complex hybrid institutions like the KEIPL leave many questions unanswered. In this complex interlinking of a cooperative with a private for-profit company, whose interests—agrarian landowners or industrialists—is the KEIPL accountable to? How are clashes in interests reconciled within the organisation? How are risks allocated among these different institutional actors? Are our current regulatory institutions—the Registrar of Cooperatives for cooperatives, the Committee for Public Sector Undertakings for public companies and the Registrar of Companies for private-sector companies—capable of regulating these complex hybrids that lie somewhere between public and private institutions? These questions form the basis for articulating criteria for evaluating the performance of regional institutions in allocating land at the trans-local scale, and I turn to this point in the concluding section.

CONCLUSION: NEGOTIATED DECENTRALISATION

The urgent demand for agricultural lands along highways to accommodate rapid urban and industrial expansions, the inability of urban and rural local governments in managing these trans-local land transformations and the agitations of a politically important constituency—the dominant-caste agrarian landowners—for inclusion in the benefits of the new highway developments are impelling local politicians and bureaucrats to experiment with new regional institutions to manage these highway urbanisations. The parastatal-mediated cooperatives are one such example in India. Other countries that are facing similar land and urbanisation challenges are also coming up with context-specific responses to these large-scale territorial transformations. For instance, joint venture companies (Ding 2004) and shareholding cooperative companies (Hsing 2010) are emerging as a common response to land conflicts in China. Similar to the dominant-caste agrarian landowners in India, the organised village collectives in China have been at the forefront of retaliations against the urban governments' requisitioning of agrarian lands from collectives for sale to industrialists and property developers. Negotiations between village collectives and urban governments have led to the reorganisation of village collectives into shareholding cooperative companies, with the urban government returning a certain percentage of appropriated, re-zoned land to these shareholding companies (Ibid.: 122–55).

These findings challenge our conventional assumptions of decentralisation, as a unidirectional devolvement of decision-making from a higher to lower level of government. Instead, I use the term 'negotiated decentralisation' to reflect the actual back and forth tug-of-war between local and regional actors in managing trans-local geographies like highway urbanisations. The negotiated solutions—like parastatal-mediated cooperatives in India and shareholding cooperative companies in China—are contingent responses to local centres of power, the institutional forms through which these local interests have historically articulated themselves, and the reworking of these existing institutions to new forms to reconcile the new challenges of urbanisation. These negotiated solutions defy our conventional categories of local–regional and urban–rural, with the emergence of leaders like Satish Magar, who straddle these categories. Instead of simplified normative abstractions, these empirical complexities can provide the grist for crafting new grounded theories on emergent phenomena like highway urbanisation and regional institutions.

NOTES

1. Studies in other sectors like health also point to the difficulties of forming new institutions. For instance, Donnegan argues that new village-level institutions to monitor India's National Rural Health Mission programme were not formed because these 'new entit[ies] imposed by upstream policy makers [are] incompatible [with] preexisting social relationships downstream' (Donnegan 2011: 63).

2. Sociologist M. N. Srinivas coined the term 'dominant caste' to describe social groups that '[preponderate] numerically over the other castes and ... [wield] preponderant economic and political power. A large and powerful caste group can more easily be dominant if its position in the local caste hierarchy is not too low.' See Srinivas (1955).

3. Interview with author, 28 April 2011.

4. Interview with author, 25 April 2011.

5. BMRDA Township brochures, copy with author.

6. Interview with author, 1 April 2011.

7. Interview with author, 1 April 2011.

8. Interview with author, 6 April 2011.

9. Interview with author, 4 April 2011.

10. Interview with author, 23 May 2011.

11. Interview with author, 15 January 2011.

12. Interview with author, 18 January 2011.

13. The Indian journal, the *Economic & Political Weekly*, launched a selection of papers on the 'urban commons'—common resources—in its 2011 Review of Urban Affairs, and some of the papers looked specifically at the depletion of water bodies and common lands because of unregulated urbanisation (*Economic & Political Weekly* 66 (50), 10 December 2011). On the government side, the Karnataka legislature set up the Karnataka Public Lands Corporation for investigating the encroachments on government lands, and for recommendations to existing laws to prevent these encroachments (Karnataka Legislature Joint House Committee 2011).

REFERENCES

Alsop, Ruth J., Anirudh Krishna and Disa Sjoblom. 2000. 'Are Gram Panchayats Inclusive? Report of a Study Conducted in Rajasthan and Madhya Pradesh'. Background Paper No. 3, *Overview of Rural Decentralization in India*, Volume 3, The World Bank. Available at http://

www1.worldbank.org/publicsector/civilservice/june2004seminar/RuralDecent.pdf (accessed on 1 August 2011).

Alternative Law Forum. 2003. *Of Master Plans and Illegalities in an Era of Transition*. Bangalore: Alternative Law Forum.

Benjamin, Solomon. 2000. 'Governance, Economic Settings and Poverty in Bangalore'. *Environment and Urbanization* 12(1): 35–56.

Besley, Timothy, Rohini Pande and Vijayendra Rao. 2007. 'Political Economy of Panchayats in South India'. *Economic & Political Weekly* 42(8): 661–66.

Burns, Nancy. 1994. *The Formation of American Local Governments: Private Values in Public Institutions*. New York: Oxford University Press.

Chamaraj, Kathyayini. 2009. 'Parastatals and Task Forces: The New Decision-Makers'. *India Together*, 22 February. Available at http://www.indiatogether.org/2009/ feb/gov-parastate.htm (accessed on 2 August 2011).

Chandra, Bipan, Aditya Mukherjee and Mridula Mukherjee. 2008. *India Since Independence*. New Delhi: Penguin Books.

Chattopadhyay, Raghabendra, and Esther Duflo. 2004. 'Women as Policy Makers: Evidence from a India-wide Randomized Policy Experiment'. *Econometrica* 72(5): 1409–44.

de Souza, Peter Ronald. 2000. 'Legislation and Administrative Reform'. Background Paper No. 1, *Overview of Rural Decentralization in India*, Volume 3, The World Bank. Available at http://www1.worldbank.org/publicsector/civilservice/june2004seminar/RuralDecent.pdf (accessed on 1 August 2011).

Dewar, Margaret, and David Epstein. 2007. 'Planning for "Megaregions" in the United States'. *Journal of Planning Literature* 22(2): 108–24.

Dhanagare, D. N. 1983. *Peasant Movements in India 1920–1950*. New Delhi: Oxford University Press.

Ding, Chengri. 2004. 'The Effects of Land Acquisition on China's Economic Future'. *Land Lines* 16(1): 11–13.

Donnegan, Brendan. 2011. 'Spaces for Negotiation and Mass Action within the National Rural Health Mission: "Community Monitoring Plus" and People's Organizations in Tribal Areas of Maharashtra, India'. *Pacific Affairs* 84(1): 47–65.

Foster, Kathryn A. 1997. *The Political Economy of Special Purpose Government*. Washington, DC: Georgetown University Press.

Ganguly, Rakesh. 2008. 'The Magarpatta Model of Land Acquisition'. *Infochange News and Views* (April).

Ghoge, Ketaki. 2009. 'A Pune Journey: Farmers to Millionaires to Unemployed'. *Hindustan Times* (March).

Hardiman, David. 1981. *Peasant Nationalists of Gujarat: Kheda District 1917–1934*. New Delhi: Oxford University Press.

Heitzman, James. 2004. *Network City: Planning the Information Society in Bangalore*. New Delhi: Oxford University Press.

Hsing, You-tien. 2010. *The Great Urban Transformation: Politics of Land and Property in China*. New York: Oxford University Press.

India Knowledge@Wharton. 2008. 'The Poor as Stakeholders: Can "Inclusive Capitalism" Thrive in India?'. November. Available at http://knowledge.wharton.upenn.edu/india/article.cfm?articleid=4336 (accessed on 6 June 2011).

Karnataka Legislature Joint House Committee. 2011. *Bangalore City/Urban District Encroachment of Government Lands*, Interim Report Parts 1 and 2. February and July.

Kidambi, Prashant. 2007. *The Making of an Indian Metropolis: Colonial Governance and Public Culture in Bombay, 1890–1920*. Hampshire: Ashgate.

Lang, Robert E., and Dawn Dhavale. 2005. 'America's Megapolitan Areas'. *Land Lines* 17(3): 1–4.

Legg, Stephen. 2007. *Spaces of Colonialism: Delhi's Urban Governmentalities*. Malden, MA: Blackwell Publishing.

Nair, Janaki. 2005. *The Promise of the Metropolis: Bangalore's Twentieth Century*. New Delhi: Oxford University Press.

National Institute of Urban Affairs. 2004. *Urban Governance Decentralization in India: A Review*. New Delhi: National Institute of Urban Affairs.

Pandey, Vikash N. 1994. 'Agrarian Transformation and Co-operatives: Continuity and Change'. *Economic & Political Weekly* 29(15): 863–69.

Pani, Narendar. 1983. *Reforms to Pre-empt Change: Land Legislation in Karnataka*. New Delhi: Concept Publishing House.

Ravindra, A., B. K. Chandrashekar, V. Govindraj and P. S. S. Thomas. 1997. *The Committee on Urban Management of Bangalore City*, Report Submitted to Government of Karnataka. Bangalore: Government of Karnataka.

Sastry, Trilochan. 2012. 'How Commodity Cooperatives Differ from Milk or Sugar Cooperatives'. Available at http://www.techsangam.com/2011/08/01/how-commodity-cooperatives-differ-from-milk-sugar-cooperatives/ (accessed on 27 July 2012).

Sivaramakrishnan, K. C. 2006. *Growth in Urban India: Issues of Governance*. New Delhi: Center for Policy Research.

Sivaramakrishnan, K. C., and B. N. Singh. 2001. *Paper on Urbanization*. New Delhi: Government of India, Planning Commission.

Sivaramakrishnan, K. C., and Leslie Green. 1986. *Metropolitan Management: The Asian Experience*. New York: Oxford University Press.

Srinivas, M. N. 1955. 'The Social System of a Mysore Village'. In *Village India*, ed. Marriot Mckim, 1–35. Chicago: University of Chicago Press.

The Hindu. 2010. 'Yeddyurappa Takes Swipe at Deve Gowda'. 5 January. Available at https://www.thehindu.com/news/national/karnataka// article60631731.ece.

UN-HABITAT. 2008. *The State of African Cities*. Nairobi: United Nations Human Settlements Program.

———. 2010. *State of the World's Cities 2010–11: Bridging the Urban Divide*. Nairobi: United Nations Human Settlements Program.

Vanaik, Achin. 1990. *The Painful Transition: Bourgeois Democracy in India*. London: Verso.

Varshney, Ashutosh. 1998. *Democracy, Development and the Countryside: Urban-Rural Struggles in India*. Cambridge: Cambridge University Press.

Vidal, John. 2010. 'UN Report: World's Biggest Cities Merging into "Mega-regions"'. *Guardian*, 22 March. Available at http://www.guardian.co.uk/world/2010/mar/22/un-cities-mega-regions (accessed on 2 August 2011).

Whyte, Willaim Foote, and Kathleen King Whyte. 1991. *Making Mondragon: The Growth and Dynamics of the Worker Cooperative Complex*. Ithaca, NY: Cornell University.

3

Scaling Up, Scaling Down

State Rescaling along the Delhi–Mumbai Industrial Corridor[1]

SHRIYA ANAND AND NEHA SAMI

> In the long run, these corridors will make a paradigm shift in India's urbanisation and manufacturing growth.
>
> —Amitabh Kant (former Chairman, Delhi-Mumbai Industrial Corridor Development Corporation) (Kant 2016)

> If you don't plan big cities well in advance, people will move to existing cities which will expand in an unplanned way, leading to a proliferation of slums. You need magnet cities that can take the influx of people looking for jobs. You need to wean them away to the new cities, so that the temptation of going to old cities will diminish.
>
> —Amitabh Kant (former Chairman, Delhi-Mumbai Industrial Corridor Development Corporation) (Bhaskar 2011)

The Indian national and state governments are actively building policies that target urban regions as potential drivers of economic growth. The government has begun to frame specific types of industrial and economic development policies that have led to the emergence of different urban forms. These include the development of Special Economic Zones (SEZs), National Investment and Manufacturing Zones (NIMZs), and new towns in and around existing urban regions that focus on specific types of industrial and economic activities. Perhaps one of the most ambitious strategies is the push to develop industrial corridors between major Indian cities, which the Indian national government has embraced as a key development strategy.

There are several other examples of industrial corridors in other parts of the world, including East Asia and the US, which were leveraged and developed to take advantage of high-density development and the clustering of businesses and labour. The Tokyo–Osaka corridor, upon which the Delhi–Mumbai Industrial Corridor (DMIC) has been modelled, is among the oldest, and was instrumental in Japan's transition to an industrial economy (Macomber and Muthuram 2014). Another Asian example comes from South Korea, where the Seoul–Busan corridor has become the country's main axis for industrial and urban development. Drawing on the Tokyo–Osaka corridor, the DMIC in India has been conceived as an industrial investment destination meant to attract domestic and international capital. Work on the DMIC is already underway while several other corridors are being planned (Department of Industrial Policy and Promotion [DIPP] 2014a).

The Government of India and its officials see the development of these industrial corridors as a means to enable India's ongoing urban transition, while simultaneously propelling economic growth by attracting domestic and international capital to invest in and along these corridor regions, as the above quotes suggest. The new industrial towns along these corridors are meant to act as magnets for migrants and job seekers, providing alternative employment locations to the older metros like Mumbai or Delhi. However, as Nair writes in the context of the Nandi Infrastructure Corridor Enterprises (NICE) corridor in Karnataka, these plans draw 'nothing from the historical failure of satellite towns or of other similar plans to act as counter-magnets to the metropolis' (2015: 58). The planning and development of large cities of an unprecedented scale, such as Dholera (Datta 2015a, 2015b), are also setting important precedents for urban governance. In Dholera, and other cities like it, there is no provision for a city government or an elected local body. These settlements will be planned and governed by a Regional Development Authority (RDA), and all the members of the RDA will be appointed by the respective state governments.[2]

In this chapter, we focus explicitly only on the planning and governance arrangements along the DMIC, focusing on two states (Gujarat and Rajasthan) through which the majority (67 per cent) of the corridor passes. In particular, we ask what the planning and implementation of megaprojects such as the DMIC implies for state rescaling in the Indian context. Recent studies in post-liberalisation India (Grant and Nijman 2004; Ren and Weinstein 2008; Kennedy 2014) have highlighted different ways in which the state in India is being restructured and rescaled. Most of the earlier work on rescaling, including the aforementioned studies, has focused on urban regions and dealt with the state restructuring in an urban context (MacLeod and Goodwin 1999; Brenner 2003, 2004, 2009a, 2009b; Jessop 2004). We take this framework and begin to apply it to the question of industrial planning and the development of mega-infrastructure projects like the DMIC.

We situate this analysis within a comparative examination of the strategies adopted by the Government of India as well as the state governments of Gujarat and Rajasthan. Since the early 1990s, there seems to have been a growing tendency away from the earlier balanced regional development strategies that the Indian government had adopted until the 1980s, and a shift towards uneven spatial development, especially in post-liberalisation India (Grant and Nijman 2004). This seems to be evident also in the case of the DMIC, as we will show later.

The rest of this chapter is laid out as follows. The next section focuses on our methodology, followed by a review of the literature that will build the theoretical scaffolding for our chapter. The remainder of the chapter is devoted to an analysis of our data to explain the changing relationship between the state and national governments and their agencies, as well as the evolving role of private sector actors in the planning process. We end with a summary of our findings and directions for future research.

METHODOLOGY

The aim of this chapter is to begin to develop a framework that helps us understand how the national and regional governments are rescaling and restructuring by studying the governance and planning arrangements of megaprojects. We are also interested in understanding relationships between various stakeholders, especially the growing role of private sector players in urbanisation and development processes. Our research involved raising questions about causes of contemporary phenomena, drawing on multiple sources of evidence, making it difficult to separate the specific set of events being studied (urban redevelopment and governance issues) from the larger context of political and economic change in India. Given these constraints, a comparative case study approach emerged as the most suitable methodology for this project (Yin 1994; Campbell 2003).

Within the larger framework of the DMIC, we focused our primary work in two states: Gujarat and Rajasthan. This was because a large majority of the corridor (67 per cent) passes through these two states, and because we expected contrasting experiences given their levels of industrialisation and urbanisation.[3] We undertook fieldwork during 2013–15 in four locations: the state capitals Gandhinagar (Gujarat) and Jaipur (Rajasthan) where much of the planning was taking place as well as two selected industrial nodes of Vadodara–Ankleshwar (Gujarat) and Jodhpur–Pali–Marwar (Rajasthan). Studying the DMIC presented an opportunity for us to interrogate the nature of planning and governance between different levels of government and explore the relationship between state and non-state actors at an early stage in the implementation of a megaproject.

Our research focused on the planning and governance arrangements for the DMIC. Although plans for the DMIC have been in place since 2007, the project itself is still at a fairly early stage in implementation, with most projects within the larger DMIC frame still at the conception, planning or approval stage. Therefore, this work is largely focused on planning arrangements, rather than studying actual impacts on the ground. It extensively uses plan and policy documents, texts of relevant Acts and press releases by the government as well as insights from over 50 semi-structured interviews with officials in different departments of local, state and central levels of government, activists, developers, lawyers, architects, academics and other knowledgeable observers. We identified a set of initial respondents through a reading of policy and government documents, as well as through our individual networks. We used a set of questions to guide the interview process, although respondents were free to direct the conversation towards their areas of expertise or knowledge. Drawing on Fainstein's methodology in *The City Builders* (2001), we used a reputational method to identify respondents, relying on them to point us to others who would be potentially valuable informants (Fainstein 2001; Sami 2012). Since several of our respondents spoke to us under conditions of anonymity, they are not directly identified in the text.

We conducted our first round of fieldwork in Gujarat (Vadodara, Ahmedabad-Gandhinagar) and Rajasthan (Jaipur) in early 2014 and pieced together a picture of institutional responsibility divisions for planning, legal matters, land acquisition and operation of the project. We followed this with a second visit in late 2014 and another in early 2015 to Ahmedabad and Gandhinagar in Gujarat, and Jaipur and Jodhpur–Pali–Marwar in Rajasthan to assess the progress that the DMIC project has made and also to probe further into the various processes and governance mechanisms that were being created as the project advanced.[4]

BUILDING THE SCAFFOLDING

Much has been written about the liberalisation of the Indian economy in 1991, and the impacts that this has had on urban regions in the country (Shaw 1999; Ahluwalia 2000; Shaw and Satish 2007). In particular, there is a growing body of work that has focused on India's urban transition and the types of new settlements that are emerging in and around metropolitan areas including new town development (see, for example, Benjamin 2006; Searle 2010; Bhattacharya and Sanyal 2011; Sami 2013), as well as the phenomenon of urban expansion particularly along transport corridors (Chattaraj 2010; Balakrishnan 2019; Coelho and Vijayabaskar 2014), sometimes using the corridor as a logic to facilitate a particular imagination of urbanisation (Nair 2015). The most recent of this work comments on the emergence of 'smart cities' in the Indian context (Datta 2015a, 2015b), especially focusing on Dholera in Gujarat, which is one of the emerging DMIC cities. There is also a wide body of literature that focuses on megaproject development in Asia and other parts of the world (see, for example, Lungo 2002; Orueta and Fainstein 2008; Shatkin 2008). However, the scale and type of megaproject discussed here is of a different order and magnitude: the DMIC is an industrial megaproject of an unprecedented scale in the Indian context. It is significantly larger than any urban or industrial project undertaken so far in terms of its physical footprint (Kumar 2015).

As these new spaces of production (Brenner 2004) emerge, new opportunities for participation are created in which non-governmental actors can assert themselves and participate in urban governance and development processes (Sridharan 2008; Sami 2012; Sundaresan 2013). Another strand of literature has examined these questions in greater detail, including the emergence of non-state, particularly private, actors in the process of planning and development, termed 'privatisation of planning' (Benjamin 2007; Shatkin 2008; Weinstein 2008; Mahadevia 2011).

Further, as the Indian economy has opened up to foreign investment, capital investments have increasingly concentrated in more economically advanced regions, like existing metropolitan areas, industrialised districts and coastal regions (Chakravorty 2000). National and state governments are increasingly setting aside the geographically balanced approach to development that they had followed until the 1980s, in favour of promoting the development of specific regions (Chakravorty 2000; Grant and Nijman 2004).

As scholars have shown (Baud and de Wit 2008; Shatkin 2013), new arrangements of state power have emerged partly as a result of this process of economic integration and globalisation with clear implications on how governments in India function. For example, with liberalisation, the Central government has considerably reduced the degree of control it has over state governments, encouraging greater state-level initiatives, especially with respect to attracting investment (Ahluwalia 2000; Kennedy 2014).

This, however, does not mean that the national government in India is 'hollowing out' (Jessop 2004). National institutions, in fact, continue to be vital to the formulation and implementation of policy. However, the principal level of political and economic coordination is shifting and being reconfigured as urban regions emerge as key sites in this process of rescaling (Jessop 1994; Roy 2003; Brenner 2004). Even as urban regions become increasingly important as 'engines of growth' (Anand et al. 2014b), the actual process of empowering local-level government agencies, however, has been slow and varies widely from state to state in India. Currently, 'municipal governments in India are *not* major actors of this evolution and city policies do not generally provide an arena for deliberation and agenda-setting about urban futures'

(Kennedy 2014: 132; emphasis in original). As state (regional) governments reinvent themselves to take advantage of these emerging opportunities, they also simultaneously resist efforts by the national government to devolve powers to the local level, through efforts such as the 74th Constitutional Amendment Act aimed at providing locally elected governments in every city.

Most of the work highlighted above has focused explicitly on trends and processes of governance and urban development within city regions. Our work extends this to industrial infrastructure projects like the DMIC, which have tremendous urban implications even though they are not planned or executed by urban development agencies. We use the framework of state rescaling to understand the reconfiguration of state power and planning priorities.

STATE RESCALING

Processes of state rescaling in the Indian context are taking place both to facilitate and as a strategic response to uneven spatial development. This resonates with literature from economic geography, which finds that in India, 'the neoliberal nation-state is simultaneously a reduced state (less concerned about promoting regional balance) and an enlarged state (directing development to selected regions)' (Chakravorty 2000: 367). In this chapter, we assess processes of state rescaling using the case of the DMIC, and by analysing the various strategies employed by the national and state governments (of Gujarat and Rajasthan) to direct capital flows. In doing this, we follow Kennedy's approach of studying 'the current spatial transformations of state power taking place in India and the implications for economic governance at various scales, offering a fresh alternative to the sterile dichotomy between decentralization and (re)centralization' (Kennedy 2014: 12).

The rescaling of state power is occurring at two levels: first, through an attempt by the national government to promote particular locations (urban or industrial, while often conflating the two) as destinations for capital accumulation while maintaining control over project financing, planning, and approvals; and second, through an increased assertion of institutions at the state (regional) level over programmes and policies introduced by the national government, especially as state- or regional-level governments and institutions are increasingly able to attract and manage forces of capital accumulation to particular locations within their territorial jurisdictions, based on either locational, resource-related, strategic or pragmatic considerations.

Echoing Brenner (2004), this process of rescaling does not imply a reduction in the power of the national government or a devolution of powers to state (regional) governments, but rather can be viewed as a process of contestation and assertion of regional governments over processes of economic governance (Brenner 2004; Kennedy 2014). In this case, state (regional) actors continue to negotiate with the central governments for particular outcomes within frameworks set by the national government as they did earlier, but they now also compete among each other to attract capital investment through high-profile investor events and institutions such as Vibrant Gujarat, as well as create new institutions (such as special purpose vehicles and RDAs) that are directly controlled by state (regional) institutions to manage the new state spaces such as SEZs and special investment regions (SIRs) that are being created through economic and industrial policies. In the next section, we begin to look specifically at how these governance arrangements play out in the case of the DMIC.

GOVERNANCE ARRANGEMENTS IN THE DMIC

The idea of the DMIC originated with two related developments: one, a memorandum of understanding (MoU) signed between the Government of India and the Government of Japan in 2006 to signal collaboration on infrastructure development in India; and two, the planned development of the Dedicated Freight Corridor (DFC) between Delhi and Mumbai by the Ministry of Railways in 2005 in response to a concern about slow average speeds of freight traffic, and an increasing share of freight moving to road (Pangotra and Shukla 2012). Motivated by the Japanese experience of the high speed rail link between Tokyo and Osaka driving economic concentration and urban megalopolis growth, the Indian government decided to develop the DMIC as a buffer region around the DFC in partnership with the Japanese government (Japan International Cooperation Agency [JICA] 2009; Mangaonkar 2009).

Spread across six states, the DMIC is being developed within a buffer region on either side of the under-development DFC between Delhi and Mumbai.[5] A project of the scale of the DMIC requires coordination across several domestic and international stakeholders from the public and private sectors. The implementation of the project spans several different ministries (ministries of finance, commerce and industry, railways, shipping, road transport and highways, civil aviation and power, urban development) and crosses several jurisdictions.[6]

The governance structure of the DMIC is consequently extremely complex. The planning and development of the corridor is managed by the Delhi–Mumbai Industrial Corridor Development Corporation (DMICDC), which was set up in 2008. As interview respondents explained to us, the DMICDC is structured as an SPV that is constituted as a public corporation. The Government of India is represented by the DIPP within this SPV as the single largest shareholder with a 49 per cent stake in the DMICDC. Other shareholders include the Japan Bank for International Cooperation (JBIC; 26 per cent), the Housing and Urban Development Corporation Ltd (HUDCO; 19.9 per cent), the India Infrastructure Finance Company Ltd (IIFCL; 4.1 per cent) and the Life Insurance Corporation of India (LIC; 1 per cent) (DIPP 2014a). In 2012, a separate DMIC Project Implementation Trust was set up to oversee project approval and to fund project implementation (Delhi-Mumbai Industrial Corridor Development Corporation 2014).

The DMIC will be built in a phased manner, with each state developing industrial areas (IAs) and investment regions (IRs) within their jurisdictions along the buffer region of the corridor.[7] With the launch of the Smart Cities Initiative and the Make in India campaign in 2014, the IAs and the IRs along the DMIC are now being imagined and planned as 'smart' manufacturing cities to attract industry and accommodate future population growth (DIPP 2014b), of which Dholera in Gujarat is the first to be developed.[8] Therefore, the plan for the DMIC explicitly intends to facilitate planned urbanisation within this buffer region by creating alternate growth centres through industrialisation. The aim is to build 24 manufacturing cities, several logistics hubs and residential townships over the course of the project (DIPP 2007). As the quotes by Amitabh Kant, former chairman of the DMICDC, at the beginning of this chapter illustrate, the vision is that these new cities will help meet pressures of urbanisation and also lead India's economic growth for the next 20–30 years.

Interviews with state government officials as well as the Cabinet Approval Note for the Development of Industrial Cities in the DMIC (DIPP 2011) show that the government plans to build and develop these manufacturing cities in a phased manner, by developing core infrastructure in a smaller area at first, and then selling the appreciated land around the core area to finance the next phase of development. As state government officials explained, the national and state governments are constrained in their ability to finance industrial infrastructure at this scale. Therefore, the national government hopes to provide seed funding for the initial phase and then finance subsequent phases through the appreciated value of the land. This is different from the earlier approach that the Government of India had adopted for the SEZ model, discussed in more detail in the following section, where the onus of building and developing core infrastructure was on private developers. The development of each node or city in the DMIC will proceed through the creation of an SPV in which the Indian national government and state governments will both hold equity. The national government's equity contribution will be capped at Rs 3,000 crore per node, while the state government's equity contribution will consist of the land required for development.

According to the Cabinet Approval Note for the Development of Industrial Cities in the DMIC (DIPP 2011), each city will take about Rs 50,000 crore to Rs 70,000 crore to construct, and 60–65 per cent of the projects will be constructed on a public–private partnership (PPP) basis. The national government will contribute Rs 2,500 crore to Rs 3,000 crore per city for the non-PPP trunk infrastructure to kick-start the first phase of around 25–50 sq km and then undertake development of subsequent phases by ploughing back the gains from the sales into the fund corpus.[9] To illustrate, the DMIC Trust approved projects worth Rs 2,784 crore for the activation area of the Dholera SIR in May 2015 (Desh Gujarat 2015; *The Indian Express* 2015).

At the state (regional) level, the management of DMIC projects is undertaken by a nodal agency within each state, which is responsible for preparing the plans for projects, securing approvals from the DMIC Trust and managing the implementation. In the case of Gujarat, the Gujarat Industrial Development Board (GIDB) was originally deputed to be the nodal agency; however, the state government has since created the Gujarat Industrial Corridor Corporation (GICC), a new agency, which will oversee the development of the DMIC within the state.[10] In Rajasthan, the Bureau of Industrial Promotion (BIP) was the designated nodal agency, but there was a proposal being tabled to create a new office under the chief minister of the state that would directly manage the development of the DMIC.

In the sections that follow, we begin to use the state-rescaling framework (Brenner 2004; Kennedy 2014) to understand how the relationships between the national and state governments are evolving through the processes of urban and industrial development.

ROLE OF THE INDIAN NATIONAL GOVERNMENT

The national government continues to assert its power over economic governance, notably through the control over choice of location of industrial development. Officials with the Dedicated Freight Corridor Corporation India Limited (DFCCIL) said that in this case, the national government has chosen to prioritise the region between Delhi and Mumbai as the first industrial corridor to be built out around planned rail infrastructure, over other locations in the country, such as the region around the Eastern Dedicated Freight Corridor or the Bangalore–Chennai Industrial Corridor. This is in direct contrast to the previous experience with SEZs, where the national and regional governments did not retain control over location decision (Kennedy 2014). Further, similar to the European context that Brenner (2004) writes about, the national government seems to be increasingly setting aside considerations of promoting industrialisation in backward regions in favour of promoting concentration in more competitive regions in order to attract capital. The selection of the location for the DMIC, benefiting one of the most industrialised regions of the country, illustrates this.

Further, within the larger regional context of the DMIC, the first concept plan prepared by the national government as well as the Infrastructure Leasing & Financial Services (IL&FS) in 2007 also identified locations for development as IAs and IRs over two phases. These included Khushkhera–Bhiwadi–Neemrana (KBNIR) in Rajasthan and Bharuch–Dahej in Gujarat. Our interviews with state government officials in Rajasthan indicated that KBNIR is already an important industrial area in the state and has grown rapidly because of its proximity to the National Capital Region. Therefore, in addition to setting location decisions at a larger regional scale (the region between Delhi and Mumbai), the national government also attempted to select locations within the states, and these were locations that were already competitive for investors. However, as we will see in the following section, this attempt to fix locations for developing nodes has been contested in both states in different ways.

In addition to control over location decisions, the national government has attempted to retain control of the vision, planning and financing of the DMIC. Interviews with private sector consultants working with the national and state governments revealed the institutional design of the project: it is managed by the DMICDC, which is largely owned and controlled by the Central government. Projects are approved and financed through the DMIC Trust, which consists of representatives of the national government. The national government appointed IL&FS as the overall project management consultant for the DMIC which developed the overall concept plan for the entire corridor in close collaboration with the DIPP at the Ministry of Commerce and Industry. Further, as interview respondents told us, IL&FS is also consulting with the individual state governments and their agencies to identify and appoint consultants for specific projects at the state level, which are also paid for by the national government.

While there is significant private sector involvement in the planning of new settlements and infrastructure along the DMIC, the extent of their involvement is very much controlled by the national and state governments and takes place within a particular framework that these governments have set. Private sector involvement in the DMIC is largely focused on providing technical capacity and expertise, as well as on implementation and project management, rather unlike in the case of the SEZ experience (Kennedy 2014).

In the case of the SEZs, the onus of land acquisition and development was on the private sector, while state governments are primarily responsible for land acquisition and development for the DMIC nodes in a phased manner.[11] For example, in the case of Dholera, the first SIR being developed under the DMIC, the state government of Gujarat is bearing the responsibility and cost of acquiring the land and the national government is financing the first phase of its development.

In this model, the state hires private consulting firms to prepare plans, implement and build projects, and also carries out projects on a PPP basis, but at its core, the state acts as the developer and benefits from the appreciation in land value. For example, IL&FS is the overall project management consultant for the DMIC and developed the overall concept plan for the entire corridor in close collaboration with the DIPP at the Ministry of Commerce and Industry. In addition, IL&FS has prepared plans for some smaller projects within the DMIC, and is also consulting with the individual state governments and their agencies to identify and appoint consultants for specific projects at the state level. In Gujarat, the planning and development of individual nodes is being handled by separate consultants.

Therefore, in the case of the DMIC, the national government hopes to provide seed funding for the initial phase and then finance subsequent phases through the appreciated value of the land instead of relying on private developers to build core infrastructure like in the SEZ model. In the case of the DMIC, it is actually the national and state governments that will realise most of the benefits from the commodification of land along the corridor and the profits that will accrue from its development.[12] This contrasts with the case of other Asian urban megaprojects that 'represent an effort to realize a privatized model of urban planning to achieve state goals of the globalization of urban economies as well as corporate goals of the large-scale commodification of urban land and the realization of unprecedented profit through real estate investment' (Shatkin 2011: 93).

In addition to negotiating with private sector actors, and state governments, the Indian national government also has to simultaneously engage with international governments and their representatives as well as donor agencies that are driving specific types of development agendas and forms and the modalities by which these are executed. The Japanese government is instrumentally involved in the visioning and financing of the DMIC and has contributed US$ 4.5 billion (about Rs 28,000 crore) as a combination of support from JBIC and Japan International Cooperation Agency (JICA). JICA is also funding the building of the Western DFC between Delhi and Mumbai through a preferential loan agreement (JICA 2009), and Japanese firms are involved with the development of the DFC (Larsen & Toubro 2014).

While the DMIC is a centrally conceived and (partially) financed programme, it faces a set of challenges to its design and implementation from both state governments as well as communities, and critically rests on the state governments for implementation.

STATE GOVERNMENTS

One of the challenges to the design of the DMIC is the response of state governments to the attempt to fix locations within the states for development. Gujarat has been more successful at incorporating its own development agenda within the national DMIC framework. The original concept plan for the DMIC developed by IL&FS with the national government had indicated Bharuch–Dahej and Vadodara–Ankleshwar as nodes to be developed in Gujarat in the first phase of the project. However, as state government officials told us, Gujarat was already engaged in planning for the development of Dholera independent of the DMIC. It was able to negotiate with the national government to replace those nodes with Dholera, which it had selected as a location for development. In addition, Rajasthan has not been able to make much progress on the KBNIR region because of difficulties with land acquisition (discussed in more detail later).

In addition to negotiating with the national government for modifications in the DMIC frame, state governments have also resisted devolving democratic power to local levels. In the context of the DMIC, this has taken place through an establishment of new institutional actors such as SPVs and RDAs that will operate in DMIC cities such as Dholera and are directly controlled by state (regional) institutions. Despite a growing involvement of the private sector and international capital in urban and infrastructure development at the local (city) level, power remains concentrated at the higher levels of government, in line with evidence from other recent research on urban governance in India (Weinstein et al. 2013; Kennedy 2014). Although urban regions are being emphasised as drivers of economic growth and job creation, urban local governments have very little power or decision-making ability to influence or leverage this growth.

In India, the emergence of new, hybrid institutional actors across scales has not taken place at the city or metropolitan level, but rather has played out at the state (regional) levels. This includes the creation of new institutions such as the GICC to implement and manage these emerging projects. Although this entity does not yet have a website, selected state officials in the GIDB have moved to a new GICC office in Gandhinagar, where we met some of our interview respondents. It is state government institutions and agencies such as these that are increasingly attracting and managing capital flows, and fixing them in what they imagine and project as globally competitive spaces—these include city regions on the one hand and industrial enclaves on the other.

Despite attempts by the Indian government since the early 1990s to cede power to local governments through the 74th Constitutional Amendment Act and the subsequent conditionalities imposed through the Jawaharlal Nehru National Urban Renewal Mission (JNNURM), planning and decision-making powers for the DMIC remain concentrated at the national and state levels. Local governments of existing cities in the corridor buffer region are largely excluded from the planning process, and existing arrangements for greenfield cities draw upon Article 243Q of the

74th Constitutional Amendment Act to mandate that these will be developed and managed by RDAs that are appointed by and responsible to state governments rather than by elected local governments. While the 74th Constitutional Amendment mandated all urban local bodies to have democratically elected governments, Article 243Q provided for an exclusion for 'industrial townships', an entity that was not clearly defined, and a clause that has been used in multiple cases by state governments, including to develop SEZs (Sivaramakrishnan 2015).

The city of Dholera is being planned and will be governed according to the provisions of the Gujarat Special Investment Region (SIR) Act 2009 (Government of Gujarat 2009), which provides for an RDA for its establishment. Even though the imagination of Dholera is that it will be a city covering 920 sq km (one and a half times the size of Greater Mumbai), there is no provision for a city government or an elected local body. According to the Gujarat SIR Act 2009, all the members of the RDA are appointed by the Gujarat state government. Since other states do not currently have legal frameworks governing the establishment of SIRs, they are relying on Gujarat's SIR Act as a model to develop their own laws, as state government officials in Rajasthan told us.[13] Therefore, Dholera is setting an important precedent for the establishment of new cities under the DMIC framework, creating spaces of exception in governance terms that will exist and function outside the purview of current urban government frameworks.

This concentration of power at the state level is also evident in the case of existing settlements along the DMIC. While the coordination mechanism between the Central government and its agencies, particularly the DMICDC, and the state governments has been worked out in detail in the DMIC policy documents, the third tier of government (i.e., at the local/city level) has largely been ignored. Central and state-level agency representatives we interviewed had very similar responses to our questions about the planning of the DMIC, the selection of sites for investment, the project influence area, the phasing and other questions related to the operationalisation of the DMIC. However, city-level planning agencies had little awareness about the plans for the DMIC, and their perceptions of the plans were often very different from those stated by the Central and state-level agencies.

This is well illustrated in the example of Vadodara, a city that falls within the buffer zone of the DMIC in Gujarat, and is close to one of the proposed industrial areas as well as an interchange location between road and rail for the DMIC. Our fieldwork showed that although the city was in the process of preparing its 20-year Master Plan when the DMIC was announced in 2007, city-planning officials had not altered their Master Plan in any way to incorporate any potential additional growth arising from the corridor and its related investments. Part of this disconnect stems from the absence of any framework governing coordination between state governments and existing cities, even though the latter are likely to experience significant impacts.

State governments have also increasingly competed with each other to attract investments. This has been evidenced by high-profile investor events such as those organised by Vibrant Gujarat, as well as meetings between state chief ministers and international investors (NDTV 2015). This has also been through an attempt at relaxing regulations such as labour laws, as interview respondents in both states told us.

But states have unequal starting points, and we find that programmes such as the DMIC reinforce these trajectories of inequality. The case of Gujarat and Rajasthan explained below illustrates what Neil Brenner refers to as 'the systemic failure of this rescaled, post-Keynesian urban policy regime to confront the polarizing, disruptive, and politically volatile effects of urban geographical development at any spatial scale' (Brenner 2004: 16–17). Gujarat, one of the most industrialised states of the country, has been able to leverage the DMIC to facilitate industrial development through the creation of new institutions such as the GICC and the leveraging of existing institutions such as Vibrant Gujarat that markets the state as an investment destination to potential domestic and international investors.

By contrast, Rajasthan has yet to fully realise its industrial development potential, and has been struggling with implementation due to institutional and resource constraints. Even though the national government has set up structures and mechanisms to enable all states to access technical and financial support through the DMIC, the case of Gujarat and Rajasthan illustrates that this type of investment has the potential to concentrate resources in more competitive regions in the short run, leading to potentially destabilising socio-political forces in the medium to long run.

A case in point is the difference between the two states in negotiating for location decisions: while Gujarat was able to replace the Central government chosen nodes with its own selection of Dholera, the Rajasthan state government is still attempting to develop KBNIR despite difficulties with land acquisition in this region. The legal framework governing land acquisition in the two states has been another key difference explaining the differential rates of project progress in the two states. During the conceptualisation of the DMIC and the preparation of original plans, governments were still acquiring land under the Land Acquisition Act, 1894, which was replaced by the Right to Fair Compensation and Transparency in Land Acquisition, Rehabilitation and Resettlement Act (LARR Act), 2013. Consequently, the rates at which governments acquired land were now four times the market value in rural areas, and two times the market value in urban areas, making it more costly for government to acquire land under the new legal framework. Gujarat has historically had an alternative framework for acquiring land, known as Town Planning (TP) schemes, which allowed the state government to acquire land, develop it and return a smaller piece of land to the original landowners, who would benefit from the appreciation in value of the developed land. Because of its ability to use TP schemes to acquire land in the Dholera region, it has been able to move forward with implementation. In the case of Rajasthan, the land around the identified KBNIR node is largely private-owned, making the land acquisition process, under the LARR bill, expensive and lengthy.

Further, Gujarat has also put in place a legal framework governing the development of these manufacturing cities in the form of the Gujarat SIR Act, 2009. The Gujarat SIR Act, 2009, is essential for the creation of new settlements along the DMIC because there is no legal precedent for this type of development in the country. While the government of Rajasthan has been debating its SIR Act since

2014, it has not passed into law at the time of writing. Therefore, Gujarat has been able to leverage its institutional capacities because of its long history of industrialisation to negotiate with the national government and to make progress on implementation. As the above examples show, the state governments differ in their ability to leverage the development of large infrastructure projects, such as the DMIC, to further their own growth.

As the examples above illustrate, these regions are therefore not blank slates or 'greenfield' sites on which the national government can implement its planned development strategies; instead it needs to contend with and accommodate existing governance structures and priorities of the state (regional) governments (Greenfield 2015). It is these transactional processes that are causing the constant negotiation between various actors at national, state and local levels, which will eventually influence the ability of this project to be implemented in the form of what Watson (2015: 37) calls 'fantasy cities', and conform to the imagination of the central state and its planners.

CONCLUSION

This chapter has focused on the planning and governance arrangements along the DMIC. Drawing on primary fieldwork in Gujarat and Rajasthan as well as an analysis of government and policy documents, we have shown how the planning and development of an industrial and urban megaproject constitutes a rescaling of power and governmental authority at the national and state scales. This is not merely a question of the national government ceding power to the regional governments, but also an illustration of the constant contestation and negotiation that state and national governments have to engage in to achieve development outcomes. It is also becoming increasingly important to acknowledge and understand the role that non-state actors are playing in the development process. In particular, these megaprojects are being increasingly planned and built by private sector consultants in the case of the DMIC. In addition, supra-national actors like international governments, such as the Government of Japan, and donor agencies such as JICA, in the case of the DMIC, are also influencing the form and types of development. There is also an increasing shift towards concentrating investment and capital in already developed regions, leading to uneven spatial development and foregoing earlier goals of balanced regional development.

The development of large projects like the DMIC is setting a precedent of developing massive urban-like settlements at a scale not seen before in the Indian context. These new settlements are emerging as spaces of exception in economic as well as governance terms, as they engender new types of planning and governance arrangements in lieu of democratically elected local government. This chapter has begun to deal with some of these issues. However, questions remain about the implication that these new forms of governance have on existing settlements, the potential economic impacts of projects like the DMIC on local and regional economies, the environmental repercussions of these developments and the community response to projects like these.

NOTES

1. This research was funded by a grant from the International Growth Centre (IGC) foundation. Parts of this chapter have been submitted to the IGC foundation as part of the project-reporting requirements. This chapter was also partially supported by the PEAK Urban programme, funded by UK Research and Innovation's Global Challenge Research Fund, Grant Ref: ES/P011055/1.

The authors would like to acknowledge the contributions of Amogh Arakali, Jyothi Koduganti and Oviya Govindan to this research. We would also like to thank Ashima Sood, Loraine Kennedy and the reviewers for their very helpful comments. Any errors remain our own.

2. The development of these corridors raises several other questions and concerns. A full discussion of these issues is beyond the scope of this chapter. For more, see Anand et al. (2014a).

3. Of the major Indian states, Gujarat had the highest level of per capita output from the industrial sector in 2011–12 at Rs 25,843 per capita (using gross domestic product [GDP] data for 2011–12 at 2004–05 constant prices, and 2011 census population). By comparison, Rajasthan was among the bottom six major states with Rs 9,418 per capita. Rajasthan has also

been part of the BIMARU grouping of poorer states—Bihar, Madhya Pradesh, Rajasthan and Uttar Pradesh. These figures are based on data from the Central Statistical Organisation, Census of India and authors' own calculations.

4. As mentioned, this research was conducted over 2013–15, but has not been updated to reflect more recent changes on the ground.

5. The six states through which the DMIC passes are Uttar Pradesh, Haryana, Madhya Pradesh, Rajasthan, Gujarat and Maharashtra.

6. In addition to the ministries listed here, the following ministries are also listed in the DMIC Concept Note as possible invitees for decision-making: ministries for environment and forests, labour and employment, petroleum and natural gas, and chemicals and petrochemicals.

7. In the original concept note, investment regions (IRs) are specifically delineated industrial regions with a minimum area of 200 sq km, while industrial areas (IAs) have a minimum area of 100 sq km. For more details, refer to the DMIC Concept Paper, and the Make in India website (www.makeinindia.com) (Department of Industrial Policy and Promotion [DIPP] 2007, 2014a).

8. Although the original plans for the DMIC were formulated by the United Progressive Alliance (UPA) government in 2007 and envisaged the development of several IAs and IRs along the corridor, the National Democratic Alliance (NDA) government that came to power in 2014 embraced this within its larger agenda of developing 'smart' cities that will attract industry and manufacturing, create employment and promote growth, especially under the recently announced Make In India campaign (DIPP 2014b). While several news announcements in 2014 claimed Dholera as India's 'first new smart city' (Datta 2015a) as well as declared several of the other planned nodes in the DMIC such as Shendra–Bidkin as smart cities, the list of cities selected under the Government of India's Smart City Mission announced in August 2015 did not include any of the DMIC cities. Prior to the announcement of the Smart City list, government officials in Gujarat had told us that CISCO and IBM have prepared an IT master plan for Dholera keeping in mind principles of smart city design, and several news stories in 2014 mentioned the same. While Dholera and other DMIC cities might not receive financing under the Smart Cities mission in its current phase, the process of planning for DMIC cities might incorporate elements of smart city design, and this will be financed in the same way as the planning of the nodes.

9. The Government of India's contribution is Rs 18,500 crore (Rs 17,500 crore for 7 cities plus Rs 1,000 crore for project development by the Delhi–Mumbai Industrial Corridor Development Corporation [DMICDC]).

10. According to interviews with officials at Gujarat Industrial Development Board (GIDB) and Gujarat Industrial Corridor Corporation (GICC), both agencies continue to be involved in the development of the DMIC. However, the exact separation of functions is unclear at this point.

11. In the case of the SEZs, there were instances where state governments themselves were developing SEZs, and also assisted private developers by facilitating land acquisition. For more on this, see Jenkins et al. 2014.

12. This does not exclude the possibility of private developers making profits from speculative real estate investments in the region of the corridor based on publicly available plans for the corridor—indeed, news stories and anecdotal evidence from our fieldwork indicate that such speculation has already begun. However, these developers are not part of the official development or planning process for the DMIC. It is therefore important to distinguish this kind of speculative private sector involvement along the DMIC from the case where private developers are directly involved in developing the projects, like in the other Asian cases mentioned earlier.

13. At the time of fieldwork, the Rajasthan government was debating the proposed SIR bill, modelled on the Gujarat SIR Act.

REFERENCES

Ahluwalia, M. S. 2000. 'Economic Performance of States in the Post-Reforms Period'. *Economic and Political Weekly* 35(19): 1637–48.

Anand, S., A. Arakali, A. Jana, J. Koduganti and N. Sami. 2014a. 'Manufacturing Cities: Industrial Policy and Urban Growth'. Indian Institute for Human Settlements and the Rockefeller Foundation, Bangalore, India.

Anand, S., A. Revi and J. Koduganti. 2014b. 'Cities as Engines of Inclusive Development'. Indian Institute for Human Settlements, Bangalore, India.

Balakrishnan, S. 2019. *Shareholder Cities: Land Transformations along Urban Corridors in India*. Philadelphia, PA: University of Pennsylvania Press.

Baud, I. S. A., and J. De Wit, eds. 2008. *New Forms of Urban Governance in India: Shifts, Models, Networks & Governance*. New Delhi, Thousand Oaks, California, London, Singapore: Sage.

Benjamin, S. 2006. 'Inclusive or Contested? Conceptualising a Globalized Bangalore via a Closer Look at the IT-dominated Territories in East and South Bangalore'. Report for the research titled 'Inclusive Mega-Cities in Asia in a Globalising World', IDPAD.

——. 2007. 'Lifestyling India's Metros: The Elite's Civic Reform'. In *Ensuring Public Accountability through Community Action: A Case Study in East Delhi*, eds R. M. Sudarshan and S. Pande, 179–208. New Delhi: Institute of Social Studies Trust.

Bhaskar, R. N. 2011. 'Delhi-Mumbai Corridor will Create New Best-in-class Cities'. *DNA*, http://www.dnaindia.com/money/report-delhi-mumbai-corridor-will-create-new-best-in-class-cities-1510755 (accessed on 9 February 2016).

Bhattacharya, R., and K. Sanyal. 2011. 'Bypassing the Squalor: New Towns, Immaterial Labour and Exclusion in Post-colonial Urbanisation'. *Economic & Political Weekly* 46(31): 41–48.

Brenner, N. 2003. 'The Formation of the Global City and the Re-scaling of the State's Space in Post-Fordist Western Europe'. *Eure-Revista Latinoamericana De Estudios Urbano Regionales* 29(86): 5–35.

——. 2004. *New State Spaces: Urban Governance and the Rescaling of Statehood*. Oxford, New York: Oxford University Press.

——. 2009a. 'Open Questions on State Rescaling'. *Cambridge Journal of Regions, Economy and Society* 2(1): 123–39.

——. 2009b. 'Restructuring, Rescaling and the Urban Question'. *Critical Planning* 16(4): 60–79.

Campbell, S. 2003. 'Case Studies in Planning: Comparative Advantages and the Problem of Generalization'. Urban and Regional Research Collaborative, Working Paper Series. Ann Arbor, University of Michigan.

Chakravorty, S. 2000. 'How does Structural Reform Affect Regional Development? Resolving Contradictory Theory with Evidence from India'. *Economic Geography* 76(4): 367–94.

Chattaraj, D. 2010. 'Roadscapes: Everyday Life Along the Rural–Urban Continuum in 21st Century India'. Ph.D. diss., Yale University, New Haven, CT.

Coelho, K., and M. Vijayabaskar. 2014. 'On the Charts, Off the Tracks, Disconnected Development in Ambur Town, Tamil Nadu'. *Economic & Political Weekly* 49 (22): 101–10.

Datta, A. 2015a. 'A 100 Smart Cities, a 100 Utopias'. *Dialogues in Human Geography* 5(1): 49–53.

——. 2015b. 'New Urban Utopias of Postcolonial India: "Entrepreneurial Urbanization" in Dholera Smart City, Gujarat'. *Dialogues in Human Geography* 5(1): 3–22.

Delhi–Mumbai Industrial Corridor Development Corporation. 2014. 'Composition of DMICDC'. 1 September, http://www.dmicdc.com/cpage.aspx?pgid=5 (accessed on 1 February 2017).

Department of Industrial Policy and Promotion. 2007. 'Delhi-Mumbai Industrial Corridor: Concept Paper'. Ministry of Commerce and Industry, Government of India, Delhi.

———. 2011. 'Details of the Cabinet Approval Accorded on 15th September, 2011 for Development of Industrial Cities in the DMIC'. Government of India, http://dipp.nic.in/English/Schemes/DMIC/Past_Activities.aspx (accessed on 23 March 2015).

———. 2014a. 'The Department of Industrial Policy & Promotion—About DMIC'. Government of India, 23 March, http://dipp.nic.in/English/Schemes/DMIC/About_DMIC.aspx (accessed on 1 February 2017).

———. 2014b. 'Make in India'. Department of Industrial Policy and Promotion, 23 December, http://makeinindia.com/ (accessed on 23 March 2015).

Desh Gujarat. 2015. 'Modi Cabinet Approves Trunk Infra Development in Dholera SIR', http://DeshGujarat.Com/author/japan3/ (accessed on 17 February 2016).

Fainstein, S. 2001. *The City Builders: Property Development in New York and London, 1980–2000*. Lawrence: University Press of Kansas.

Grant, R., and J. Nijman. 2004. 'The Re-Scaling of Uneven Development in Ghana and India'. *Tijdschrift voor Economische en Sociale Geografie* 95(5): 467–81.

Greenfield, A. 2015. 'Zeroville-on-Khambhat, or The Clean Slate's Cost'. *Dialogues in Human Geography* 5(1): 40–44.

Government of Gujarat. 2009. Gujarat Act No. 2 of 2009. January, Gandhinagar.

Japan International Cooperation Agency (JICA). 2009. 'Japanese ODA Loan Agreement with India'. Dedicated Freight Corridor Project (Phase I)—Promoting Renovation of India's Infrastructure through the Delhi-Mumbai Industrial Corridor. Available at https://www2.jica.go.jp/yen_loan/pdf/en/5965/20091027.pdf (accessed on 23 June 2022).

Jenkins, R., L. Kennedy and P. Mukhopadhyay. 2014. *Power, Policy, and Protest: The Politics of India's Special Economic Zones*. New Delhi: Oxford University Press.

Jessop, B. 1994. 'Post-Fordism and the State'. In *Post-Fordism: A Reader*, ed. A. Amin, 251–79. Oxford; Cambridge, MA: Blackwell.

———. 2004. 'Hollowing out the "Nation-state" and Multilevel Governance'. In *A Handbook of Comparative Social Policy*, ed. P. Kennett, 11–25. Edward Elgar Publishing: Cheltenham.

Kant, A. 2016. 'Make in India: India's Vision for Manufacturing', http://www.amitabhkant.in/images/amitabh/interviews/Binder2.pdf (accessed on 9 February 2016; link discontinued).

Kennedy, L. 2014. *The Politics of Economic Restructuring in India: Economic Governance and State Spatial Rescaling*. Oxon, UK and New York, USA: Routledge.

Kumar, R. 2015. 'The World's Largest Infrastructure Project is Being Built in India—Stretching from Delhi to Mumbai'. *Scroll*, http://scroll.in/article/746736/the-worlds-largest-infrastructure-project-is-being-built-in-india-stretching-from-delhi-to-mumbai (accessed on 19 February 2016).

Larsen & Toubro (L&T). 2014. 'India's Largest and the First-of-Its-Kind Project in the Rail Sector'. Sojitz-L&T Consortium. Western Dedicated Freight Corridor Project, L&T, https://www.lntecc.com/homepage/multislug/demos/images/ti/sojitz.pdf (accessed on 23 October 2015).

Lungo, M. 2002. 'Large Urban Projects. A Challenge for Latin American Cities'. *Land Lines*, http://www.lincolninst.edu/pubs/PubDetail.aspx?pubid=544 (accessed on 6 August 2009).

Macleod, G., and M. Goodwin. 1999. 'Space, Scale and State Strategy: Rethinking Urban and Regional Governance'. *Progress in Human Geography* 23(4): 503–27.

Macomber, J., and V. Muthuram. 2014. 'Delhi-Mumbai Industrial Corridor: India's Road to Prosperity?' Harvard Business School, Boston, MA.

Mahadevia, D. 2011. 'Branded and Renewed? Policies, Politics and Processes of Urban Development in the Reform Era'. *Economic & Political Weekly* 46(31): 56–64.

Mangaonkar, R. 2009. 'DMIC Modelled along Tokyo–Fukuoka'. *Times of India*, 3 January 2009.

Nair, J. 2015. 'Indian Urbanism and the Terrain of the Law'. *Economic & Political Weekly* 50(36): 54–63.

NDTV. 2015. 'Rajasthan Chief Minister Vasundhara Raje Meets Japanese Prime Minister Shinzo Abe', http://www.ndtv.com/india-news/rajasthan-chief-minister-vasundhara-raje-meets-japanese-prime-minister-shinzo-abe-753041 (accessed on 16 February 2016).

Orueta, F. D., and S. Fainstein. 2008. 'The New Mega-Projects: Genesis and Impacts'. *International Journal of Urban and Regional Research* 32(4): 759–67.

Pangotra, P., and P. Shukla. 2012. 'Infrastructure for Low Carbon Transport in India: A Case Study of the Dedicated Freight Corridor'. United Nations Environment Program (UNEP) and Indian Institute of Management (IIM) Ahmedabad.

Ren, X., and L. Weinstein. 2008. '"Metropolitanizing" the State: Scalar Transformations and Mega-Project Development in Shanghai and Mumbai'. American Sociological Association Annual Meeting, Sheraton Boston and the Boston Marriott Copley Place, Boston, MA.

Roy, A. 2003. *City Requiem, Calcutta: Gender and the Politics of Poverty*. Minneapolis: University of Minnesota Press.

Sami, N. 2012. 'Building Alliances: Power and Politics in Urban India'. Ph.D. diss., University of Michigan, Ann Arbor.

——. 2013. 'From Farming to Development: Urban Coalitions in Pune, India'. *International Journal of Urban and Regional Research* 37(1): 151–64.

Searle, L. G. 2010. 'Making Space for Capital: The Production of Global Landscapes in Contemporary India'. Ph.D. diss., Department of Anthropology, University of Pennsylvania, Philadelphia.

Shatkin, G. 2008. 'The City and the Bottom Line: Urban Megaprojects and the Privatization of Planning in Southeast Asia'. *Environment and Planning A* 40(2): 383–401.

——. 2011. 'Planning Privatopolis: Representation and Contestation in the Development of Urban Integrated Mega-Projects'. In *Worlding Cities: Asian Experiments and the Art of Being Global*, eds A. Roy and A. Ong, 77–97. Oxford, UK: John Wiley & Sons.

——, ed. 2013. *Contesting the Indian City: Global Visions and the Politics of the Local*. West Sussex, UK: Wiley Blackwell.

Shaw, A. 1999. 'Emerging Patterns of Urban Growth in India'. *Economic & Political Weekly* 34(16–17): 969–78.

Shaw, A., and M. K. Satish. 2007. 'Metropolitan Restructuring in Post-liberalized India: Separating the Global and the Local'. *Cities* 24(2): 148–63.

Sivaramakrishnan, K. C. 2015. *Governance of Megacities: Fractured Thinking, Fragmented Setup*. New Delhi: Oxford University Press.

Sridharan, N. 2008. 'New Forms of Contestation and Cooperation in Indian Urban Governance'. In *New Forms of Urban Governance in India: Shifts, Models, Networks & Governance*, eds I. S. A. Baud and J. De Wit, 291–311. First edn. New Delhi, Thousand Oaks, California, London, Singapore: Sage.

Sundaresan, J. 2013. 'Urban Planning in Vernacular Governance: Land Use Planning and Violations in Bangalore'. Ph.D. diss., Department of Geography and Environment, The London School of Economics, London.

The Indian Express. 2015. 'NDA Government Approves Rs 2784 cr Worth of Trunk Infrastructure for Dholera SIR'. 30 May, Ahmedabad.

Watson, V. 2015. 'The Allure of "Smart City" Rhetoric: India and Africa'. *Dialogues in Human Geography* 5(1): 36–39.

Weinstein, L. 2008. 'Mumbai's Development Mafias: Globalization, Organized Crime and Land Development'. *International Journal of Urban and Regional Research* 32(1): 22–39.

Weinstein, L., N. Sami and G. Shatkin. 2013. 'Contested Developments: Enduring Legacies and Emergent Political Actors in Contemporary Urban India'. In *Contesting the Indian City: Global Visions and the Politics of the Local*, ed. G. Shatkin, 39–64. West Sussex, UK: Wiley Blackwell.
Yin, R. K. 1994. *Case Study Research: Design and Methods*. Thousand Oaks: Sage.

4

Roads to New Urban Futures

Flexible Territorialisation in Peri-urban Kolkata and Hyderabad

SUDESHNA MITRA

Peri-urban areas of metropolitan cities have attracted significant land and real estate interests in the decades following liberalisation. This chapter examines high-speed, limited-access road projects promoted by state governments in the geographic peripheries of metropolitan cities. It not only interrogates their role in shaping peri-urban real estate markets, but also unpacks them as territorial strategies of state governments, trying to woo external investors, in the post-liberalisation milieu.

The chapter focuses on the peri-urban road projects promoted in Kolkata and Hyderabad. Both cities, as state capitals, received a significant proportion of 'place-making' attention from their respective state governments after liberalisation. These efforts were aimed at creating destinations to attract and anchor domestic and foreign corporates, developers and investors, in exclusive townships, Special Economic Zones (SEZs), campuses for information technology (IT), biotechnology, pharmaceutical research and development, finance, specialty healthcare, higher education, etc. (Denis 2011; Kennedy and Sood 2016), in peri-urban areas where land was cheaper and easier to alienate (Shaw 2005; DuPont and Sridharan 2007). Within a context of state rescaling, which culminated in state governments materialising post-liberalisation economic growth agendas at the city-scale (Kennedy 2014), these 'place-making' efforts were more than localised strategies (Shaw and Satish 2007). They ran concurrent to state-level strategies such as accelerated timelines to implement investor and developer-friendly policies and projects, as well as inter-state competitive tactics (Kennedy 2007). These were often led by chief ministers themselves, and enacted across domestic and international investor meets, marketing road-shows and specially organised homecoming events for the diaspora (Kohli 1989; Naidu and Sevanti 2000; Basu 2007; Bose 2007). In both cities, the road projects provided critical support to state governments' efforts to transform urban peripheries into externally legible destinations and changing market perceptions about what constituted the cities' 'urban' regions.

A closer examination of these road projects offers the opportunity to examine the role of the state in remaking peri-urban areas, with an emphasis on the 'optics' of connectivity and external legibility in discursive imaginaries of the urban and urban futures, played out through billboards, project marketing, investor meets and city-branding exercises (Kennedy 2007; Bhattacharya and Sanyal 2011). Beyond the optics these projects offer the opportunity to examine how the state's territorial strategies engendered real estate markets, leveraged finance for hyper-modern projects in peri-urban/rural locations and facilitated a range of institutional modalities, including public–private partnerships. These road projects highlight that the spatial contours and transactional dynamics of peri-urban land transformations have not been natural, incidental or inevitable effects of natural growth and/or 'free market' pressures. Rather, these projects reveal the state's flexible territorialisation strategies at the city scale, and highlight implicit state guarantees extended to private investment interests in land via infrastructure, post liberalisation.

Using a comparative, inter-city relational frame, the chapter undertakes a three-part reading of Kolkata and Hyderabad's peri-urban road projects: (1) as inter-scalar spatial strategies of the state that privileged 'optics' of delineation and legibility, and deviated from practices of expanding urban limits via extension of urban boundaries and jurisdictions; (2) as state guarantees into peri-urban real estate markets that facilitated new modalities of peri-urban governance, including public–private development partnerships, constituted around land management, land delivery and land leveraging; and (3) as inter-scalar state strategies, which legitimised state governments intervening at the city-level, within a context of competitive dynamics of economic and political regionalism.

The chapter starts with a brief contextualisation with reference to conceptual frames used to understand India's dramatic post-liberalisation peri-urban land transformations. In the second section the road projects in Kolkata and Hyderabad are situated within the post-liberalisation context of political and economic regionalism. After an introduction to the two road projects, the subsequent sections are organised into a three-part reading of the projects. The chapter concludes with reflections on changes in forms and modalities of urbanisation and urban governance that these projects implicate.

The chapter represents part of the work undertaken during the dissertation research on peri-urban transformations in Kolkata and Hyderabad. Twelve months of fieldwork was undertaken in 2008–09, followed by two months of fieldwork in 2012. Over 80 interviews were conducted with officials in state government departments, city development authorities, developers, real estate consultants, property brokers, representatives of business associations, displaced persons, academics and activists. The research included review of relevant legislations, policy reports, consultant reports, court cases, local archives maintained by displaced persons and media reports. For this chapter some information has been updated via secondary research.

THEORETICAL CONSIDERATIONS

The encounters and experiences associated with the rapid influx of urban real estate market dynamics in peri-urban areas of metropolitan cities, post liberalisation, have attracted a lot of contemporary research. These encounters are caught between discursive narratives that reference transnational scales of investor networks and capital accumulation strategies on one hand and messy material realities that comprise of local, often 'under the radar' (Vijayabaskar and Menon 2018), nexus of local politicians, brokers, middle men, touts, developers that mediate and negotiate with landowners, development authorities, parastatals (with eminent domain powers[1]), and new public–private partnerships (PPPs) and special purpose vehicles (SPVs) (with mandates to manage and deliver land), on the other hand. Deregulation, post liberalisation, has made it considerably easier for foreign investors to enter the Indian real estate sector. As such, India has experienced an influx of financial capital from 'insurance companies, investment banks, sovereign funds, family offices and other hedge funds' (Rouanet and Halbert 2016: 6). While acknowledging the role of external investors in the liberalised land markets in India, Rouanet and Halbert warn against assuming a 'mechanistic link between investor expectations and the newly-built urban landscapes' (ibid. 2016: 4). Rather than having a top–down effect on Indian urban real estate, foreign investment interests have been mediated by local developers, embedded in local land and political networks, with capacities to navigate the Indian urban institutional terrain (Searle 2014; Rouanet and Halbert 2016). As such, state governments' efforts to woo investors have included significant numbers of domestic investors looking to expand. As such, the term 'external' investor is more useful than the term 'foreign' investor in this context. Moreover, foreign investors are frequently involved only in the projects' 'last mile' (Rouanet and Halbert 2016), that is, the construction phase, rather than land aggregation and property title clearance stages. These times are when contextual 'risks', including pushbacks from farmers unwilling to sell, ambiguity of property papers, cost and project over-runs due to delays, etc., are higher. This too has significance for the investment and development profiles in peri-urban areas, as foreign investments play a role predominantly in built-up phase of projects, which comprise a small proportion of peri-urban real estate markets, otherwise dominated by land transactions. Raman (2016) and Vijayabaskar and Menon (2018) add to this global–local complexity of scale by highlighting the importance of small-scale real estate transactional dynamics in peri-urban transformations. Vijayabaskar and Menon (2018) link their overall argument to the state's neglect of the agricultural sector, which shapes the underlying structural conditions within which farmers are made to 'voluntarily' or 'coercively' part with their land, a binary that does not always hold as separate and discrete categories in actual experience.

Another set of research approaches peri-urban transformations not from the perspective of investors and developers, but rather state–market relationalities. Goldman (2010) and Shatkin (2016) emphasise that the post-liberalisation real estate turn cannot be seen simply as a market phenomenon, but rather needs to be examined in relation to the state and modalities of urban governance facilitating these dynamics. Goldman uses the term 'speculative urbanism' while Shatkin refers to the 'real estate turn in policy and planning' to highlight that separations between state and market have become porous with regimes of urban development revealing 'privatised' objectives and modalities. Levien (2012) and Vijayabaskar and Menon (2018) link the deployment of such new regimes of governance, especially in predominantly rural areas, to dynamics of land grabs and 'accumulation by dispossession' (Harvey 2003).

In Kennedy (2007) and Kennedy and Sood (2016), the state's contemporary practices to accommodate investors in zones and investment regions, by making land, infrastructure and simpler regulatory regimes available, are discussed with reference to Ong's (2006) conceptual frame of 'spaces of exception'. These spaces allow firms and developers to be shielded from local political and economic realities, allow bypass of existing regulations and facilitate expedited clearances. Levien (2012) argues that use of eminent domain to aggregate land for such zones makes the state a 'land broker' to private interests. Some direct mediations by the state to anchor foreign corporates have been iconic as success stories, such as Chandrababu Naidu (former chief minister of Andhra Pradesh [united]) negotiating with globally well-established technology companies to set up their international offshore research and development centres and campuses in Gachibowli, in the periphery of Hyderabad. However, more frequently, direct and absolute territorial claims of the state in the post-liberalisation period have encountered significant pushbacks, as the examples of Singur, Nandigram, Maha Mumbai SEZ, Goa SEZs highlight. This has led to the replacement of the colonial era Land Acquisition Act, 1894, with the Right to Fair Compensation and Transparency in Land Acquisition, Rehabilitation and Resettlement Act, 2013.

This chapter also focuses on the state and the implications of peri-urban road projects as state strategies. The key argument is that the peri-urban road projects in Kolkata and Hyderabad represent substantive but flexible territorialisation strategies deployed by the state, which are in contrast to the use of eminent domain, designation of 'zones of exception' and even explicit expansions of city boundaries as municipal and/or development areas—where expressions of the state's territorial powers are absolute. As expensive infrastructure interventions, the road projects are substantive and they signal clear state intent regarding the transformation of the cities' peri-urban areas. They extend a form of state guarantee to real estate interests in these areas. At the same time, they are flexible as they are operationalised through a range of governance and financing modalities, including SPVs and PPPs. The flexibility is also linked to the range of local actors as well as foreign corporates and investors, looking for 'available' and peri-urban land, that these strategies speak to, without directly undertaking land acquisitions and/or zone demarcations (although in both cities, these direct strategies were also deployed). The projects segue well into the state government's discursive practices, that is, marketing and branding of the cities as investment destinations, through billboards, brochures and powerpoint presentations in investor meets, playing on optics of connectivity and legibility. They also facilitate fragmented and messy material practices across multiple real estate intentionalities and actors, as referenced by Raman (2016) and Vijayabaskar and Menon (2018) in their work on Chennai's peripheries.

Kolkata and Hyderabad's peripheries, emerging as IT hubs, are characterised by iconic buildings of well-known global and national technology companies, whose spectacular structures are amplified by the large swathes of undeveloped land around them. The land is caught up in volatile and frequently violent real estate dynamics with pushbacks from residents against state-led land acquisitions, and the presence of local developers, politicians, middle-men, touts and residents, and frequent aggregations and transactions (Mitra 2018). These volatile and uneven geographies highlight that peri-urban transformations cannot be examined in terms of only the observable and visible built forms. Rather, it is important to understand both the representational optics deployed as well as the emergent 'invisible' layers of urban territorialisation, including governance forms and processes, project financing and reclamations from other resource footprints, particularly 'marginal' lands such as marshy lands, rocky outcrops, drainage channels, dry tank beds and other forms of 'waste' lands. A territorialisation lens allows complexities of deploying global spatial imaginaries on a terrain comprised of complex and unclear property tenure relationships, tied into complex urban–peri-urban systems of waste, water, food and energy (Ghosh and Sen 1987; Bunting et al. 2005; Dey 2008), to be considered.

This chapter takes a closer look at the state's territorial strategies, implicated by the peri-urban road projects in Kolkata and Hyderabad, in terms of the spatial guarantees they signal. It examines the road projects both in terms of their discursive deployment in marketing and branding exercises, as well as the material dynamics of territorialisation that they have facilitated on ground.

ECONOMIC AND POLITICAL REGIONALISM IN INDIA POST LIBERALISATION

The scalar significance of the peri-urban road projects in Kolkata and Hyderabad has to be read within the larger context of political and economic regionalism (Sinha 2004), post liberalisation. Liberalisation in 1991 coincided with an intense period of political volatility and six changes of the national government between 1989 and 1998. The national elections did not deliver a clear majority to any political party and there were frequent making and unmaking of political coalitions to form the government. Regional political parties, which emerged in response to Congress-I's hegemonic national and state presence post Independence, were key to these political barters and gained voice at the national scale despite regional constituencies and agendas. Thus, economic regionalism was strongly affected by political regionalism (Corbridge and Harriss 2000). Inter-state competition for investments, since 1991, have exhibited a performative side, with roadshows and state investor meets being used by state governments to make claims and counter-claims about regional superiority, with socio-culturally coloured 'homecoming' appeals to the diaspora, for investments. The claims and appeals have frequently bordered on regional chauvinism. With liberalisation, state governments assumed more responsibilities for economic growth agendas, including policies to induce private sector investments and gain fiscal autonomy (Kohli 1989; Joshi and Little 1996). Limited internal capacities and compressed timelines facilitated ingress of private sector consultants, particularly global firms, with experience in IT hubs in the Global North, as well as Singapore and other parts of South-East Asia, along with new civil society groups and corporate business associations, which represented limited sections of the society and the market (Pedersen 2000), to devise state and city reform agendas. It marked a shift from an era of state-led planning to an era of consultant-led visioning exercises (Reddy 1999; West Bengal Electronics Industry Development Corporation Limited [WEBEL] n.d.).

Kolkata and Hyderabad's experiences echo the pressures and eventually the choices that many lesser known Indian cities encountered, wherein state governments devised competitive, often aggressive, strategies to remake particular cities into 'globally' relevant investment destinations to be inserted into national and transnational flows of capital (Jessop 2002; Harvey 2006). They also echo the experiences of most state capitals in the country that became default and priority locations of their respective state governments' post-liberalisation enthusiasm.

PERI-URBAN ROADS TO NEW URBAN FUTURES IN KOLKATA AND HYDERABAD

The two road projects used as cases in this chapter include the East West Road Corridor (EWRC) project in New Town–Rajarhat in Kolkata and the Outer Ring Road (ORR) project in Hyderabad. The EWRC project, a 6.5-km stretch of a 10-lane arterial road, proposed as a high-speed corridor, between Action Area ID in New Town and Shikarpur Kulti Canal Road created a critical link between the New Town–Rajarhat urban extensions and Kolkata's international airport at Dum Dum. The ORR project is at a much grander scale. It is a 159-km long, eight-lane road project, with a design speed of 120 kmph, encircling Hyderabad, connecting the new international airport at Shamshabad to SEZs, Cyberabad, the Financial District and other destinations (Hyderabad Metropolitan Development Authority [HMDA] 2016).

The peri-urban context of the EWRC project was New Town planned over 3,780 hectares (Mitra 2002) and Rajarhat designated across roughly 2,400–2,800 hectares of land (West Bengal Housing

Infrastructure Development Corporation [WBHIDCO] 2018). New Town was conceptualised as a self-sufficient mixed-use township, planned around IT and other knowledge economy sectors. These areas were extensions of the IT hub in Sector 5 in Bidhannagar, and located on Kolkata's eastern periphery (Bunting et al. 2005; Bose 2008). Kolkata's Basic Development Plan designates the city's eastern periphery as a no-development zone because of its wetland characteristics (Bagchi 1987). To bypass these regulations, New Town was planned and developed by the West Bengal Housing Infrastructure Development Corporation (WBHIDCO) (constituted under the Companies Act) and Rajarhat was put under the jurisdiction of the Bhangar-Rajarhat Area Development Authority (BRADA), which was created in 2007 under the Housing Department (rather than the Urban Development Department, as is the common practice).

The EWRC was under the planning control of the WBHIDCO and developed via an external contractor. Originally it was planned as a 10-lane arterial road, and estimated to cost Rs 40.65 crore by the West Bengal Housing Directorate (estimates were done in December 2004) (Comptroller and Auditor General [CAG] 2007). However, the work was taken up on fast-track in March 2005 to facilitate bulk land-buyers in the New Town area who wanted the road to be developed before their land deals with the government were finalised and project specifications were changed to that of a six-lane road. The Housing Directorate was bypassed and as the CAG (2007) report highlights, the contractor was given the project, without a tender, for a price of Rs 16.6 crore, rather than Rs 17.66 crore, as estimated. The CAG highlights multiple concerns including cost overruns, project delays, temporary exit of the contractor from the project, non-payment of compensation, poor quality materials, non-coordination with government bodies in laying infrastructure along the road, selection of contractor without a tender and bypassing of the Housing Directorate in decision-making.

The ORR project in Hyderabad also started in 2005. It was proposed by Y. S. R. Reddy (of Congress-I), who took over as chief minister after Chandrababu Naidu (and the Telugu Desam Party) was voted out in 2004. It is difficult to find a consistent project valuation of the ORR project; however, a project appraisal report prepared by The Government Performance Group (TGPG) at the Indian School of Business (ISB) put estimates above Rs 6,000 crore (Indian School of Business [ISB] 2010) for the first three phases of the project, accounting for approximately 54 per cent of the project. Nallathiga (2014) mentions a cost of approximately Rs 7,400 crore. The governance of the ORR (design, bid management, financial mobilisation) was operationalised via an SPV, constituted by the Government of Andhra Pradesh, called the Hyderabad Growth Corridor Limited (HGCL), under the Companies Act 1956. Initially, the equity partners included the Infrastructure Corporation of Andhra Pradesh (INCAP) with a 40 per cent stake and the Hyderabad Urban Development Authority (HUDA) with a 60 per cent stake. Now INCAP has a 26 per cent share and the Hyderabad Metropolitan Development Authority (HMDA), which subsumed HUDA, holds a 74 per cent stake (HMDA 2016). The construction of the ORR project, divided into two phases, has leveraged a mix of state investments, long-term loans from national banks (with HMDA's land bank held in mortgage), PPP models with annuity repayment, funding from the Japan International Cooperation Agency (JICA), etc. (ISB 2010; Nallathiga 2014). The CAG (2018) report highlights over-payments to concessionaires. The project has faced controversies around land acquisition (Nallathiga 2014) and frequent (115 instances) alignment changes (*The Hindu* 2006; Nallathiga 2014),[2] which have made surrounding land markets volatile. The alignment changes drew a Central Bureau of Investigation (CBI) enquiry and were scrutinised by a special high court bench, with Chandrababu Naidu levelling charges of corruption against Y. S. R. Reddy (*The Times of India* 2006).

As per the ORR website,

> the Outer Ring Road should be viewed as road-cum-area development project... (it) creates options for development of further satellite townships, provides quick access to the International Airport from strategic parts of the city, connects various new urban nodes outside the city like Hi-Tech city, Games village, IIIT, ISB, Hardware Park, Singapore Township Financial district etc... The proposed corridor is designed to be fully access controlled and limited access is to be provided

> at NH/SHI Major road crossings (Government of Andhra Pradesh 2009).

Although the two projects differ significantly in alignment length, technical design and their scale of peri-urban intervention, they are similar in their basic objective of connecting the city's international airport to new peri-urban locations. Both represent direct involvement of the state governments in peri-urban city-scale strategies.

SPATIAL STRATEGIES OF DELINEATION AND LEGIBILITY VIA ROAD PROJECTS

Both road projects have facilitated high-speed entry and exit to peri-urban destinations via the cities' international airports, bypassing the main cities' economies and resident populations.[3] As marketing of peri-urban destinations continues to occur in investor meets and road shows, not only in domestic locations but also Dubai, Singapore, etc., the 'optics' of connectivity that these roads facilitate continue to be relevant. The success of the roads as territorial delineation strategies, especially for the 'external' gaze, may also be read into the successful finance leveraging exercise by HGCL to secure interest in the ORR project from private concessionaires, domestic national banks and from a multilateral funding agency such as JICA. In Kolkata, a similar success may be read in relation to the urgency with which the EWRC project was pushed through at the behest of bulk land-buyers in New Town, who were eager for the road to be completed before finalising their land deals.

These road projects reveal a new logic of spatially delineating the 'urban' that deviates from the state's traditional relationship to territoriality. State claims to territoriality have commonly been enacted via boundaries and bounded jurisdictions. Master plans and notified 'development areas' have been used to expand metropolitan limits (Kumar 2006). Such delineations affirm/reaffirm the regulatory role of the state, reconfigure governance responsibilities and signal the state's acknowledgement that urbanisation trends have spilled beyond existing boundaries, and there is need for development controls and new urban infrastructures in the expanded areas. However, in both Kolkata and Hyderabad, the road projects were infrastructure interventions that preceded statutory jurisdictional expansions, which eventually rationalised the cities' expanded urban limits (discussed in more detail in the section 'State Rescaling and Its Modalities of Governance'). Both roads were key instruments that 'unlocked' a mostly rural periphery as urban real estate and 'delineated' new expanded urban regions in terms of market perceptions. Both roads allowed the state to territorialise and spatially reconfigure the peri-urban via new pathways that opened up areas, as if they were otherwise an indistinguishable hinterland/frontier, bypassing their values and legibility as rural economies, shaped by urban–peri-urban exchanges of food, water, waste and energy. Kennedy and Sood (2016) refer to this as a *Tabula Rasa* imagination. Flyvbjerg et al. (2003: 2) highlight that in such deployments infrastructure is not just a 'simple precondition for production and consumption', but rather 'at the very core of these activities'.

This highlights that in the post-liberalisation milieu state strategies have become increasingly cognizant of investor perceptions and private developers' expectations from the state, and in time are aligning with 'market' practices of colonisation as the way to materialise urban expansion. The explicit optics geared towards an external audience in both road projects reveal that both state governments believed they were ultimately dependent on investors to deliver on their claims of economic growth.

ROAD PROJECTS AS STATE GUARANTEES FOR REAL ESTATE MARKETS

Fernand Braudel highlights that the state can play the role of a regulator to control the private sector's appetite for profits (Wallerstein 1991). It can also assume the role of a facilitator and become a guarantor for private interests and profits. He theorises that exceptional private profits are not possible without the state rescinding its role as regulator and without explicit state guarantees bolstering the private sector. Braudel's thesis provides a provocation to examine the state's territorialisation of peri-urban areas via road projects, in terms of its implications on the state's role as regulator versus a facilitator and guarantor in the post-liberalisation milieu.

First, the state guarantees implicated by these road projects emerged from the substantive state investments, ranging from about Rs 40 crore in the EWRC in Kolkata to more than Rs 6,000 crore in the ORR in Hyderabad. The state's commitment and priority about developing the peri-urban areas were further showcased by the state's willingness to be institutionally flexible and using a private company mode to govern the build-phase of these road projects and fast-track their development—both the WBHIDCO in case of the EWRC and the HGCL in case of the ORR project were state agencies, constituted under the Companies Act. Most importantly, the state's own peri-urban stake was clarified (in case of the ORR) by the flows of finance that the state leveraged and directed into the road project, including loans from domestic banks and development funding from JICA, an international development agency.

Also significant were the ways in which the state itself leveraged land around these road projects, highlighting the state's own interest in these areas as land supplier/developer, another signal of state guarantee. The ORR alignment is in effect a 'growth corridor', which encompasses one kilometre of land on either side of the road (Municipal Administration and Urban Development Department [MAUD] 2008),[4] covering nearly 56,656 hectares (*Deccan Chronicle* 2017). In 2017, HMDA proposed to expand this 'corridor' to 5 km on either side of the ORR as per the direction of Chief Minister K. Chandrashekhar Rao, and hired two consultants to undertake a market research of the real estate potential of the 2,170 sq km of area that this would bring in (*The Hans India* 2017). In addition, the ISB (2010) report highlights that the ORR is associated with real estate developments across 10 intersections, each of which has just over 100 hectares of land available for commercial development, as well as a further 12 locations where HUDA has land banks. In an article Gupta (2017) wrote,

> ORR development in Hyderabad has transformed old villages into new real estate destinations. Shamirpet, Kokapet, Puppalaguda used to be rural areas but now they are witnessing the rampant construction of residential buildings, projects,

> townships due to their proximity to the IT corridor of Hyderabad via ORR. While Shamirpet has its own biotechnology park coming up, Kokapet and Puppalaguda are receiving housing demand from IT workforce. Apart from this, Gandipet, Kollur, Chandanagar, Adibatla and Pocharam are other areas that have come up as prominent markets for buying properties.

In New Town–Rajarhat the implementation of the EWRC was fast-tracked by WBHIDCO to facilitate bulk land sales (CAG 2007). Moreover, WBHIDCO held monopoly on land supply and price in New Town. On one hand, they tried to leverage this monopoly. Some researchers characterised WBHIDCO's pricing as the steepest mark-ups in Asia (Sengupta and Tipple 2007). On the other hand, the CAG (2007) highlights how the WBHIDCO significantly misused the chairman's quota to preferentially accommodate corporates, which were being otherwise wooed to invest in West Bengal, at minimal prices in New Town. If land supply and price were used to signal the state government's commitment to place in New Town, in the 7,000-hectare Rajarhat area the commitment was expressed by allowing private developers a free-for-all green light to aggregate land from farmers directly under the jurisdiction of the newly constituted BRADA, which did not set in place any regulations for the private sector's land aggregations. Rajarhat's 'laissez faire' land market encouraged widespread violence and coercions, especially as land prices increased significantly. Mamata Banerjee dismantled BRADA in 2011, soon after Trinamool Congress won the state elections and she became the chief minister. As Dey et al. (2013: 211) note, the effects of dismantling of BRADA were immediate on land prices: 'land off the main road which used to cost Rs 7 lakh a cottah has come down to Rs 2.25 lakh a cottah overnight. Even in the remoter areas under BRADA the price of land was anything between Rs 1 lakh and Rs 5.5 lakh till yesterday.' These price drops highlight the critical role of state guarantees in bolstering peri-urban real estate markets.

Field research revealed that urban real estate dynamics in the peripheries attracted city brokers and 'fixers', and created a new generation of agents and aggregators from amongst the original residents in both cities. Also, local actors were tied to local political parties and politicians in both cities, and there were multiple stories of personal fortunes that were made as well as stories of personal fortunes that were lost in frequent cycles of land transactions, aggregations and land price volatilities. Displaced households highlighted how land loss affected the ways in which they had used land as a financial social security net to navigate the times when agricultural yields were low. In both cities, the relatively well-off landowners who received compensation highlighted that the money had eventually run out and they were left with few options afterwards. These land markets irretrievably altered the land use and land value regimes associated with these peri-urban locations even when they did not translate eventually to built-up developments. In Kolkata, New Town and Rajarhat displaced farming and fishing activities and affected the waste treatment capacities of the location's geo-hydrological formations. In Hyderabad, the ORR created financial incentives that led to rapid abandonment of arid agricultural practices and associated groundwater recharge practices (Van Rooijen et al. 2011). This exacerbated the drought-like conditions in Hyderabad.

STATE RESCALING AND ITS MODALITIES OF GOVERNANCE

The changing relationalities of the state to territoriality and new state priorities embedded in these relationalities played out in terms of new authorities and multiple transitions in jurisdictions in the peri-urban areas of both cities and the two peri-urban road projects.

The creation of new authorities served many purposes. In its simplest form it allowed project implementation to be fast-tracked, as exemplified by the SPV created for the ORR in Hyderabad—HGCL—and the private company status of WBHIDCO in Kolkata, overseeing the implementation of the EWRC. More complex reasons included accommodating preferred private partners as was the case when the company developing the Hyderabad International Airport was given 2,224 hectares as a land bank to be developed for real estate purposes. The company developed 607 hectares of this land as an Airport City, which accommodates two SEZs of just over 100 hectares each. The remaining 405 hectares are to be developed as per 'themes' or sectors, including a 'healthport' and 'eduport' (GMR 2016). In many cases, new authorities allowed new master plans and new development areas to be designated. For example, the Cyberabad Development Authority (CDA) created a master plan for Cyberabad, the BRADA facilitated laissez faire land aggregation in Rajarhat, and the WBHIDCO prepared and implemented its own master plan for New Town that allowed the urbanisation of the city's eastern periphery, which had been deliberately left out of the Kolkata Metropolitan Development Authority's Basic Development Plan (Bagchi 1987). However, across the many authorities, many jurisdictions and multiple instrumentalities that the peri-urban areas of Kolkata and Hyderabad experienced, some common thematics emerge—flexible territorialisation of the peri-urban and fragmented spatiality of multiple jurisdictions. While such 'jurisdictional creep' strikes a discordant note in relation to traditional expectations of coherent metropolitan boundary expansions and planning concepts such as metropolitan regions, such incrementalism dovetails well with market-led land colonisation patterns and speaks to Braudel's thesis regarding the state assuming regulatory versus facilitatory roles.

Over time the spatially fragmented jurisdictions of new peri-urban authorities in both cities were consolidated/rationalised. In peri-urban Hyderabad, the Greater Hyderabad Municipal Corporation (GHMC) was created in April 2007, based on a government order issued in 2005, which proposed to consolidate the Municipal Corporation of Hyderabad (MCH) area with the areas of 12 surrounding municipalities and 8 gram panchayats. The consolidation was made possible by a High Court judgement in 2007, as the consolidation was opposed across party lines (Kennedy 2014; Sood 2016). The Hyderabad Metropolitan Development Authority (HMDA) was constituted in 2008 by consolidating the areas under multiple authorities, including the HUDA, CDA and the Hyderabad Airport Development Authority (HADA). In Kolkata, the New Town area has also seen governance transitions from the WBHIDCO (constituted under the Companies Act) initially designated as the planning and development authority. In 2007, the New Town Kolkata Development Authority (NKDA), constituted under the New Town, Kolkata Development Authority Act, 2007, took over from the WBHIDCO. In Rajarhat, the BRADA was created in 2007 under the Housing Department. BRADA was dismantled in 2011 and the land was transferred to the jurisdiction of WBHIDCO. In 2012, the WBHIDCO created a Land Use and Development Control Plan (LUDCP) for the area previously under BRADA.[5] In 2015, an expanded municipal body called the Bidhannagar Municipal Corporation was constituted for Salt Lake city as well as areas previously under BRADA (My Estate Point 2015). The multiple cycles of jurisdictional changes are now invisible as are the conflicts between different state bodies that were functional in these areas. The current consolidated jurisdictions fit with planning conceptions of a metropolitan region. However, the history of institutional conflict, negotiations, frequent changes in jurisdictions and use of institutional modalities for varying objectives from project management to land acquisition to land price setting to regulation to effect statutory bypass of existing regulations highlight how flexible the state's territorial strategies have been in these peri-urban areas. The institutional history experienced by the two cities in their peripheries remains critical for understanding the politics and increasing flexibility of state territoriality, which were facilitated by the modality of territorial delineation that new roads allowed in the peri-urban expansions of both cities.

The thesis regarding state rescaling highlights the essentially politicised processes (often in response to new economic and political imperatives) through which the state reorganises its systems of power and authority across scales of governance (Brenner 2004), often involving introduction of new authorities, removal of others, revival of yet others and sometimes a restructuring of the scale and jurisdictional powers of particular authorities. The multiple jurisdictions deployed in both cities, some with new structures and some with new roles (such as the Housing Department rather than the Urban Development Department overseeing New Town's development), highlight the significant ways in which the state governments reinserted themselves into city-scale strategies, over and beyond existing authorities, including parastatals. Citing examples from Bangalore and Pune, Balakrishnan (2013) terms the emergence of institutional forms beyond parastatals as forms of 'negotiated decentralization'.

Rescaling in the Indian context has been analysed in terms of state governments increasingly leveraging land, a state subject in the Constitution, as they engage in strategies of capital accumulation (Gupta and Sivaramakrishnan 2011; Kennedy 2014). There is also clear acknowledgement that rescaling has not trickled down to the municipal level, which continues primarily as provider of basic services (Kennedy and Sood 2016), even as cities are inserted into discourses and practices of being 'growth engines'.

I argue that the Indian dynamics of state rescaling have also been intensely political and associated with significant flexibility of territorial strategies and institutional modalities. For one, regional political parties and regional agendas have played a significant role in shaping rescaling dynamics. This can be observed in West Bengal and Andhra Pradesh (united). Both state governments faced legacy economic and political challenges post liberalisation. West Bengal under the Communist Party of India (Marxist) (CPI[M]) was seen as the hub of union politics and general unfriendliness towards private capital (Pedersen 2001; Banerjee et al. 2002). Andhra Pradesh (united) under Telugu Desam Party (TDP) and then Congress-I had to consolidate its regional Telugu constituency, including its caste dimensions, and its proud links to irrigation-fed agriculture on one hand, and the global IT industry on the other (Kohli 1988; Srinivasulu and Sarangi 1999), even as they tried to become 'globally' relevant. In both states, the state capitals were critical sites to reconcile state-level legacy issues (Basu 2007). The road projects in particular played a critical role in these inter-scalar and state rescaling dynamics. Hyderabad's peri-urban land market anchored and accommodated the demand for urban real estate that emerged from agricultural surpluses for people from coastal Andhra, who did not have a landed interest in Hyderabad for historical reasons (Upadhya 1988; Luther 2006). As such, Hyderabad's peri-urban market was active since the 1980s. However, these real estate market dynamics saw a dramatic expansion post liberalisation in the late 1990s in areas such as Madhapur and Gachibowli. The ORR consolidated these dynamics via new IT campuses, educational campuses and the Financial District in these locations. In West Bengal, the CPI(M) tried to change investor perceptions by promoting 13 new PPPs between leading local developers and the state government (Sengupta 2006, 2007). These new entities were involved with housing projects in Kolkata and these developers became de facto advisors to the state government and played an active role in the New Town–Rajarhat areas, particularly land aggregations in Rajarhat.

CONCLUSIONS

This chapter privileges a particular empirical and analytic entry point of peri-urban road projects into the phenomenon of peri-urban transformations of metropolitan cities in India, post liberalisation—a phenomenon that has otherwise attracted substantial research. The decision to enter via the road projects is a conscious attempt to make explicit the mode of territorialisation that has been associated with the state's interventions in peri-urban areas. Notions of connectivity and legibility are by now familiar discourses. On one hand, the definitional ambit of these notions is expanding. The material connectivity promised by road projects is expanding into 'infrastructure corridors' that promise pathways to facilitate digital, infrastructural, material and investment flows. On the other hand, these notions are also being depoliticised, accepted and eventually normalised. For example, enhancing the digital footprint of our cities, which otherwise lack infrastructure and are held together by complex and fragmented systems of governance and legality (Kennedy and Sood 2016), is now accepted as a key component of national urban missions such as 'Smart Cities'. It may therefore be imperative to move beyond an analysis of the discourses themselves and unpack the material modalities of urban territorialisation, the nature of emergent urbanisation and changes in governance they are facilitating.

The experiences with the peri-urban road projects in both Kolkata and Hyderabad highlight that the state's priorities to encourage developers and investors (as well as brokers, touts and middlemen) rather than regulate them has meant that the state has taken on a much clearer role of providing guarantees to mitigate the market's perceptions of risks but these guarantees have been subject to political cycles, and has implicated the state's power to provide a balance to an unregulated regime of coercions, violence and volatility around land transfers. Ultimately, this not only makes emerging urbanisation and its associated economies more directly vulnerable to shifts in investor perceptions and subject to the flow and ebb of investments, but also facilitates a structurally violent process of dispossession as productive rural economies transition into undeveloped real estate.

The fragmented and incremental spatiality of multiple jurisdictional boundaries associated with corridor-led urban growth highlight urbanisation patterns where traditional core–periphery spatialities are disrupted. With in-place urbanisation encouraged by roads and corridors, the question is not just limited to the challenges of rural populations moving to urban areas, but is also one of urban dynamics moving to rural areas. Ultimately this means there may be a need to rethink the definition of the 'urban' itself. Apart from the theoretical work that such patterns of urbanisation demand, there are implications for urban infrastructure delivery, economic transitions and spatialities of urban governance.

Both peri-urban road projects discussed in this chapter have been followed by larger and even more ambitious plans and corridor projects. In Hyderabad, now situated in Telangana, a new proposal floated in 2014 by the state government proposed the development of 13 mini-cities (or investment regions) along the ORR (*Deccan Chronicle* 2014). Even more ambitiously, in 2017 a new 340-km-long Regional Ring Road (the ORR is 159 km) was announced, also encircling Hyderabad and located even further out than the ORR, to connect key locations in surrounding districts and national highways (*Eenadu* 2017). In Kolkata, the objective of connecting the city's eastern periphery has gone beyond the EWRC. The ambitious East–West Metro Corridor, planned over two phases and sponsored by JICA, has become the new eastern corridor.

The questions and provocations in this chapter find wider relevance with the proliferation of pan-regional infrastructure corridors across the country, which implicate significant changes in the country's economic geography. For example Sampat (2016) raises concerns about 'rentier' economies emerging along the Delhi–Mumbai Industrial Corridor (DMIC), Dholera in particular. The footloose nature of investments is a genuine concern. However, in the Indian context these aspirational scales of investments have often not materialised. Rather, there has been a proliferation of multi-scalar politicised real estate nexuses. In addition, there is an even more fundamental concern about state–market relationality here. What do these corridors signal about the extent to which the state is willing to retreat from regulatory imperatives and jurisdictional boundaries via flexible territorialisation? In effect, these corridors could be institutionally designed to act as 'pipelines' that allow the state to funnel access to land, labour, credit, approvals, infrastructure and exemptions, across and beyond direct deployment of eminent domain and beyond existing scales of governance and jurisdictional boundaries. The economic geography likely to emerge from these dynamics and mitigating responses, if any, remain to be seen.

EPILOGUE

The fragmented spatial development patterns and institutional terrains that initially emerged along the roads have experienced a slow and incremental consolidation. The consolidation has been aided by renewed private investments as circuits of real estate financing in India have stabilised after the global crisis in 2008–09 (Goldman and Narayan 2021). State strategies to consolidate private investments through infrastructure and new governance institutions have been supplemented by interventions to link policies and circuits of capital associated with 'smart' technologies (including green technologies) and finance.

New Town, Kolkata, has emerged as a recognisable, even aspirational, destination, with upper middle-class housing and high-end commercial projects (Anarock Property Consultants Private Limited 2018). The area has the aesthetics of planning with wide roads, roadside herbage and skyscrapers. Recurrent and severe flood episodes in the area annually, affecting roads and building-level water and power supplies, have not significantly changed perceptions about New Town being a well-planned area. The flooding episodes have high visibility across social media platforms and are not hidden or invisibilised, as they once were, when the area was being opened up to private land consolidations and investments. However, private investor interest has not been affected and has been shored up by the steady state-facilitated investments into infrastructure, beautification and tourism in the area. State responses to flood conditions have assumed local, small-scale, retrofitted solutions, operating on temporal cycles of the everyday, such as new pumping stations, deployment of pumps and opening of utility access holes. Infrastructure plans to promote growth in the area are, in contrast, large-scale, ambitious, radical and tied into long-term cycles of multilateral financing. The work on the EWRC has been completed and the alignment augmented by a co-located Metro line that brings in Rs 3,268 crore from the Ministry of Railways,[6] Rs 1,148 crore from the Ministry of Housing and Urban Affairs[7] and a loan of Rs 4,158 crore from JICA.[8] JICA has provided an Official Development Assistance Loan of Rs 1,600 crore for an East-West Metro Corridor to link this area to Howrah.[9] The city's first under-river tunnel is under construction for the Howrah connection. The future plans for New Town are premised on remaking it as a 'smart city' (Antenucci 2021) and a 'green city' where broad-based transitions to electric vehicle-based transportation modes are planned. It has become the first Indian city to commit to the United Nations 'energy compact' pledge.

In Hyderabad, the spatial consolidation has been more fragmented as the ORR has a larger spread. However, it has been more focused on priority areas and strategic in its reach towards global connections. The Financial District, located at Nanakramguda, along the ORR, for example, has ambitious plans for second phase expansion. It hosts a number of major corporates, which are part of the knowledge economy and finance sectors. In 2019, one of the world's largest e-commerce companies opened its first (and its largest) office outside the US in the Financial District. There has been focused attention from the state government on investing in additional transportation infrastructure to priority areas. Parastatals like the Hyderabad Road Development Corporation Limited (HRDCL), the Hyderabad Unified Metropolitan Transport Authority (HUMTA) and the Hyderabad Metro Rail Limited (HMRL), in coordination with (and in some cases funding from) the GHMC and HMDA, have plans for additional roads and a Light Rail Transit System to better connect areas like the Financial District and Hi-Tech City to the main city. There have also been state attempts to use land value capture (LVC) instruments to earn from the peri-urban growth along the ORR. Mahendra et al. (2020) reviewed LVC instruments being used, including the special development charges (SDCs) and the development deferment charges (DDCs). As a part of the SDCs, the city charges up to 1.25 times the normal fee for building permissions along the ORR Growth Corridor (MAUD 2016). The DDCs are fee-based and punitive. They are collected by the HMDA on land where development has been deferred by the developer and transferred to the village local bodies. Revenues from SDCs and DDCs have been minimal so far, relative to the overall HMDA budget (ibid.). However, they have been significant in reorganising the micro-politics of real estate developments and governance along the ORR (ibid.). In Hyderabad too, the continued real estate and infrastructure investment interests remain unabated by concerns such as flood resilience (Sehra and Punia 2020) and impacts of the ORR and real estate developments in its influence zone on the local system of tanks that the city of Hyderabad continues to be dependent on for its water security (Reddy et al. 2019).

NOTES

1. Eminent domain refers to the powers of the state to acquire land for 'public purpose' using the statutory provisions of certain acts, such as 'The Right to Fair Compensation and Transparency in Land Acquisition, Rehabilitation and Resettlement Act, 2013'. This power may be wielded only by certain government bodies that are identified in the relevant acts. For a detailed analysis of the history, practice and limitations of eminent domain in India, see Sampat (2013).

2. Ramachandraiah (2009) is a useful parallel reference here since it highlights how the alignment of the Hyderabad Metro project given to a private company, for infrastructure development, was closely tied to the real estate interests of the company.

3. For example, both roads lacked public transportation systems in initial years. For many years, a system of private chartered buses and

mini-vans plied on the Outer Ring Road (ORR) to bus in people from the city to new peri-urban employment hubs.

4. A list of the relevant government orders is available at https://www.hmda.gov.in/pdf/G.O.Ms.No.%20470%20%20%20dt-%2009-07-08.pdf (accessed on 5 July 2022).

5. Available at http://www.wbhidcoltd.com/uploads/reports/report11.pdf (accessed on 5 July 2022).

6. See https://www.pmindia.gov.in/en/news_updates/cabinet-approves-revised-cost-for-kolkata-east-west-metro-corridor-project-for-kolkata-city-and-surrounding-urban-areas/ (accessed on 5 July 2022).

7. Ibid.

8. Ibid.

9. See https://www.jica.go.jp/india/english/office/topics/press180928_02.html (accessed on 5 July 2022).

REFERENCES

Anarock Property Consultants Private Limited. 2018. 'Rajarhat New Town, Kolkata: An Emerging Commercial Hub in the Eastern Fringes: Micromarket Overview Report'. Available at https://api.anarock.com/uploads/research/Rajarhat%20New%20Town%20-%20Micro%20Market%20Overview%20Report.pdf (accessed on 5 July 2022).

Antenucci, I. 2021. 'Infrastructures of Extraction in the Smart City Zones, Finance, and Platforms in New Town Kolkata'. *International Journal of Communication* 15: 2652–68. Available at https://www.researchgate.net/profile/Ilia-Antenucci/publication/355105323_Digital_Infrastructure_Liminality_and_World-Making_Via_Asia_Infrastructures_of_Extraction_in_the_Smart_City_Zones_Finance_and_Platforms_in_New_Town_Kolkata/links/61ae2272ca2d401f27cdb8e2/Digital-Infrastructure-Liminality-and-World-Making-Via-Asia-Infrastructures-of-Extraction-in-the-Smart-City-Zones-Finance-and-Platforms-in-New-Town-Kolkata.pdf (accessed on 5 July 2022).

Bagchi, A. 1987. 'Planning for Metropolitan Development: Calcutta's Basic Development Plan, 1966–86: A Post-mortem'. *Economic & Political Weekly* 22(14): 597–601.

Balakrishnan, S. 2013. 'Highway Urbanization and Land Conflicts: The Challenges to Decentralization in India'. *Pacific Affairs* 86(4): 785–811.

Banerjee, A., P. Bardhan, K. Basu, M. D. Chaudhuri, M. Ghatak, A. S. Guha, M. Majumdar, D. Mookherjee and D. Ray. 2002. 'Strategy for Economic Reform in West Bengal'. *Economic & Political Weekly* 37(41): 4203–18.

Basu, P. 2007. '"Brand Buddha" in India's West Bengal: The Left Reinvents Itself'. *Asian Survey* 47(2): 288–306.

Bhattacharya, Rajesh, and Kalyan Sanyal. 2011. 'Bypassing the Squalor: New Towns, Immaterial Labour and Exclusion in Post-colonial Urbanization'. *Economic & Political Weekly* 46(31): 41–48.

Bose, P. S. 2007. 'Dreaming of Diasporas: Urban Developments and Transnational Identities in Contemporary Kolkata'. *TOPIA: Canadian Journal of Cultural Studies* 17: 111–30.

Bose, S. 2008. 'Adaptive and Integrated Management of Wastewater and Storm Water Drainage in Kolkata—Case Study of a Mega City'. In *Adaptive and Integrated Water Management: Coping with Complexity and Uncertainty*, eds C. Pahl-Wostl, P. Kabat and J. Moltgen, 341–55. Berlin, Heidelberg: Springer Verlag.

Brenner, Neil. 2004. 'Urban Governance and the Production of New State Spaces in Western Europe, 1960–2000'. *Review of International Political Economy* 11(3): 447–88.

Bunting, S. W., N. Kundu and M. Mukherjee. 2005. 'Peri-urban Aquaculture and Poor Livelihoods in Kolkata, India'. In *Urban Aquaculture*, eds B. Costa Pierce, A. Desbonnet, P. Edwards and D. Baker, 61–76. Cambridge: CABI Publishing.

Comptroller and Auditor General (CAG). 2007. *West Bengal Report*. New Delhi: CAG. Available at https://www.cag.gov.in/sites/default/files/old_reports/state/West_Bengal/2007/Commercial/com_chap_2.pdf (accessed on 10 July 2018).

———. 2018. *Report No. 1 of 2018 (Public Sector Undertakings, Chapter III: Hyderabad Growth Corridor Limited)*. New Delhi: CAG. Available at https://cag.gov.in/sites/default/files/audit_report_files/9%20Chapter-IIIfm.pdf (accessed on 2 October 2018).

Corbridge, S., and J. Harriss. 2000. *Reinventing India: Liberalization, Hindu Nationalism and Popular Democracy*. Cambridge, UK: Polity Press.

Deccan Chronicle. 2014. 'Thirteen Urban Centres to Come Up on Outskirts of the Hyderabad'. Available at https://www.deccanchronicle.com/141021/nation-current-affairs/article/13-urban-centres-come-outskirts-hyderabad (accessed on 10 July 2018).

———. 2017. 'Move to Expand Outer Ring Road Corridor'. Available at https://www.deccanchronicle.com/nation/current-affairs/120917/move-to-expand-outer-ring-road-corridor.html (accessed on 2 October 2018).

Denis, E. 2011. 'Financing Land in Egyptian and Indian Megacities: The Frontiers of Urban Liberalization'. *Revue Tiers Monde* 2011/2(206): 139–58.

Dey, D. 2008. 'Sustainable Development and Wastewater in Peri-urban Wetlands: A Case Study on East Kolkata Wetland'. In *Water and Urban Development Paradigms: Towards an Integration of Engineering, Design and Management Approaches*, eds J. Feyen, K. Shannon and M. Neville, 441–45. Boca Raton, FL: CRC Press.

Dey, I., R. Samaddar, and S. K. Sen. 2013. *Beyond Kolkata: Rajarhat and the Dystopia of Urban Imagination*. New Delhi: Routledge India.

DuPont, V., and N. Sridharan. 2007. 'Peri-urban Dynamics: Case Studies in Chennai, Hyderabad and Mumbai', Working Papers id: 974: eSocialSciences. Available at https://ideas.repec.org/p/ess/wpaper/id974.html (accessed on 10 July 2018).

Eenadu. 2017. '12 Logistic Parks to Come Up Around Hyderabad'. Available at http://www.eenaduindia.com/states/south/telangana/telangana-hyderabad-city/2017/10/06213327/12-logistic-parks-to-come-up-around-Hyderabad.vpf (accessed on 10 July 2018).

Flyvbjerg, B., N. Bruzelius and W. Rothengatter. 2003. *Megaprojects and Risk: An Anatomy of Ambition*. United Kingdom, New York: Cambridge University Press.

Ghosh, D., and S. Sen. 1987. 'Ecological History of Calcutta's Wetland Conversion'. *Environmental Conservation* 14(3): 219–26.

GMR. 2016. 'GMR Aero Space Park—About Us'. Available at http://www.gmraerospacepark.in/about-us/asip/ (accessed on 2 October 2018).

Goldman, M. 2010. 'Speculative Urbanism and the Making of the Next World City'. *International Journal of Urban and Regional Research* 35(3): 555–81.

Goldman, M., and D. Narayan. 2021. 'Through the Optics of Finance: Speculative Urbanism and the Transformation of Markets'. *International Journal of Urban and Regional Research* 45(2): 209–31.

Government of Andhra Pradesh. 2009. 'Project Features'. Available at http://www.hyderabadringroad.com/html/project_features.htm (accessed on 17 June 2011).

Gupta, A., and K. Sivaramakrishnan, eds. 2011. *The State in India after Liberalization*. London and New York: Routledge.

Gupta, S. 2017. 'Here's How Outer Ring Road is Pushing Hyderabad Real Estate'. Available at https://www.proptiger.com/guide/post/heres-how-outer-ring-road-is-pushing-hyderabad-real-estate? (accessed on 2 October 2018).

Harvey, D. 2003. *The New Imperialism*. Oxford: Oxford University Press.

———. 2006. *Spaces of Global Capitalism*. New York: Verso.

Hyderabad Metropolitan Development Authority (HMDA). 2016. 'Outer Ring Road'. Available at https://www.hmda.gov.in/orr.aspx (accessed on 2 October 2018).

Indian School of Business (ISB). 2010. 'Project Appraisal of the Hyderabad Outer Ring Road Project'. Available at https://www.google.com/url?sa=t&rct=j&q=&esrc=s&source=web&cd=3&cad=rja&uact=8&ved=2ahUKEwjrnN-9tujdAhUMcCsKHafiDRsQFjACegQIAxAC&url=http%3A%2F%2Ftgpg-isb.org%2Fsites%2Fdefault%2Ffiles%2Fpolicy-paper%2F11.%2520Project%2520Appraisal%2520of%2520Hydrabad%2520Outer%2520Ring%2520Road%2520Project%2520%2528ORR%2529.doc&usg=AOvVaw0y2S1iqIMF1aj_zwnz4ZOF (accessed on 2 October 2018).

Jessop, B. 2002. 'Time and Space in the Globalization of Capital and Their Implications for State Power'. *Rethinking Marxism* 14(1): 97–117.

Joshi, V., and I. M. D. Little. 1996. *India's Economic Reforms, 1991-2001*. New York: Oxford University Press.

Kennedy, L. 2007. 'Regional Industrial Policies Driving Peri-urban Dynamics in Hyderabad, India'. *Cities* 24(2): 95–109.

——. 2014. *The Politics of Economic Restructuring in India: Economic Governance and State Spatial Rescaling*. London: Routledge.

Kennedy, L., and A. Sood. 2016. 'Greenfield Development as Tabula Rasa'. *Economic & Political Weekly* 51(17): 41–49.

Kohli, A. 1988. 'The NTR Phenomenon in Andhra Pradesh: Political Change in a South Indian State'. *Asian Survey* 28(10): 991–1017.

——. 1989. 'Politics of Economic Liberalization in India'. *World Development* 17(3): 305–28.

Kumar, A. 2006. 'Trends of Planning and Governance in Metropolitan India'. *Institute of Town Planners India* 3(2): 10–20.

Levien, M. 2012. 'The Land Question: Special Economic Zones and the Political Economy of Dispossession in India'. *The Journal of Peasant Studies* 39(3–4): 933–69.

Luther, N. 2006. *Hyderabad: A Biography*. New Delhi: Oxford University Press.

Mahendra, A., R. King, E. Gray, M. Hart, L. Azeredo, L. Betti, S. Prakash, A. Deb, E. Ashebir and A. Ibrahim. 2020. 'Urban Land Value Capture in Sao Paulo, Addis Abbaba and Hyderabad: Differing Interpretations, Equity Impacts, and Enabling Conditions'. Working Paper WP20AM1, Lincoln Institute of Land Policy and World Resources Institute. Available at https://www.lincolninst.edu/sites/default/files/pubfiles/mahendra_wp20am1.pdf (accessed on 5 July 2022).

Mitra, Sanjay. 2002. 'Planned Urbanisation through Public Participation: Case of the New Town, Kolkata'. *Economic & Political Weekly* 37(11): 1048–54.

Mitra, S. 2018. 'A "Peripheries" View of Planning Failures in Kolkata and Hyderabad in India'. In *Routledge Companion to Planning in the Global*

South, eds G. Bhan, S. Srinivas and V. Watson, 79–90. Oxon, New York: Routledge.

Municipal Administration and Urban Development Department (MAUD). 2008. Abstract, Government of Andhra Pradesh, 9 July. Available at https://www.hmda.gov.in/pdf/G.O.Ms.No.%20470%20%20%20dt-%20 09-07-08.pdf (accessed on 5 July 2022).

———. 2016. 'Amendments to Special Development Regulations of Hyderabad Outer Ring Road Growth Corridor—Orders—Issued'. Government of Telangana. Available at https://tsiic.telangana.gov.in/wp-content/uploads/2017/07/2016MAUD_MS9.pdf (accessed on 5 July 2022).

My Estate Point. 2015. 'Challenge for New Civic Body: Uniform Land Rule in West Bengal'. Available at http://news.myestatepoint.com/news/kolkata/challenge-for-new-civic-body-uniform-land-rule-in-west-begal/ (accessed on 2 October 2018).

Naidu, C., and N. Sevanti. 2000. *Plain Speaking*. New Delhi: Viking.

Nallathiga, R. 2014. 'An Assessment of Land Acquisition Under Hyderabad Outer Ring Road Project'. Available at https://www.researchgate.net/profile/Ramakrishna_Nallathiga/publication/268153283_An_assessment_of_land_acquisition_under_Hyderabad_Outer_Ring_Road_Project/links/54991f610cf2c5a7e342cc4a.pdf (accessed on 5 July 2022).

Ong, A. 2006. *Neoliberalism as Exception: Mutations in Citizenship and Sovereignty*. Durham: Duke University Press.

Pedersen, J. Ø. D. 2000. 'Explaining Economic Liberalization in India: State and Society Perspectives'. *World Development* 28(2): 265–82.

———. 2001. 'India's Industrial Dilemmas in West Bengal'. *Asian Survey* 41(4): 646–68.

Ramachandraiah, C. 2009. 'Maytas, Hyderabad Metro and the Politics of Real Estate'. *Economic & Political Weekly* 36(40): 36–40.

Raman, B. 2016. 'Reading into the Politics of Land: Real Estate Markets in the South-west Peri-urban Area of Chennai'. *Economic & Political Weekly* 51(17): 76–84.

Reddy, D. N. 1999. *Vision 2020: Myths and Realities*. Seminar papers, Sundaratta Vignanakendra, Hyderabad.

Reddy, R., P. Narender Babu and E. Srinivas. 2019. 'Urbanisation and Tank Systems Adjoining Hyderabad—A Rapid Assessment Using Remote Sensing Techniques'. In *Proceedings of International Conference on Remote Sensing for Disaster Management*, eds J. Rao, K. N. Rao and S. Kubo, 91–99. Cham, Switzerland: Springer.

Rouanet, H., and L. Halbert. 2016. 'Leveraging Finance Capital: Urban Change and Self-empowerment of Real Estate Developers in India'. *Urban Studies* 53(7): 1–23.

Sampat, P. 2013. 'Limits to Absolute Power: Eminent Domain and the Right to Land in India'. *Economic & Political Weekly* 48(19): 40–52.

——. 2016. 'The Emperor's New City'. *Economic & Political Weekly* 51(17): 59–67.

Searle, L. G. 2014. 'Conflict and Commensuration: Contested Market Making in India's Private Real Estate Development Sector'. *International Journal of Urban and Regional Research* 38(1): 60–78.

Sehra, V., and M. Punia. 2020. 'Overcoming Barriers to Urban Flood Resilience: A Case of Hyderabad, India'. In *Flood Impact Mitigation and Resilience Enhancement*, ed. G. Huang, 37–52. London: IntechOpen.

Sengupta, U. 2006. 'Government Intervention and Public-Private Partnerships in Housing Delivery in Kolkata'. *Habitat International* 30(3): 448–61.

——. 2007. 'Housing Reform in Kolkata: Changes and Challenges'. *Housing Studies* 22(6): 965–79.

Sengupta, U., and A. G. Tipple. 2007. 'The Performance of Public-Sector Housing in Kolkata, India, in the Post-Reform Milieu'. *Urban Studies* 44(10): 2009–27.

Shatkin, G. 2016. 'The Real Estate Turn in Policy and Planning: Land Monetization and the Political Economy of Peri-Urbanization in Asia'. *Cities* 53: 141–49.

Shaw, A. 2005. 'Peri-urban Interface of Indian Cities: Growth, Governance and Local Initiatives'. *Economic & Political Weekly* 40(2): 129–36.

Shaw, A., and M. K. Satish. 2007. 'Metropolitan Restructuring in Post-Liberalized India: Separating the Global and the Local'. *Cities* 24(2): 148–63.

Sinha, A. 2004. 'The Changing Political Economy of Federalism in India: A Historical Institutionalist Approach'. *India Review* 3(1): 25–63.

Sood, A. 2016. 'Emerging Megacities: Hyderabad and Bangalore'. *Sociology of Urban Transformations*. Available at https://www.researchgate.net/publication/323265010_EMERGING_MEGACITIES_HYDERABAD_AND_BANGALORE_A_module_prepared_for_the_Urban_Transformations_curriculum_for_EPG-Pathshala (accessed on 5 July 2022).

Srinivasulu, K., and P. Sarangi. 1999. 'Political Realignments in Post-NTR Andhra Pradesh'. *Economic & Political Weekly* 34(34/35): 2449–58.

The Hans India. 2017. 'HMDA to Develop Growth Corridor'. Available at http://www.thehansindia.com/posts/index/Telangana/2017-09-07/HMDA-to-develop-growth-corridor/324761 (accessed on 2 October 2018).

The Hindu. 2006. 'ORR Alignment Changed 115 Times: Devender Goud'. Available at http://www.hindu.com/2006/08/31/stories/2006083111520400.htm (accessed on 10 July 2018).

The Times of India. 2006. 'CBI Probe Ordered'. Available at https://timesofindia.indiatimes.com/city/hyderabad/CBI-probe-ordered/articleshow/2030263.cms (accessed on 2 October 2018).

Upadhya, C. 1988. 'The Farmer-Capitalists of Coastal Andhra Pradesh'. *Economic & Political Weekly* 23(28): 1433–42.

Van Rooijen, D., A. Evans, J. P. Venot and P. Drechsel. 2011. 'Cities, Agriculture and Environment—Sharing Water In and Around Hyderabad, South India'. In *Water Resources Planning and Management*, eds R. Q. Grafton and K. Hussey, 367–79. New York: Cambridge University Press.

Vijayabaskar, M., and A. Menon. 2018. 'Dispossession by Neglect: Agricultural Land Sales in Southern India'. *Journal of Agrarian Change* 18(3): 571–87.

Wallerstein, I. 1991. 'Braudel on Capitalism, or Everything Upside Down'. *The Journal of Modern History* 63(2): 354–61.

West Bengal Housing Infrastructure Development Corporation (WBHIDCO). 2018. 'About Us'. Available at http://www.wbhidcoltd.com/org_desc.php?pg=invcommon&typ=common&tag=aboutus_com (accessed on 2 October 2018).

West Bengal Electronics Industry Development Corporation Limited (WEBEL). n.d. 'West Bengal's Policy on IT Enabled Services'. Kolkata: Government of West Bengal. Available at http://www.webel-india.com/pdf-download/west_bengal_ites_policy.pdf (accessed on 10 July 2018).

PART II

DYNAMICS

LAND AND REAL ESTATE

5

Dholera

The Emperor's New City

PREETI SAMPAT

In mid-2009, the Gujarat government converted 22 villages along the Gulf of Khambhat into the Dholera Special Investment Region (DSIR). The 920–sq km DSIR is constituted under the Gujarat Special Investment Region (SIR) Act 2009, and home to a predominantly agrarian population of about 39,300. Dholera is slated to be the first 'smart city' (referred to as *samrat sheher* in local parlance) along the Delhi–Mumbai Industrial Corridor (DMIC).[1] As 340 sq km of the project area falls under the coastal regulation zone, the 'developable land area' of the project is 580 sq km. This massive conversion of agrarian land into a 'greenfield' (new) city is an exercise in government planning not unlike the halcyon days of state-led development planning, albeit with newer legal mechanisms and private bodies in partnership.

The central contention of this chapter is that a growing 'rentier economy' is driving urbanisation infrastructure projects since the mid-2000s in India, ostensibly to attract economic growth. This rentier economy brings within its purview, in varying combinations, policy, speculative land markets, real estate and other urban infrastructure investments by global and domestic investors, private consultants and developers, interests within the state at various levels, and (usually large) landowners willing and able to benefit from rentier activity (at least temporarily). The rentier economy hinges crucially on ownership of land, or access to it. There is a need to distinguish rent-driven urbanisation infrastructure projects from industrialisation and concomitant job creation despite their conflation in policy rhetoric. The transition to industrialisation and jobs that such projects promise to unleash remains elusive as rentier-driven dispossession threatens productive political economics around land.

As a greenfield city-making project, Dholera offers insights into the scale and implications of this rentier economy in the countryside. Its planning regime grafted existing and purportedly voluntary legal mechanisms like 'land pooling' to new policies for industrial corridors and SIRs, involving private planners and developers. As this study demonstrates, the absence of investor interest, the state's inability to establish consent for the proposed transformation of existing agrarian relations and elite circuits of rent render the future of Dholera uncertain. Its realisation hinges on anticipated and precarious futures of investment and rent.[2] Investment is expected to arrive once basic infrastructure is in place, and rent is expected to accrue as land and eventually real estate prices appreciate with the 'development' of the area into a 'smart city'. I argue that these precarious futures and circuits of rent are salient features of India's growing rentier economy.[3]

The study was undertaken over a period of four months from March to July 2015 and subsequently in November 2021, and uses ethnographic and archival materials. I interviewed bureaucrats, developers, academics, journalists, lawyers and activists in Delhi, Ahmedabad, Gandhinagar, Vadodara as well as residents in the villages of the Dholera SIR area. I also participated in seven public meetings in and around the Dholera area dealing with the question of dispossession caused by the project. As these villages are sensitive areas of resistance fraught with tensions over 'outsider' access, my access to the area was mediated by the non-governmental organisation Khedut Samaj, the state-wide land-rights campaign *Jameen Adhikar Andolan Gujarat* and local *Bhal Bachao Samiti* activists. My fieldwork in the villages was not comprehensive and was mediated by those opposing the project, but it should be noted that my objective here is not to document the extent of dissent or analyse in detail the organisational dynamics of the social movement in the area. The material I present instead demonstrates the inability of the state to establish consent for the project, and counters official claims of 100 per cent consensual land pooling for Dholera.

INSTITUTING DHOLERA SMART CITY

The Gujarat SIR Act 2009 was enacted to institute 'investment regions' and 'investment areas' feeding growth along the DMIC.

The SIR law allows for the use of both the Central land acquisition law and the Gujarat Town Planning and Urban Development Act (GTPUDA) 1976 for land consolidation. Perhaps as a demonstration of commitment to voluntary land consolidation, or to avoid the political resistance to forcible land acquisition (or both), the state government initially invoked land pooling in Dholera, but with unsuccessful attempts at pooling, shifted to land acquisition under the GTPUDA.[4] The state has historically used the town planning law for the conversion of rural-agrarian land for the expansion of existing cities. Through the SIR Act, the town planning law's scope was extended to greenfield cities. Typically, such cities are instituted as public–private partnerships (PPPs) between the state government, and private investors and developers. Dholera envisaged such partnership from its inception.

The development plan for the Dholera SIR was elaborated by a UK-based global consultancy firm for the Government of Gujarat in 2010 (Datta 2015), and subsequently sanctioned and rendered operational by 2012. A global infrastructure giant was then awarded a $30-million five-year extendable contract by the DMIC Development Corporation in mid-2013 for full programme management services in Dholera. The Dholera SIR Authority was in charge of implementing the project phase-wise over 30 years, in three development phases of 10 years each. It formed the special purpose vehicle (SPV) Dholera Industrial City Development Limited (DICDL) in 2016 with 51 per cent state equity (in the form of land) and 49 per cent Central government equity to execute the project. DICDL is initially developing trunk infrastructure such as roads, water, sewage and power supply systems in an 'activation zone' of 22.54 sq km on land it already possesses. As we see later, there has been trouble in securing more land for the project because of popular resistance in the area.

The proposed land use in Dholera includes residential, industrial, tourism, commercial, information technology, recreation sports and entertainment zones. Under the provisions of the town planning law, land for the Dholera SIR was to be consolidated via a 'pooling' mechanism: 50 per cent of the land of each owner in the Dholera area was to be 'deducted' at market price from the owners, the rest returned to them as 'developed' plots in re-designated zones under the new plan criteria. A 'betterment charge' was levied on the original owners for the provision of new infrastructure facilities, further deducted from the compensation award for 50 per cent of the land. Each affected family was promised one job per family in the Dholera SIR. While the town planning law contains provisions for the participation of local bodies and residents in the determination of compensation and award, it made no provisions for ascertaining consent to land pooling for the project. In a change from earlier policy, indicative of the challenges of pooling land in Dholera, the managing director of DICDL clarified in a November 2021 interview that Dholera's land is being aggregated from farmers under the GTPUDA. While the compensation package remains the same as under pooling, the land acquisition framework of the town planning law is now being used for the project.

The land pooling mechanism was premised on the principle that the development authority in charge of undertaking planned urban development temporarily brings together a group of landowners for planning a region's development. As there is no forcible acquisition or 'transfer of ownership', the case for compensation under the national land acquisition law does not arise, except for the proportion of the land deducted for basic infrastructure provision. The rest of the land remains with the original landowner, and the 'benefit' of development in terms of the increment in land value after development accrues to the owner rather than to the development agency. The original owner continues to enjoy access to the land without being displaced (Ballaney 2008), at least on paper. Irrespective of the land consolidation mechanism, the incorporation of the town planning law into the SIR Act in Gujarat for a greenfield city poses significant issues (see discussion later).

The planning for Dholera was conceived in distinct phases under the GTPUDA: a development plan was initially prepared for the entire area affected by the project, followed by several smaller town planning schemes (TPSs) for smaller portions of the project development area. The initial draft plan was kept open for public inspection for two months, inviting objections and suggestions to its terms. Procedurally, the plan could then be modified and published again, inviting further objections and suggestions for incorporation, and the state government may suggest further modifications before the final plan is prepared. The TPSs are the micro plans for the development of smaller areas as per the final plan, and each scheme similarly allows 'consultation' and 'participation' in its drafting and implementation.

One issue that comes up with reference to the use of a town planning law for greenfield urbanisation is that the extent of land required for a new city invariably results in the loss of a far greater extent of land than in the course of expansion of an existing city. Additionally, with the re-zoning of land according to the new development plan, owners do not retain their original agricultural plots and must relocate. With the development of a new city (or the expansion of an existing city), even if village settlements are protected with buffer zones, conditions invariably develop to prevent older rural settlements from continuing in the same form. This forces the original inhabitants to move in search of livelihoods, or as they are priced out, for affordable living options. Moreover, the disruption of the agrarian economy and the re-zoning and subdivision of plots result in severe temporal and physical dislocation of agricultural livelihoods, and only large farmers with the holding power to wait the years for development of the re-zoned plots and with enough surplus land may retain their hold on cultivation and allied agricultural activities. Agrarian livelihoods and resources also experience a severe contraction with the growth of industry, tourism, construction and other related economic activities. With immediate attractive returns, the push is towards sale of land and rentier incomes as land values appreciate. With productive agricultural activity decreasing, this further raises issues of livelihood and food security from the local to regional scales. Finally, developing and returning 50 per cent land to the original owners can presumably take several years. In the interim, the livelihood and food security options available for local residents significantly dependent on land are unclear.

There are also significant issues with 'consent'. Despite provisions for consultation, Dholera's plan and its schemes contain no procedure for ascertaining consent for the proposed development. In fact, there was an a priori assumption of consent built into the land pooling mechanism (see Sampat and Sunny 2016). Even under the land acquisition framework currently being used, there is no clarity as to how the consent from landowners is being established for the project. On paper, the state government has already transferred the land to the DSIR Authority. On the ground, as we see later, there is little clarity on how and when consent was established, and the transfer is challenged by local residents and peasants in an ongoing case challenging the constitutional validity of the SIR law in the Gujarat High Court (HC). Under the 2013 land acquisition law as well, in PPP projects, consent of 70 per cent of original landowners is required before a project can be undertaken. The pooling mechanism circumvented consent-based development through the disingenuous language of consultation and voluntary pooling. The current mechanism does not specify what consent provisions are to be used for the forthcoming TPSs. The language of pooling is officially substituted with that of acquisition under the GTPUDA, but consent provisions were neither specified nor followed before the official land transfer was made on paper. Ongoing resistance to the project must be situated in the context of all of these issues.

Land Relations and Dissent

The 22 villages in the Dholera SIR area are a vibrant landscape of existing relations around land and various local resources. A thriving agrarian political economy cultivating rain-fed wheat (the coveted *bhaliya ghaun* for which the region is known), cotton, cumin and jowar as well as rearing milch cattle complements livelihood strategies with other diverse occupations in the region, including diamond polishing. The majority community in the area are Koli Patels (roughly 62 per cent of the population), who own a majority of marginal to medium landholdings that many received, ironically, through redistributive land reforms. The next community are the large landholding Darbars (kshatriyas, 11 per cent), followed by a smattering of other communities, including those dependent on the commons like the Bharwads (pastorals), Scheduled Caste (SC) communities, Muslims and barely, if any, Scheduled Tribes (ST) (SENES Consultants India Pvt. Ltd 2013). Many milch cattle-owning

Table 5.1 Land area of 22 villages under DSIR

Name of district	Name of taluka	Name of revenue villages			
		Sr. no.	Name of village	Total survey nos.	Total area of land in sq km
Ahmedabad	1. Dhandhuka	1	Bavaliyari	1204	111.2724
		2	Bhadiyad	1908	49.7331
		3	Bhangadh	620	83.0777
		4	Bhimtalav	223	7.4042
		5	Dholera	969	45.8145
		6	Gorasu	1219	31.1763
		7	Kadipur	648	27.3509
		8	Khun	227	38.2968
		9	Mahadevpura	179	22.5431
		10	Mingalpur	261	33.0813
		11	Mundi	316	17.8054
		12	Otariya	801	18.0975
		13	Panchi	360	13.9638
		14	Rahatalav	2336	63.4464
		15	Sandhida	517	18.6401
		16	Zankhi	389	22.0941
		17	Ambli	1084	55.2044
		18	Cher	464	16.2436
		19	Gogla	385	55.4426
	2. Barwala	1	Hebatpur	1086	72.6594
		2	Sangasar	790	35.4928
		3	Sodhi	588	40.4975
	Total			**16574**	**879.3377**

Source: Dholera Special Investment Region Development Authority (DSIRDA) (2013).

villagers are members of flourishing milk cooperatives in the area. Table 5.1 gives the total land area of the 22 villages under the DSIR.

In 2018, the Dholera SIR Development Authority (that set up the DICDL) also successfully gained approval from the state's Coastal Zone Management Authority to obtain clearance from the Ministry of Environment, Forests and Climate Change, Government of India, for the development of a 5,000-megawatt solar park and a 200-megawatt wind power project along 110 sq km of coastal lands adjoining Dholera. In early 2019, the ministry approved phase one of the project for a 1,000-megawatt solar project. When the state invited bids for solar power generation in the first phase of the project in March 2020, however, there were no takers for it.

Additionally, in terms of land use, the Velavadar National Park is a blackbuck sanctuary adjacent to the DSIR.[5] By law, the park has to be protected by a 10-km buffer zone around it, but the Dholera development plan violates this stipulation, focusing instead on providing wildlife crossings and flood mitigation as compensation measures to protect the wildlife of the area from the urban centre. The national environment ministry's 2019 approval letter for the first phase of the solar project noted on the basis of documents submitted by the Dholera authority that: 'There are no eco-sensitive areas within 2–3 kilometers of the site. The nearest eco-sensitive site of Velvadar [sic] blackbuck sanctuary is about 4 kilometers south-west from the nearest solar plot planned' (MOEFCC 2019: 5).

According to official figures, dryland farming is the source of livelihood for nearly 70 per cent of the local population, while more than 56 per cent depend on livestock rearing and 23 per cent on farm labour (being part of one livelihood category does not imply exclusion from another category; see Table 5.2; also see SENES Consultants India Pvt. Ltd [2013] for more details).

The literacy rates in the entire DSIR area are worth noting, with just over 35 per cent of the population non-literate, 44 per cent with primary education, just under 15 per cent with secondary education, 3 per cent with higher secondary and 3 per cent with college education (SENES Consultants India Pvt. Ltd 2013). As I recount later, several residents I interviewed in Bavaliyari and Ambli villages argued that agricultural work does not require specialised skill sets of the kind that other urbanised and industrial

Table 5.2 Livelihood pattern in the DSIR area

Village	No. of Reported HH	Dry land Farming	Livestock Rearing	Farm Labour
INNER-COASTAL ZONE				
Bavaliyari	408	299	355	95
Bhangadh	326	272	203	10
Bhimtalav	23	8	4	12
Khun	200	122	194	49
Mahadevpura	251	211	81	40
Mingalpur	556	185	203	0
Rahtalav	443	378	307	110
Zankhi	186	80	46	50
Total	2393	1555	1393	367
% of Total		65	58.2	15.3
TRANSITIONAL ZONE				
Ambali	212	97	86	120
Dholera	591	217	152	302
Gogala	224	164	160	55
Hebatpur	677	623	471	108
Kadipur	133	88	92	56
Mundi	82	46	48	9
Panchi	123	123	116	0
Sandheda	158	114	100	0
Total	2200	1472	1225	650
% of Total		67	56	30
OUTER ZONE				
Bhadiyad	489	306	146	128
Cher	53	46	46	8
Gorasu	226	136	85	74
Otariya	240	218	82	15
Sangasar	177	171	118	11
Sodhi	373	358	325	150
Total	1558	1235	802	386
% of Total		79.3	51.5	24.8
All Zones Total	6151	4262	3420	1403

Source: Adapted from SENES Consultants India Pvt. Ltd (2013).

work may. The offer of one job per affected family will thus not compensate others in a family rendered without work. Residents expressed anxiety that losing land and commons to the Dholera SIR would render them without livelihoods and future security.

The 22 villages also fall within the Narmada river canal command and have been waiting for over a decade for canal water. The villages were 'decommanded' in 2014 in the wake of the DSIR, but residents fought for reinstatement and the area was subsequently 'recommanded' in 2015. As of late 2021, the canal infrastructure had reached the villages but they still awaited water. According to the residents, if the water reaches the villages, the fertile soil will give them two or three yearly crops of wheat, cotton, cumin and jowar, enriching the local agrarian economy. Given existing skills, literacy and education levels, in nearly all interviews and meetings, irrespective of community and socio-economic status, residents expressed the desire for greater state support in strengthening the existing agrarian economy with the provision of canals and other agrarian infrastructure to create overall prosperity and development in the region. In the following, I represent key concerns articulated by residents across community and socio-economic status from Bavaliyari and Ambli panchayats.[6]

Voices from Bavaliyari and Ambli[7]

Champa ben Pratap Singh of Bavaliyari is a non-literate landless Koli Patel peasant who cultivates others' lands with her husband, Pratap Singh, in exchange for 25–30 per cent share of the produce. The couple have two school-going sons and a daughter. They have three buffaloes that suffice for their family's needs and allow for minor sale of milk. During an interview, Champa ben asked if non-literates like her would be given jobs in the new smart city with her skills of cotton picking, cleaning and growing other crops. The SC community in Bavaliyari has a *mandali*, a collective landholding of around 500 acres allotted by the state that is divided among the SC households in the village for cultivation. Jayantibhai Solanki has a 16-acre share in the mandali. He also bought 10 acres of land in 1982 and owns a tractor. One of his sons studies in college while the other farms, and three of his daughters are married. According to Manju ben, his wife, there should first be a clear guarantee of work for the locals and then alone should land be taken by the state for a project. She added that the canal water from the Narmada will be of use to them and that 'in the village there can be no development without farming'. Even if one has to go out to a city for work temporarily, she pointed out, at least there is the security of land to return to in the village, while the city is too expensive to sustain oneself in. If an industry comes to the area, she asked, 'What will we do in case it closes? On the land, we can grow food and eat and sustain other livelihood activities.'

Similarly, Darshanbhai Chonchla from Bavaliyari is a Bharwad and reveals that he has approximately 6 acres as share in the 400 acres of land owned by the *gopalak* mandali (cow-herder collective). He has 20 buffaloes and 7 cows and reveals that there are around 5,000 cattle in the entire village. He asked, 'If a company comes to the village, where will the cattle and people go? As we are not educated, how will we get jobs?'

Pradyumna Singh Chudasama, a large landholding Darbar with 54 acres of land (and an additional 35 acres in his wife's name) is a retired officer from the state education department from Bavaliyari and a key organiser in the anti-DSIR movement. Chudasama has collated details of the DSIR project through several applications under the Right to Information Act 2005 and maintains the documents and records of all project details, petitions, appeals, communications and relevant press cuttings for the Bhal Bachao Samiti. Chudasama is also involved in the writ petition challenging the DSIR in the Gujarat HC. While taking me through his meticulously maintained files, Chudasama argued that agricultural work offers gainful employment to all people irrespective of their abilities and capacities. The aged as well as people with special physical and mental abilities can find gainful work in agriculture, but a factory will not hire everyone and will require specific skill sets. Several petitions have been made to the DSIR authorities and the state government requesting the cancellation of the project. According to Chudasama, the petitions of the villagers opposing the project have not been taken into account officially.

Lalitaben Bana Jadav of Sarasla village in Ambli panchayat is also a Koli Patel and has a small plot of about 3 acres as her husband Bana Jadav's share among three brothers. She used to work as an agricultural labourer but injured her back two years ago. Her husband works at a hotel on the highway outside the village and they have two sons and two daughters, one of whom is married. While performing her chores in the kitchen garden outside her house, she explained that they (the villagers) do not want a city and the women of the area will fight as the entire village is against giving the land for the project. If the project comes, she argued, people will die as what jobs will the uneducated get in the project? She argued that it is a lie that they will prosper with land values appreciating, as the land being allotted is close to the sea and flood-prone. Besides, with a majority of the population in the area non-literate, she expressed scepticism about creating locally owned tourism and other service-oriented businesses. She added that the farmers of the area need Narmada canal water to enhance productivity.

Salimbhai Maru is a Muslim from Dodhiya Para in Ambli panchayat and shares about 40 acres of land with four brothers. He has five cows. In his interview he complained that the rate of compensation fixed for the 50 per cent of land sought by the DSIR is very low at Rs 70 per bigha compared to the market price in the area of Rs 400 per bigha. Additionally, he raised the issue that if the other half of the land is to be developed and returned to the original owners in 15 years, what are people supposed to do for livelihood in the meanwhile?

Like Lalitaben, several residents claimed that the developed plots allotted to them are within the flood-prone areas where they will not be able to live, graze cattle or cultivate fields. Indeed, the development plan shows tourism and residential zones on areas reclaimed from the sea. Landless agricultural workers further pointed out that while they had no land to lose, the proposed project was unlikely to hire non-literate unskilled labourers and thus be of little aid in their development.

Residents opposed the economic overhaul of the region proposed by the DSIR, but they did not argue that 'development' is not important or necessary in the villages. Rather, they argued for the need to strengthen existing agrarian infrastructures and to develop other support mechanisms. This shows that the contest in Dholera is over defining the terms of development and its beneficiaries. As resistance continues, contingent alliances across caste, class, community and gender hierarchies coalesce in confrontation with interests promoting the DSIR. While not radically egalitarian, these alliances nevertheless open possibilities for articulations of 'development from below' (Sampat 2015a).

LOCAL RESISTANCE AND CONFLICTING NARRATIVES ABOUT PUBLIC CONSULTATION

The Bhal Bachao Samiti, a committee with representatives of the 22 impacted villages, was formed by local residents to resist the project, with each village reportedly constituting a sub-committee. Approximately 100 people were detained and several arrested in February 2014 when protesting land acquisition (Chavda 2014; Jameen Adhikar Andolan Gujarat [JAAG] 2014a, 2014b). Local residents also filed a writ petition in the Gujarat HC challenging the takeover of their productive agricultural land by the state under the GTPUDA. A 2015 HC order stayed proceedings for land consolidation as the matter was under consideration in the court (*Gujarat Khedut Samaj and Others v Gujarat State and Others* 2015). As of late 2021, the legal status quo remains in place. However, as the latest developments around the construction of a new highway in the region show (see later), this is interpreted in very different ways by the DICDL officials and the local residents.

The Gujarat Infrastructure Development Board (GIDB) is the apex authority under the SIR Act 2009 and functions as the regulatory board for all SIR projects in the state. In a 2015 interview, the chief executive officer of the GIDB claimed no knowledge of resistance in the DSIR area and further claimed that adequate public consultations had been undertaken in the region regarding the project.[8]

An official of the Gujarat Industrial Corridor Corporation (GICC, constituted in 2009 for the implementation of the DMIC projects in Gujarat) overseeing the DSIR described the project as a 'nation-building exercise' and claimed that 140 public consultations had already been undertaken in the area that include consultations in every village affected by the project. In my interviews, GICC officials initially claimed that people had been 'educated' and any resistance had been addressed and resolved successfully. After some persistent questioning, however, the officials conceded that if indeed there is opposition on the ground, the project may have to be cancelled.[9]

A town planning officer in Dholera at the DSIR authority office responsible for the implementation of a TPS also denied the presence of any local opposition in the DSIR villages and claimed that surveys were being successfully undertaken by a private contractor for the Town Planning Office to ascertain plot survey numbers and titles in the area.[10]

In his November 2021 interview, the managing director of DICDL was quick to point out that the only opposition to the project was from a handful of farmers who had filed a case against the project in the Gujarat HC. The rest of the locals, he claimed, supported the project.

My interviews with villagers ran counter to these assertions. They claimed that only preliminary meetings introducing the project were held in the area, and attendance was officially assumed to imply consent. They also maintained that no officials were being allowed to enter the DSIR villages and all official surveys stood suspended. Anxiety and opposition over loss of land and livelihoods in the region has been palpable, and ongoing opposition renders the future of the project uncertain.

In October 2021, under heavy police protection, the National Highways Authority of India (NHAI) initiated digging for a 90-km stretch of land for a new highway from Ambli to Bavaliyari. Crossing fields under preparation for the winter crop, the highway is part of the DSIR, but the local residents claimed that no prior consultation was held for the highway nor was their consent sought for it. The NHAI claims that the land has been officially given to it by the state government, while the residents claim that initiating the highway is a violation of the status quo mandated by the Gujarat HC. The residents have organised sit-ins, protest actions and public meetings opposing the highway, and have filed a contempt petition in the HC. Even as the court summoned concerned officials in early 2022 (*The Indian Express* 2022) amid a fresh wave of the COVID-19 pandemic, case hearings were reportedly deferred with the advocate general of the state representing the officials requesting more time, a common feature in Indian litigation. According to Pradyumna Singh Chudasama, highway authorities also continued to dump fresh mud along sections of the highway falling on village common lands that are officially state-owned, despite the ongoing litigation.[11] The NHAI intended to initiate road construction by December 2021, even as local residents organise opposition.

Opposition to Dholera must be understood in the wider ferment over land in Gujarat and across the country. Not too far from Dholera, the 50,884 hectare Mandal-Becharaji SIR (MBSIR) in the Saurashtra region of Gujarat was one of the first 'nodes' to begin implementation along the DMIC. It faced immediate resistance from the 44 villages coming under it (Shivadekar 2013). When agitations intensified in 2013–14, the then Chief Minister of Gujarat Narendra Modi, probably fearing electoral repercussions in a sensitive election year, cancelled the notification for 36 MBSIR villages.[12] The resistance to MBSIR was largely successful in forcing the state to withdraw in the face of electoral contingencies, a tendency witnessed in other states as well (Bedi 2013; Sampat 2015a).[13]

In the fraught landscape of widespread resistance to land acquisition over infrastructure projects across the country since the mid-2000s, public consultation and prior informed consent for development projects assumed significance as never before. In 2015, this resulted in the failure of the ordinances and the amendment bill proposed to the national 2013 land acquisition law by the National Democratic Alliance (NDA) government.[14] The opposition in Dholera points to the salience of informed consent in infrastructure projects. The imagined futures that moor Dholera smart city are tenuous and rife with possibilities of resistance and breakdown. These futures can then be pursued only with resort to force and violence by the state, which must in turn account for electoral contingencies.

Precarious Geographies of Rent and Resistance in Dholera

Chudasama pointed out that in 2011 the revenue department sold land under its possession to the DSIR Development Authority at Rs

20 per sq m, and the SIR authority is now attempting to sell this land to industry at Rs 600 per sq m. The difference is retained by the development authority. Added to this are other political and economic elite investing in land around Dholera in anticipation of future land price appreciation. By several local accounts, powerful politicians have already invested in the land around Dholera, presumably adding to the impetus behind the smart city project. While rent from real estate is anticipated, much like investment in industry, rentier gains from land prices are an active constituent of the region's anticipated economic transformation.

The final development plan for the DSIR reveals the active role of rent in the compensation envisaged in the project for landowners:

> The land owners provided with readjusted land would need to be trained to negotiate with the industry/developers for giving land for industrial use on lease rental basis rather than outright sale basis; or industrial houses setting-up industries could be encouraged to provide certain share-holding to the land owner. It would help the land owner to ensure regular income from the land allotted to them (Dholera Special Investment Region Development Authority [DSIRDA] 2013: 150).

The plan adds:

> The owners could also be encouraged to invest in housing and commercial uses to have an opportunity for rental incomes, for which people would need to be supported through appropriate capacity building measures (ibid.).

The plan also reserves a token place for agriculture in the DSIR schema:

> Facilitating agricultural training for improved productivity for farmers left with part of their agricultural land and extension of facilities for seeds and fertilisers for improved productivity (ibid.).

At the same time, there is little actual private investment on the ground in Dholera. State-level bureaucrats in charge of facilitating the development of Dholera claim that investors 'will come only when there is something on the ground'.[15]

A highly placed corporate source brokering land deals in the region revealed in 2015 on request of anonymity that while several attempts have been made with advertisements and field-trips for investors from Dubai, Mumbai and elsewhere, no investor is interested in the area as there is 'nothing' on the ground. The only 'stray buyers' of land around the Dholera SIR were those parking excess money to gain from future appreciation, many allegedly powerful politicians or those who could not afford to buy plots near Ahmedabad.[16] Representatives of two prominent real estate developers I interviewed in Ahmedabad at the time also expressed unwillingness to invest in Dholera due to lack of demand.[17] With no significant rise in investor interest in the ensuing period, there has only been a total of three projects, two involving water sewage and treatment plants, and one a forthcoming lithium plant, investing in the activation zone by late 2021.

The anticipated futures of Dholera have thus to contend with the unwillingness of local residents to give up their land and the unwillingness of investors and developers to invest in Dholera's fortunes. It is in the gap between the absence of investor interest and the anticipated rentier gains envisaged as compensation and opportunity for economic growth that a precarious rentier economy (rather than productive industrialisation) emerges as the driving force for instituting Dholera smart city.[18] I contextualise in the following the developments in Dholera within the emergence of what I call 'India's rentier economy' since the mid-2000s.

INDIA'S RENTIER ECONOMY

According to the erstwhile Planning Commission of India:

> 300 million Indians currently live in towns and cities. Within 20–25 years, another 300 million people will get added to Indian towns and cities. This urban expansion will happen at a speed quite unlike anything that India has seen before. It took nearly 40 years for India's urban population to rise by

> 230 million. It could take only half the time to add the next 250 million (Government of India 2013a).

India's policy impetus for urbanisation increasingly encompasses the outskirts of existing cities and new cities and urbanisation infrastructures in industrial corridors such as Dholera and Shendra-Bidkin (also along the DMIC), Special Economic Zones (SEZs) and other PPP initiatives such as Andhra Pradesh's proposed capital city at Amaravati. Policy emphases on urbanisation infrastructures rely on rent-driven logics of land commodification. Differential rent accrues to land depending on its qualities, location, use(s) and existing infrastructures (Marx 1992; Lefebvre 2016). Differential rent from the conversion of agricultural land to urban infrastructures and real estate reconfigures the political economy of land in greenfield urbanisation project areas.

In his analysis of Indian land markets, Chakravorty (2013) argues that land prices in India have risen phenomenally and growing real estate prices reflect the rise in the price of land, given the construction costs have grown stably along the consumer price index. He points out that current urban land prices range from $833 to $33 million per acre[19] and the price of urban land has increased five-fold in the period 2001–11. Agricultural land prices in some rural areas have increased by a factor of five to ten in the decade following the early 2000s, higher in urban peripheries than in interior districts. Prices vary, Chakravorty suggests, in relation to productivity and income from land, how active local land markets are, and the scarcity of land supply and fragmentation. These factors have combined with the post-liberalisation expansion of money supply to result in phenomenal land prices. Money supply has grown in this period through expanding credit markets, income growth for some sections (who in turn invest in land and property as status markers), rise in 'black' money (see also Nijman 2000; Weinstein 2008) and foreign investment from non-resident Indians. Chakravorty misses the crucial point, however, that these are elite and precarious circuits of money supply fuelling rentier investments.

If the official predictions of the massive movement of 300 million people from rural to urban areas over two decades bear out, there will be serious implications for dispossession and uprooting of rural populations, agrarian livelihoods and cultures, and large-scale land-use change with consequent conflict and stresses on the environment and food security. As agriculture is rendered less profitable, agrarian infrastructures and relations are devalued. With the appreciation of land prices as projects are announced, farmers who are able to profit from rentiering 'buy in' or 'give up' land for immediate returns (Sampat 2015b). The capacity to profit from rentiering hinges on ownership of or access to land. If agrarian relations are already skewed against the small peasantry,[20] rising rent from land price appreciation through urbanisation projects can only make inequalities worse. As discussed earlier, active encouragement of rentier activity accelerates pressure on existing agrarian relations to change land use, even in relatively fertile regions. This 'creative destruction' of existing productive agrarian relations in anticipation of rent from future investments in urbanisation projects is, at best, officially unacknowledged and, at worst, actively silenced.

CONCLUDING REMARKS

Investments in urbanisation infrastructures are critical for the constant absorption and expansion of surplus value (in other words, economic growth). They facilitate the 'annihilation of space by time' for faster movements of goods, services, information and money flows (Harvey 1982). The diversification of several large global and domestic business houses and finance capital into housing, infrastructure and retail construction points to the significance and scale of this 'fix' for capital, irrespective of the realisation of the promise of industrialisation. Investors and builders may or may not have direct stakes in potential productive linkages emerging from real estate creation (the small number of operational SEZs despite generous concessions is instructive).

While industrialisation plays a significant role in the imaginary of Dholera and the DMIC, it is worth noting that manufacturing in India has stagnated at 15 per cent to 16 per cent of the gross domestic product since 1980 (Government of India 2011).

Interestingly, in an interview with a senior industry representative in Ahmedabad in 2015, the industrialist candidly acknowledged that land and infrastructure are not the critical issues for boosting manufacturing as serious industrialists are not looking for concessions from the government. He pointed out that it is real estate interests that seek subsidised access to land from the state. What industry requires instead, he argued, is a focus on 'soft infrastructures' and an easing of bureaucratic procedures and rules.[21]

Even as manufacturing stagnates in the country, the construction sector is booming. The growing share of construction in the national economy underscores the significance of this sector. In 2011–12, the shares of real estate and construction together accounted for 19 per cent of the Indian economy, growing from 14.7 per cent in 2000–01 (Government of India 2013b; see Table 5.3). More remarkably, in 2009–10, the construction sector formed the second largest employer of workers in India, employing 11 per cent of the workforce after agriculture, which employed 36 per cent (Soundararajan 2013). This growth is the backdrop for the recent policy push towards urbanisation infrastructures in India. Land, and by extension real estate, is 'like gold with yield' in so-called emerging economies (cf. Fairbairn 2014).[22]

Table 5.3 Share and growth of real estate and construction sectors

	2000–01	2005–06	2006–07	2007–08	2008–09	2009–10	2010–11	2011–12	2017–18
Real estate, ownership of dwellings and business services	8.7 (7.5)	9.1 (10.6)	9.3 (9.5)	9.6 (8.4)	10.3 (10.4)	10.4 (8.3)	10.4 (6.0)	10.8 (10.3)	Figures unavailable
Construction	6.0 (6.1)	7.9 (12.8)	8.2 (10.3)	8.5 (10.8)	8.5 (5.3)	8.2 (6.7)	8.2 (10.2)	8.2 (5.6)	7.8 (3.6)

Source: Adapted from Central Statistics Office in Government of India (2013b, 2018). Shares are in current prices and growth in constant prices. Figures in parentheses indicate growth rate.

A 2012 report by a real estate consulting company ranked India twentieth among the current top real estate investment markets globally, with an investment of $3.4 billion (*The Economic Times* 2013). Another study further predicted that India will become the world's third largest construction market by 2025, adding 11.5 million homes a year to become a $1 trillion-a-year market (Sen 2013). Foreign investments in real estate and land remain regulated, although three real estate investment trusts have entered the market by 2021. It is largely through partnership investments in urbanisation infrastructures (for smart cities, industrial corridors and other PPPs) that global finance fuels the rentier economy.[23] For instance, in addition to the involvement of global consultancy and infrastructure giants for Dholera, mentioned earlier, other global partnerships to develop the DMIC infrastructure include Japanese loans, investment by Japanese firms and Japan depository receipts issued by Indian companies. A number of national, regional, state and local developers and consultants, along with fly-by-night operators, brokers and dealers out to make a quick buck, join the ranks in fuelling the rentier-driven commodification of land and built space.

Through categorisation into 'barren lands' or 'backward areas', existing agrarian relations and infrastructures are rendered 'unproductive' discursively, so they can be converted to high-end urban enclaves. Official accounts often describe Dholera as 'barren' and 'backward'; bureaucrats used these terms in official presentations and interviews as well. Repeated claims that 'there is nothing on the ground' by state officials and private developers disclosed bias against agriculture, and in favour of urbanisation. However, urbanisation infrastructures index rentier investments without 'productive linkages' with industrialisation critical for wider distributive effects of transition.[24] In the absence of productive investment in industry, and the deeply unequal geography of rent, the peasantry (large and small) emerges as an 'absolute surplus population' (Smith 2011)[25] that is irrelevant to accumulation[26] in the rentier economy, except as an obstacle.

The refusal of residents in the Dholera SIR (and elsewhere) to consent to their dispossession by urbanisation infrastructures challenges these rentier-driven logics of accumulation. Interests within the state promoting urbanisation infrastructures must contend with electoral fallouts of such dissent, as evidenced in the MBSIR area. Meanwhile, the rentier economy, with its elite circuits of money and rent, lack of productive linkages with industrialisation, challenges of access to land and its sheer anticipated futures is a precarious model of growth. Left unfettered, and implemented through forcible acquisition where 'consent' is not forthcoming, it will destroy existing productive agrarian relations and dispossess agrarian populations with little option for sustainable livelihoods or food security.

NOTES

1. The Delhi–Mumbai Industrial Corridor (DMIC) itself spans 1,483 km and is officially expected to 'impact' 180 million people across six states—Uttar Pradesh, Delhi, Haryana, Rajasthan, Gujarat and Maharashtra. According to the then DMIC Chief Executive Officer Talleen Kumar, smart cities along the DMIC will have integrated communications technology as one of the components for improving life; infrastructure will operate through sensors sharing information in real time and this will make for efficiency. Smartness will include hard and soft infrastructure, including flood control, drainage, sewage and drinking water provisions, developed with extensive back-office work in project development. Special purpose vehicles (SPVs) will be responsible for the implementation of the cities. Planned industrial cities will address the growth and employment needs of the country and turn India into a manufacturing and investment destination. They will address rural to urban migration and help pull thousands of people above poverty line (interview with the author, 13 May 2015).

2. In his work examining the Andhra Pradesh Special Economic Zone (SEZ), Cross refers to SEZs as 'uniquely charged objects of conviction and anxiety' (2014: 4) that are 'made into particular places for capital by planners and politicians, corporate managers and executives, farmers, workers and activists as they pursue different futures' (ibid.: 5) built on an 'economy of anticipation' (ibid.: 6). My aim in invoking the anticipated nature of investments in Dholera is more modest, and points only to the tenuousness of the futures invoked by the planners and promoters of the project, in this case various state agencies and private planners.

3. It should be noted that while real estate plays a significant role in the *imaginary* of Dholera, real estate developers are not a driving force in its institution. This is different from many large and medium SEZs in India

that have courted controversy as real estate grabs (see Banerjee-Guha 2008; Levien 2012; Cross 2014; Jenkins et al. 2014; Sampat 2015a).

4. There has been a phenomenal rise in the scale of protests against forcible land acquisition in the country since the early 2000s (see Basu 2007; Banerjee-Guha 2008; Levien 2012; Bedi 2013; Chakravorty 2013; Sampat 2013; Jenkins et al. 2014). Jenkins et al. (2014) also discuss the provisions of the 2013 land acquisition law as a response to these grievances (see also Sampat [2013]). For a critique of land pooling in Dholera, see Sampat and Sunny (2016).

5. Blackbucks are a species of antelope indigenous to the Indian subcontinent, and listed as 'near threatened' by the International Union for the Conservation of Nature in its Red List since 2003.

6. This is not to obscure caste, gender and other deeply entrenched pernicious hierarchies across communities in the area. However, as in other areas of such resistance, contingent alliances among unequal social forces are emerging under threat of dispossession.

7. The interviews in this section were conducted by the author in Gujarati in May 2015.

8. Interview with chief executive officer (CEO), Gujarat Infrastructure Development Board (GIDB), 29 April 2015.

9. Interview with officials of Gujarat Industrial Corridor Corporation (GICC), 29 April 2015.

10. Interview with Town Planning Officer, Dholera Special Investment Region (DSIR), 22 May 2015.

11. The details regarding the deferment of case hearings and the dumping of mud are reported by key informants.

12. The remaining eight villages continue to resist the institution of an automobile plant on the pasture lands of the traditional cattle-rearing *Maldhari* community. See *The Indian Express* (2013).

13. Bedi (2013) argues that the fortunes of localised struggles are contingent upon 'viewings of the accessible state' by social movement activists. While this is undoubtedly one of the factors aiding the success of resistance in some areas, anti-SEZ oppositions, for instance, have successfully mobilised despite violent repression by the state, such as in Nandigram in West Bengal and Raigad in Maharashtra. In many of these areas, peasants' and citizens' groups risked their lives and livelihoods, irrespective of state receptivity, to assert rights over land and resources (Sampat 2015a).

14. Two key controversial amendments proposed by the central government in the 2013 land acquisition law included the exemption

of industrial corridors and SIRs from prior informed consent and social impact assessments.

15. Interview with Shardul Thakore of GICC, 29 April 2015.

16. Interview, 25 May 2015.

17. Interview, 28 May 2015.

18. While rentier interests within the state constitute an important tier in Dholera's rentier economy, the state itself is not amenable to the descriptor 'rentier state'. The significant role of interests within the state rentier activity from land consolidation and acquisition processes has led some to describe the Indian state as a 'speculative state' (Goldman 2011), a 'land-broker state' (Levien 2012) or an 'entrepreneurial state' (Datta 2015). However, as I discuss in my work elsewhere, interests within the state are often working at cross-purposes and respond to political contingencies and possibilities in complex ways (Sampat 2016).

19. At dollar–rupee rate Rs 60 = $1.

20. Peasantry here refers to small and marginal landowning farmers with less than 10 acres and 2 acres of land respectively, landless agrarian workers, pastoralists, fisher folk, forest dwellers and other petty commodity producers.

21. Interview, 23 April 2015.

22. Fairbairn (2014) has used this phrase in relation with recent investments by global finance in agrarian land for agriculture. I extend her argument here to investment in land for rent from price appreciation and real estate development.

23. Such partnerships, however, are not without their problems. See Searle (2014) for conflicts over issues like land valuation, power, prestige and business practice that form critical stumbling blocks for international financing in infrastructure projects.

24. Hirschman defines 'linkage effects' as 'investment-generating forces that are set in motion, through input-output relations, when productive facilities that supply inputs to that line or utilise its outputs are inadequate or nonexistent. Backward linkages lead to new investment in input-supplying facilities and forward linkages to investment in output-using facilities' (1981: 65).

25. Smith (2011) argues that the growing impoverishment of people confronted with capitalist growth is creating an absolute surplus population that can no longer engage in a 'politics of negotiation' to the terms of a project, but instead create a non-negotiable 'counterpolitics' of resistance.

26. Levien (2012) finds a similar indifference to local populations in the institution of an SEZ in Rajasthan, albeit without alliances of resistance to the project.

REFERENCES

Ballaney, S. 2008. *The Town Planning Mechanism in Gujarat, India*. Washington, DC: The World Bank.

Banerjee-Guha, S. 2008. 'Space Relations of Capital'. *Economic & Political Weekly* 43(47): 51–59.

Basu, P. 2007. 'Political Economy of Land-grab'. *Economic & Political Weekly* 42(14): 1281–87.

Bedi, H. 2013. 'Special Economic Zones: National Land Challenges, Localised Protest'. *Contemporary South Asia* 21(1): 38–51.

Chakravorty, S. 2013. *The Price of Land: Acquisition, Conflict, Consequence*. New Delhi: Oxford University Press.

Chavda, H. 2014. 'Dholera Special Investment Region Protests: 18 Arrested'. *The Times of India*, 10 February.

Cross, J. 2014. *Dream Zones: Anticipating Capitalism and Development in India*. London: Pluto Press.

Datta, A. 2015. 'New Urban Utopias of Postcolonial India: "Entrepreneurial Urbanisation" in Dholera Smart City, Gujarat'. *Dialogues in Human Geography* 5(1): 3–22.

Dholera Special Investment Region Development Authority (DSIRDA). 2013. Final Development Plan—DSIRDA: Report One. Gandhinagar: DSIRDA. Available at https://dholerasir.com/wp-content/uploads/2019/01/2.-DP-Report-1.pdf (accessed on 5 June 2022).

Fairbairn, M. 2014. '"Like Gold with Yield": Evolving Intersections between Farmland and Finance'. *The Journal of Peasant Studies* 41(5): 777–95.

Goldman, M. 2011. 'Speculative Urbanism and the Making of the Next World City'. *International Journal of Urban and Regional Research* 35(3): 555–81.

Government of India. 2011. Press Note No. 2 (2011 Series). New Delhi: Government of India. Available at http://nmcc.nic. in/pdf/National_Manufacturing_Policy_ 25October 2011.pdf (accessed on 6 October 2015).

———. 2013a. 'The Challenges of Urbanisation in India'. Approach to the 12th Plan. Available at http://12th plan.gov.in/forum_description.php?f =17 (accessed on 18 November 2013).

———. 2013b. *Economic Survey 2012–13*, 213. Available at http://indiabudget.nic.in (accessed on 18 November 2013).

———. 2018. *Economic Survey 2017–18*, Volume II. Available at http://mofapp.nic.in:8080/economicsurvey/pdf/000_Preface_Ten_Facts_2017-18_Vol_1-18_pages.pdf (accessed on 3 June 2019).

Gujarat Khedut Samaj and Others v Gujarat State and Others. 2015. Oral Order Pronounced in Writ Petitions 227 of 2014 and 57 of 2015. 10 December.

Harvey, D. 1982. *The Limits to Capital*. New York: Verso.
Hirschman, A. O. 1981. *Essays in Trespassing: Economics to Politics and Beyond*. Cambridge: Cambridge University Press.
Jameen Adhikar Andolan Gujarat (JAAG). 2014a. 'Once Again, the Voice of Dissent is Sought to be Suppressed in Gujarat. Leaders of DSIR Arrested from a Public Sammelan'. Press release, 9 February.
——. 2014b. 'DSIR: Meetings Being Held in the Villages; Affidavits Being Prepared'. Press release, 28 April.
Jenkins, R., L. Kennedy and P. Mukhopadhyay, eds. 2014. *Power Policy and Protest: The Politics of India's Special Economic Zones*. New Delhi: Oxford University Press.
Lefebvre, H. 2016[1956]. 'The Theory of Ground Rent and Rural Sociology'. *Antipode* 48(1): 67–73.
Levien, M. 2012. 'The Land Question: Special Economic Zones and the Political Economy of Dispossession in India'. *The Journal of Peasant Studies* 39(3–4): 933–69.
Marx, K. 1992[1894]. *Capital*, Volume III. London: Penguin.
MOEFCC. 2019. 'Minutes of the 207th Meeting of the Expert Appraisal Committee for Projects Related to Coastal Regulation Zone Held on 25th January, 2019 at Indira Paryavaran Bhawan, Ministry of Environment, Forest and Climate Change, New Delhi'. Available at http://environmentclearance.nic.in/writereaddata/Form-1A/Minutes/01022019LEMK1QX7FINALMINUTES207MEETINGJANUARY252019.pdf (accessed on 5 June 2022).
Nijman, J. 2000. 'Mumbai's Real Estate Market in 1990s: De-Regulation, Global Money and Casino Capitalism'. *Economic & Political Weekly* 35(7): 575–82.
Sampat, P. 2013. 'Limits to Absolute Power: Eminent Domain and the Right to Land in India'. *Economic & Political Weekly* 48(19): 40–52.
——. 2015a. 'The Goan Impasse: Land Rights and Resistance to SEZs in Goa'. *The Journal of Peasant Studies* 42(3): 765–90.
——. 2015b. 'Growth for Few, Loss for Many'. *The Hindu*, 28 March.
——. 2016. 'Infrastructures of Growth, Corridors of Power: The Making of the SEZ Act 2005'. In *Political Economy of Contemporary India*, eds R. Nagaraj and S. Motiram, 230–59. Cambridge: Cambridge University Press.
Sampat, P., and S. Sunny. 2016. 'Dholera and the Myth of Voluntary Land Pooling'. *Socio-Legal Review* 12(2): 1–17.
Searle, L. 2014. 'Conflict and Commensuration: Contested Market Making in India's Private Real Estate Development Sector'. *International Journal of Urban and Regional Research* 38(1): 60–78.

Sen, S. 2013. 'India to be World's 3rd Largest Construction Mkt by 2025'. *Economic Times*, 1 July.

SENES Consultants India Pvt. Ltd. 2013. List of Annexure for Environmental Impact Assessment of Dholera Special Investment Region (DSIR) in Gujarat. New Delhi: Delhi Mumbai Industrial Corridor Development Corporation Ltd. (DMICDCL). Available at https://www.gpcb.gov.in/pdf/DMICDC_DHOLERA_SPECIAL_INVEST_DSIR_EIA.PDF (accessed on 1 April 2016).

Shivadekar, S. 2013. 'Industrial Plan Hits Road-block'. *The Times of India*, 12 July.

Smith, G. 2011. 'Selective Hegemony and Beyond—Populations with "No Productive Function": A Framework for Enquiry'. *Identities: Global Studies in Culture and Power* 18(1): 2–38.

Soundararajan, V. 2013. 'Construction Workers: Amending the Law for More Safety'. *Economic & Political Weekly* 48(23): 21–25.

The Economic Times. 2013. 'India Ranked 20 among Global Real Estate Market, Says C&W'. 25 March.

The Indian Express. 2013. 'Govt Gives in to Farmers, Withdraws 36 Villages from Mandal-Becharaji SIR'. 15 August.

———. 2022. 'Farmland for Expressway: Dholera SIR CEO Tenders Apology in Gujarat High Court'. 4 January.

Weinstein, L. 2008. 'Mumbai's Development Mafias: Globalisation, Organised Crime and Land Development'. *International Journal of Urban and Regional Research* 32(1): 22–39.

6

Industrial Zone to New Skycity

The (Un)Making of India's First Aerotropolis

GOPA SAMANTA AND AKASH BANERJEE

With the enormous increase in the mobility of both goods and passengers in a globalising world, the aerotropolis or airport city is a new trend in urban development discourse. India, being no exception, with the increased trade and investment after the liberalisation of economy in the 1990s, has also started to develop large infrastructure projects such as aerotropolises and smart cities.

Such urban megaprojects as aerotropolises are not new in India and were earlier seen in the form of planned city-building in the post-Independence phase in places such as Chandigarh and Durgapur. The new characteristic is the development of such megaprojects either by private firms or under the public–private partnership (PPP) model (Kennedy 2007; Kennedy and Sood 2016), and their explicit profit-oriented and commodified nature (Ramachandraiah 2016). Besides 54 urban agglomerations with more than 1 million population and 100 proposed smart cities, such airport cities will dot the Indian urban territory along with thousands of small cities and towns.

Considering airports as growth centres with immense potential for regional development, in June 2016 the Government of India also launched a programme called *Ude Desh ka Aam Naagrik* (UDAN) to build new regional airports and enhance existing ones in smaller cities under the Regional Connectivity Scheme (RCS) of the Ministry of Civil Aviation. The objectives of this programme are to boost economic development and to enhance job growth in the regional centres outside metropolitan areas with the assumption that 'every 100 rupees spent on air transport contributes to 325 rupees worth of benefits, and every 100 direct jobs in air transport result in 610 jobs in the economy as a whole' (Government of India 2016: 5). Thus, these new large transport infrastructures and smart urban development agenda in the form of aerotropolises are rooted in the understanding that airports can act as growth poles in a fashion similar to metropolises. A similar argument is also made by the promoters of the aerotropolis project examined here.

Andal Aerotropolis, locally called Andal airport city, is the first development initiative of its kind taken up by the Government of West Bengal. On 7 September 2007, the West Bengal government decided to build this aerotropolis megaproject covering an area of 1,616 sq km in the midst of an old mining-cum-industrial zone of the Paschim Bardhaman district under the planning area called Asansol Durgapur Development Authority (ADDA). The very decision raises the question of why a debt-ridden state and one that performs poorly on all financial indicators (Mathew 2018) was motivated to build an airport city just 200 km away from the well-connected Kolkata International Airport.[1]

Against the backdrop of a new urban frontier in India (Kennedy and Sood 2016), this chapter explores the process of the building of urban integrated megaprojects (Shatkin 2011), especially aerotropolises, under private ownership. This chapter focuses especially on the viability of such a project in the midst of a region known for mining and heavy industries. It examines the problems inherent in private planning, which applies a top-down approach without completely understanding the ground reality. It also discusses the major hindrances to the success of the aerotropolis project besides analysing how it has impacted the local economy. The speculation of land has been set in motion not only within the aerotropolis project area but in the surrounding areas as well. Although the scale of the speculation may not match that of some other cases in India, such as the Bangalore airport project (Goldman 2011), prices of land have increased to very high levels. An informal land market has also developed in the surrounding area through micro-networks (Raman 2016) of local middle-class people, businessmen and real estate agents. The chapter thus also addresses the complexities and uncertainties of both the intended and unintended impacts of building large infrastructure projects on the local area.

The chapter is based on an analysis of policy documents available on the website of the Bengal Aerotropolis Project Limited (BAPL), the private company in charge of building the Andal Aerotropolis, an exhaustive review of newspaper articles and field research in two phases: April 2015 and March–April 2018. The authors conducted fieldwork with the help of semi-structured and open-ended interview methods in the local villages surrounding the aerotropolis. Residents across different interest groups were interviewed. These included farmers and sharecroppers, employees of a coal mining company, local schoolteachers and businessmen in the Raniganj market (one of the major markets in the vicinity of the aerotropolis). Our business enterprise survey encompassed managers of branded stores, hotel and restaurant owners, owners of cloth and garment stores, and retail stores selling grocery items. The owner of a private institution offering spoken English courses was also interviewed. The fieldwork also reached out to a construction contractor, two construction workers within the aerotropolis area, several people engaged in the real estate business, besides the villagers who had knowledge about the change of land value in the area. The questions for these 23 interviews were focused on the making and viability of the greenfield aerotropolis project.

INTRODUCING THE ANDAL AEROTROPOLIS PROJECT

Although the aerotropolis has been called a greenfield airport, it is not located in an isolated territory; rather, it is being developed as an expansion of an already developed urban industrial region. The existing density of population in the ADDA area is 3,594 persons per sq km with more than 77 per cent of its total population (2.4 million) already living in urban areas in 2011 (ADDA n.d.).

Following the decision made by the Government of West Bengal (then led by the Communist Party of India-Marxist [CPI-M]), an independent private company called BAPL was established and empowered to build the entire project in 2007. BAPL is a specialised infrastructure company engaged in building aerotropolises in India. It has five major stakeholders, both Indian and foreign. Three Indian individual promoters of BAPL have expertise in different components necessary for developing an aerotropolis, such as developing large-scale infrastructure, experience in financial markets and working with government entities. BAPL signed a joint venture development agreement with the West Bengal Industrial

Development Corporation Limited (WBIDC). Initially the stake of WBIDC was 11 per cent but in September 2017, the West Bengal government paid Rs 180 crore to BAPL, which increased its stake to 26 per cent (Majumdar 2017).

The aerotropolis is built around the Kazi Nazrul Islam (KNI) Airport, also called Durgapur Airport by the Airports Authority of India. Located in the peri-urban area of Durgapur city, the aerotropolis comprises an industrial skyzone, a logistics skyhub, an information technology (IT) skypark and a township called Sujalaam Skycity. All these activities depend on the viability of the airport. The aerotropolis is based on the idea that the airport will act as the growth centre for all kinds of development activities and will ultimately boost the development of the entire region.

LOCAL ECONOMY AND ITS CHANGING DYNAMICS

The aerotropolis is situated in the middle of the Asansol–Durgapur mining and industrial belt. Coal mining and associated manufacturing industries have been the backbone of the regional economy since before Independence. Numerous mining towns or collieries such as Moira, Khandra, Chak Bankola, Khas Kajora and Central Kajora, in association with heavy manufacturing industries in the Andal–Durgapur region such as Durgapur Steel Plant (DSP), Durgapur Steel Thermal Power Station (DSTPS) under the Damodar Valley Corporation (DVC), Durgapur Projects Limited (DPL), NTPC-SAIL Power Co. Ltd and Alloy Steel Plants are located in the area surrounding the aerotropolis. The DSTPS, commissioned in 2012 in Andal, is the most recent addition to the large-scale heavy industries in the area surrounding the aerotropolis. This has generated substantial employment opportunities for the locals as industrial labour and staff. Another glass manufacturing unit has also come up in Khandra. Employment of a significant number of local people in these recently built industries also influences the growth of housing and businesses in the area around the aerotropolis.

Two industries had also started to operate within the industrial and logistics hub of the aerotropolis. Both were running at a small scale and had not yet developed to their full capacities. One of them had also stopped operating for some time. A leading paints manufacturer developed a warehouse inside the aerotropolis area, which has also been closed for a significant period.

The heavy industries of the Durgapur–Asansol region under public sector companies—such as iron and steel, machine manufacturing and mechanical engineering—received a serious setback in the 1980s, with the closure of many industries and declaration of many others as sick public sector undertakings. Since then, the new industries that have developed in the region are predominantly small scale and under private ownership. Though activities such as coal mining, mining-associated heavy industries and construction activities still constitute the dominant economies in this region, there has been noticeable growth of the service sector here since the beginning of the twenty-first century. A gradual shift from mining activities towards service sector employment among the local youth in the first two decades of the twenty-first century was observed during the field survey in the surrounding villages.

Farming activities were getting replaced as more and more farmlands were put to non-agricultural uses and transformed into built-up areas. Trade and business activities are intensifying along with the development of both road and rail transport networks. Rapid infrastructural development in the region has influenced the expansion of business and commercial complexes in Andal and Ukhra. It has also contributed to the level of economic diversification in the villages surrounding the aerotropolis. These developments together have boosted the urbanisation process in the entire area. It is expected that Andal Aerotropolis will continue to influence the level of urbanisation here in the near future and will drive Andal and its surroundings to merge with Durgapur in the east and Asansol in the west, forming a continuous built-up urbanised area along National Highway 2 and Andal–Ukhra road.

The development of the service sector, especially the IT sector in the surrounding regions, was not at a stage where it could act as an incentive for the development of a world-class aerotropolis in 2007. At the same time, the sector was not completely undeveloped either. Durgapur is developing as an IT hub and the recent development in this sector is much more pronounced than ever before. The IT sector is also developing in Asansol, but not at the same scale as

Durgapur. Basic IT training centres, both under public and private enterprises, are frequently found throughout the region. All of them have come up since 2010.

In our assessment, although there has been an increasing trend of social infrastructure development, the scale of operations may not be enough to make the airport sustainable. The area surrounding the aerotropolis is also developing as an education hub, as more and more schools, colleges, institutions of management studies and skill development centres are coming up there. Most of these educational institutions are privately owned. They target the upper middle class and the rich. All these seem to have altered the regional economy from a secondary to a tertiary one. It is expected that this change in the regional economy would attract large domestic as well as foreign investments in both industrial and corporate business sectors in this region. Therefore, the operation of uninterrupted flights at Durgapur/Andal Airport would appear to be of utmost necessity for the development of the entire area into an aerotropolis-centred mega urban–industrial region.

TOP-DOWN PLANNING AND VIABILITY OF KNI AIRPORT

The airport lies at the centre of the success of aerotropolis project and that is why we need to look at the viability of the airport as estimated in the project planning. This section also explores the gap between the estimated and actual prospects for an airport located not far from the Kolkata international airport.

The Durgapur/Andal airport was inaugurated on 19 September 2013 by West Bengal's Chief Minister Mamata Banerjee. It was named after the famous Bengali poet Kazi Nazrul Islam, who hailed from that area of erstwhile Bardhaman (*The Hindu BusinessLine* 2013). Commercial flight operations started from 18 May 2015—a 48-seater ATR-42 aircraft was used for the inaugural commercial flight. The flight was then scheduled to operate every day except Friday between the KNI Airport in Durgapur and the Kolkata airport, with a travel-time of 35 minutes (*The Indian Express* 2015a).

The Kolkata–Durgapur–New Delhi flight was inaugurated on 7 December 2015 and started operating from 21 December 2015. This time flight services were operational with a 122-seater aircraft in this sector thrice a week, every Monday, Wednesday and Friday. It was then the only flight operating from the airport (*The Indian Express* 2015b). However, from 17 June 2016, flight operations from KNI Airport were cancelled due to the lack of passengers on a daily basis. This caused financial losses to the national airline. On an average, the number of passengers on the Durgapur–Kolkata sector was in single digits while around 50 passengers used the Durgapur–Delhi sector on a daily basis (*The Hindu BusinessLine* 2016).

Having been dropped off the aviation map for about eight months, the airport once again came into operation when another airline, India's newest full-service carrier, started daily scheduled operations in the Delhi–Kolkata–Durgapur–Delhi sector from 15 February 2017, with a 50-seater Bombardier CR-J 200 aircraft. The flight was scheduled to take 30 minutes to travel between Kolkata and Durgapur with a fare of Rs 1,000, and 1 hour and 40 minutes to travel between Durgapur and Delhi with a fare of Rs 3,500 (*The Times of India* 2017a). On the first day, about 30 Delhi-bound passengers got on board from Durgapur, as the remaining seats were booked from Kolkata (*The Times of India* 2017b). In an interview with *The Hindu Business Line*, the managing director of BAPL claimed that the flights were operating at 95 per cent occupancy (Bose 2017). However, from July 2017, the airline stopped its flight service.[2] Once again, flight services from the airport had come to a halt.

At the time of conducting this study, flight service at KNI Airport had once again resumed from 15 April 2018 after a long gap of about nine months. A 122-seater flight had been scheduled to operate on the Durgapur–Delhi sector four days a week (Sunday, Monday, Thursday and Friday) from the KNI Airport (ABP News 2018). This was the most recent and ongoing operation at the KNI Airport.

The airport thus came into operation twice and stopped twice before the most recent phase of operations. Each time, flight services did not last for more than six months. According to the agreement between the airline and BAPL, the principal stakeholder of the Andal Airport and Aerotropolis project, the latter had to pay subsidies to the airline for the unsold seats during the first phase of operation (December 2015 to June 2016). Besides citing lack of passengers on a daily basis as the main reason behind cancelling flight service, the airline also accused BAPL of not paying the subsidy amount on time (*The Hindu BusinessLine* 2016). On the other hand, BAPL blamed flight delays and costly operations for the losses suffered by the airline (Bose 2017).

This detailed account of the recent history of airline services at Durgapur Airport shows that the viability of airlines utilising this airport is still a big issue. Different airlines started their businesses here and stopped due to lack of demand. Samanta (2015) had raised the question of sufficient number of passengers available from the area long before operations started at this airport. She raised this issue on two grounds: first, the KNI Airport is located just 200 km from the Kolkata International airport. Second, Kolkata airport is well connected with this region by both road transport through the Durgapur expressway, and also by train services to Howrah.

The field research indicated that the local middle classes, consisting of those engaged in business and service sector activities, the prospective customers of the airlines, thought that the operation of flights between Delhi and Durgapur alone was not viable. According to them, Delhi was not a business centre in high demand among the local people, although the importance of Delhi was growing as a centre of service sector employment. Interviewees from middle-class households in nearby places thought that there was much higher demand for airline services to Bengaluru and Chennai, where people went for better health services. Other places in south and west India such as Hyderabad, Pune, Mumbai, Ahmedabad and Jaipur were popular destinations as the local businesspeople often had professional connections there, and several families had enrolled their children in private colleges and universities in these cities. They thus opined that operations only to Delhi could not ensure the viability of the airport. In addition to expanding their reach to more destinations, the airlines would have to operate with smaller aircraft which would reduce the quantum of loss from non-filling of seats. The interviewees also demanded operation of flights on the weekends, especially Sundays, which would help them to start work at the destination—whether related to business, education or health services—from Monday. These observations raised the issue of how planning is done and for whom. Participatory planning could have helped make the airport viable for operation.

Uncertainties are endemic in large infrastructure projects. Whatever the sector—public, private or PPP—the record of delivery on large infrastructure cost and performance promises is observed to be dismal (Flyvbjerg et al. 2009). The problem at the KNI Airport was also one of overestimation of air traffic demand and cost overruns. The progress and problems in making the airport viable also suggested that unless BAPL mended the gap between the estimated and the actual air traffic volumes as well as the nature of demand, it was heading towards an uncertain predicament of the kind observed in many other megaprojects in different parts of the world.

LAND ACQUISITION AND KEY ROLE OF REAL ESTATE DEVELOPMENT

Situated between Durgapur (15 km) and Asansol (25 km), in the heart of the mining and industrial belt in West Bengal, Andal Aerotropolis named as 'Sujalaam Skycity' by BAPL, and as 'Golden Industrial Town' by the Government of West Bengal, proved to be the best location for such an initiative from the point of view of land acquisition. There was no settlement in the entire area and the agricultural land was not highly productive. Other than the airport, the area is sanctioned to be used for industrial houses (distribution and logistics centres, office buildings, light manufacturing firms, convention centres, service industries), institutional and social infrastructure development (IT, financial, educational and health care institutions), commercial and business complexes, residential areas and for common areas.

In September 2007, the Union Civil Aviation Ministry and the West Bengal government announced plans to set up a new airport—along with a township, IT and logistic hub at Andal. Following that decision, the state government empowered the WBIDC to acquire land as WBIDC was the only entity in the state that could purchase large tracts of land after successful implementation of land reform measures in the state in 1980s. Moreover, acquisition by WBIDC had one added advantage. It could easily reclassify the land from agricultural to industrial use with the direct help from district land records office. The land acquisition process was relatively peaceful and after the acquisition was over, the land was handed over to the BAPL, the special purpose private company, to develop the entire area, including the airport and the skycity.

A survey report from the area (Adhikar n.d.) said that out of the total acquired land under this project, only 56.53 acres was vested land remaining under government control, while the remaining 2,306.31 acres was under agricultural use. According to this report, in the 12 *mouzas*[3] coming under the project, there were 18,000 farmers of different categories and there was no record of sharecroppers and non-recorded *bargadars*.[4] Thus, the tension between sharecroppers and landowners, which usually makes the issue of land acquisition complex in West Bengal (Banerjee 2006), did not have any impact in the initial phase of this megaproject.

The landowners of this area did not protest much. The bloodshed and political turmoil that occurred in Singur and Nandigram, the other two well-known land acquisition cases of West Bengal, were not witnessed here. The major reason behind this was the difference in the quality of land from the point of view of agricultural productivity. Here, the entire area was under rain-fed single crop land without much irrigation support. Only big landholders had small water tanks to supplement the water deficiency from rainfall in the monsoon season, as well as to be used for the second and sometimes third crops in winter and summer respectively. Although many small farmers and sharecroppers were reluctant to give the land for the 'greater common good', big landholders considered it wise to give up the land as it was not very productive. The then government was able to resolve the issue quite peacefully with the help of local political leadership under the CPI-M. Most of the people accepted the compensation money at the rate of Rs 4 lakh to 10 lakh per acre in 2009–10 (Niyogi and Chakraborty 2011).

Major hurdles to land acquisition came from Coal India as the land holds coal blocks under the surface in many places, and Coal India wanted to mine the high-quality Raniganj coal from the area. After long negotiations with Coal India, the issue got resolved and Coal India had to close three mines in the area. However, it is also notable that people from nearby villages did not want this huge area to be transformed into a mining area, which is often accompanied by pollution, land degradation and anti-social activities linked with the illegal coal trade. Landholders of a few villages such as Tamla and Andal Gram were not ready to give the land for mining but they easily accepted the deal with BAPL for the development of the aerotropolis. From the intensive interviews with the previous landowners, it was understood that due to unwillingness of owners to sell the land for coal mining, BAPL had got a competitive advantage over Coal India in acquiring the land for the project (Niyogi and Chakraborty 2011).

Although the land acquisition for the Andal Aerotropolis had been done mostly without dispute, a small number of sharecroppers and agricultural labourers of Dakshinkhanda, Khandra, Bhadur, Andal Gram, Amloka and Tamla villages protested against the land acquisition time and again between 2010 and 2011 and on a number of occasions stalled work at Andal airport, demanding higher and faster compensation (Chatterjee 2011). They demanded higher compensation as they had earlier experience of negotiations with Durgapur Project Limited, the thermal power company, which had installed its new unit in the Andal area. Their protests were based on two major questions: first, how could lands located far away from the roadside and those located on the roadside be offered the same compensation; second, when the market price of their land was already Rs 3 lakh per *katha*,[5] then why would they give the land at the rate of Rs 2.5 lakh per *bigha*.[6] That dispute was finally resolved with a relatively higher compensation package for them.

At the time of the study, there was no conflict over the land acquisition for Andal Aerotropolis between the landowners, farmers and the stakeholders of the project. There had been no unrest or protest on this issue since 2015–16. Field interactions with some of the landowners and farmers whose lands had been acquired for the project against compensation revealed that the landowners got full compensation amount for their land and 25 per cent of the value of each land occupied by the sharecroppers and bargadars was paid by BAPL separately to them in addition to the landowner. However, they now regret giving their land at a very cheap rate as they could easily have gotten higher compensation if they had carried on their non-violent protest for longer and in a united way.

A contractor who was engaged in the construction work of the aerotropolis told us that the land inside the aerotropolis area was then priced at about Rs 6 lakh to Rs 8 lakh per katha. He added that some of the roadside plots had been purchased by BAPL later on at a price of Rs 2 lakh per katha after the protest here and now the stakeholder was selling those plots at a price of Rs 8 lakh per katha. Most of the lands inside the aerotropolis had already been purchased by corporate entities and business houses, while some plots were still unsold. He also mentioned that as the project still had not flourished significantly since the inauguration of the airport, no real estate builder or corporate house was willing to invest there right now. BAPL seemed more interested in the profit it made from the real estate business than operating the airport on a regular basis.

EVALUATING THE PROGRESS OF THE AEROTROPOLIS

As of late 2018, apart from the airport, no other construction work in the skycity was complete. The main road extending from the main entrance of the airport at Dubchuria crossing towards the terminal building was the only road in good condition. All the other roads which were constructed during the initial phase were in a bad condition and needed immediate repair. Vast areas were lying covered with bushes and some structures had been under construction for the last five years. The number of construction workers, including contractors and supervisors, engaged in such a vast project appeared to be very small. The only construction company present on the site was working on the entire aerotropolis area. The construction was progressing at an abnormally slow speed.

Although some length of covered drainage-cum-sewerage and the footpath had been constructed, it appeared insignificant when compared with the total length planned. The construction company stopped work on grounds of not receiving payments from BAPL. The mammoth electrification programme, moving all the overhead lines in the aerotropolis area to the other side of the Andal–Ukhra road, had been completed. Initially, there was some protest about the acquisition of land for replacing the electric post to the other side, but those issues were resolved and the work was completed.

The only visible nearly completed constructions in the area were two schools in the educational hub of the skycity under institutional area of the plan. Although the construction was not complete, the schools had already started operation at a small scale. In addition, one charitable school was also being established nearby.

No building work had started in the plots assigned for residential and commercial uses yet (Figure 6.1). Some of the residential plots had been planned out, marked by partially completed lanes with covered drains. Even after four to five years of commencement of the project, there was little progress. One could see vast vacant lands filled with weeds, along with a few building structures here and there and a few men working in the area demarcated as Andal Aerotropolis. The form did not match the dream-project as propounded by BAPL. The pace at which construction activities were being carried out raised serious doubts about the future of Sujalaam Skycity.

The problem lay in the conceptualisation of the timeline of the project. Whereas in large infrastructure projects, the normal timeline is fairly long, that is, 20–30 years (Salet et al. 2013), BAPL planned to finish the project in just 13 years (2007 to 2020). During the field investigation in 2018, just before two years of the expected completion of the project, it was observed that except

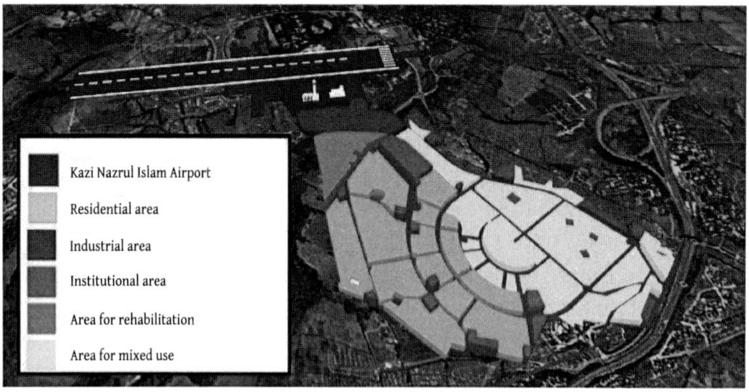

Figure 6.1 General layout of Andal Aerotropolis

Source: www.bengalaero.com (accessed on 22 October 2018)

the airport area, none of the other planned zones were even partially near completion.

SPECULATION AND CHANGING LANDSCAPES AROUND THE AEROTROPOLIS

Although there was not much change within the demarcated area of Andal Aerotropolis, things were changing a lot around it. In particular, the pace of infrastructural development in Andal, Kajora, Dubchuria, Dighnala, Dakshinkhanda, Moira, Khandra and Ukhra areas had been accelerated since the inception of the aerotropolis project. Significantly higher level of infrastructural development in association with greater degree of transformation of greenfields into residential, institutional and commercial areas had taken place in those areas, especially in the preceding five years. During interviews, the residents of nearby villages opined that the ongoing development of the aerotropolis had surely been a major factor behind this development and the transformation of landscapes there.

Land speculation and consequent inflated demand are on the rise in the entire area, thus leading to the development of a small-scale informal land market, as is seen in many other cases in India such as Chennai (Raman 2016) and Amaravati (Ramachandraiah 2016). The demand for land by the local people as well as by the promoters expecting future real estate development raised the value of the land to very high levels after the inauguration of KNI Airport (Table 6.1).

However, the quantum of transaction of lands did not increase uniformly in the area surrounding the aerotropolis. Rather, it increased more along the already existing transport lines such as Andal–Ukhra road, especially at the more connected points such as the area surrounding Andal crossing, the area in between Moira and Khandra, and the area in between Khandra and Ukhra. The price of land in these particular places surrounding the aerotropolis has been noticeably increasing since 2008. According to local respondents, before 2008, not many people of this area had been interested in purchasing land along this stretch either for residential or for commercial uses. Most of these lands used to be mono-crop agricultural fields and barren lands.

Table 6.1 Average rates of land (Rs in lakh per katha) in areas surrounding Andal Aerotropolis since 2005–06

Years	Zones Demarcated on the Basis of Land Value							
	Zone A: Andal		Zone B: Dakshinkhanda		Zone C: Moira–Khandra		Zone D: Khandra–Ukhra	
	Roadside	Away from road	Roadside	Away from road	Roadside	Away from road	Roadside	Away from road
2005–06 (Before Aerotropolis)	0.60–0.70	0.30–0.50	0.01–0.05	0.01	0.01–0.03	0.005–0.01	0.40–0.50	0.30
2010–11	1.30–2.20	0.80–1.20	0.15–0.30	0.10–0.15	0.10–0.30	0.05–0.15	1.00	0.70
2013–14	2.50–3.00	2.00–2.50	0.60–0.80	0.30–0.50	0.60–0.80	0.30–0.50	2.00–2.50	1.50–2.00
2015–16	5.00	4.00	2.00	1.50	1.50–2.00	1.00–1.50	3.50	2.50–2.70
2017–18	7.00–8.00	4.80–5.50	3.00–4.00	2.00–3.00	2.50–3.50	1.50–2.00	4.00–6.00	3.00–4.00

Source: Field survey, April–May, 2018.

But the initiation of the BAPL project has altered the scene entirely. These lands have now been transformed into compact settlement areas with the growth of complexes and institutional buildings. Now the demand for land in these locations, especially in the surroundings of Andal and Ukhra, for residential, institutional and commercial uses has increased, as is commonly seen in cases of other urban megaprojects (Ramachandraiah 2016; Raman 2016).

Field observations along the Andal–Ukhra road and conversations with the local people revealed that the newly built settlement areas in Andal and between Khandra and Ukhra had been both densifying and expanding since 2015. Different institutions such as private English-medium schools and skill development institutions have also come up. The vacant area between Khandra and Ukhra is being filled up with individual houses. In Andal, expanding housing complexes include both residential flats and societies built by real estate agents and individual housing. Many walled land parcels were also noticed along this stretch, especially in between Andal and Dakshinkhanda and between Moira and Khandra, indicating 'speculative urbanisation' in the surroundings of the aerotropolis.

Local people predicted that growth of Andal, Dakshinkhanda, Moira, Khandra and Ukhra villages along this road would lead to the development of a continuous built-up area within the next 10–12 years if the aerotropolis developed as planned. Consequently, investments would get intensified in the area. Though the enthusiasm for purchasing land in Dakshinkhanda and Moira plateaued over the two years before 2018 due to the limited success of the aerotropolis project, the price of land did not decrease in the locations along the Andal–Ukhra road. Nor has interest in purchasing lands in Andal and Ukhra diminished. Retired people from colliery areas such as Moira, Dakshinkhanda and Kajora have started to build their houses in Andal and Ukhra, contributing to the densification of the area. Although the processes of growth have slowed down due to ineffectiveness of airport operations, land value either has remained the same or has risen due to speculation of future growth.

At present, the growing market, business and industrial activities in Ukhra and Andal along with higher level of connectivity seem to be more significant factors than the presence of the aerotropolis to attract more people towards these two nodal locations. Efficient and frequent transport connectivity along the Andal–Ukhra road is critical for the local people to commute as it connects with National Highway 2, and the Andal Railway (Junction) Station and Ukhra Railway Station. People are also settling near the Andal crossing and Ukhra Railway Station to avail these transport connections more easily.

However, conversations with the real estate agents, corporate houses, business enterprises, local traders and also the local residents buying land in these areas showed that the location of Andal Aerotropolis and the development of the project had always been at the back of their minds while purchasing land in the surrounding areas. Our interviewees showed optimistic views on the development of the aerotropolis. They believed it would help them either develop their own activities or at least benefit from selling the lands to other enterprises to make high profits in the near future.

HURDLES FACING THE AEROTROPOLIS

Funding the project seemed to be one of the major problems faced by BAPL. As we learnt from the contractors, BAPL was not paying the construction company on time and that was why some of the construction activities had stopped. Construction workers said that the company could not pay their salaries on time. Thus, a suppressed tension existed between the stakeholders. Although in its vision statement BAPL claimed that by 2020 it would be among the top best employers in India and would add value to all stakeholders on a sustained basis, the work on the ground was unlikely to be finished by 2020.

The Government of West Bengal had rolled back its policy of providing subsidies for unsold seats on flights operating from smaller airports like those in Cooch Behar and Andal after realising the inefficiency of such payouts to make routes viable (Mandal 2017). Previously, according to the agreement, the subsidies were paid by BAPL in collaboration with the state government to the airline in the first phase of flight service at KNI Airport. After this decision of the state government, funding the airport and aerotropolis seemed to be more problematic given that the project was already not in a good financial position.

More direct flights were being demanded by the local people, but airlines wanted to route flights via Kolkata airport to reduce their risk of not having enough passengers from Andal. However, our field survey shows that people do not want to pay more for the flights via Kolkata. The area is well-connected with Kolkata airport through frequent rail and bus services which are much cheaper than flights and take only about three hours to reach. At the time of the survey, the fare of a luxury air-conditioned bus from Durgapur to Kolkata was about Rs 300–400, and that of an air-conditioned railway chair car was Rs 355, which was much less than the flight fare in this sector—Rs 1,000 or even higher. Hence, unless they have an emergency, people will not avail these flights to Kolkata and prefer direct flights to other destinations.

Following the UDAN scheme of the Union government which aimed to connect different smaller and regional airports of the country via flight service, another smaller airport was proposed to be developed in Burnpur where there is an existing airport operated by the Steel Authority of India. The distance between Burnpur and Andal airports is only 40 km. If the Burnpur airport gets connected to other cities by smaller flights, it would affect the flight services of the already non-profitable Andal Aerotropolis. The chance of cross-cutting of the benefits and profitability of two nearby airports brings into light another conflict of interest between the multiple government institutions. Here, these are the state government and the Central government. Burnpur is being developed under the Central government's UDAN scheme whereas the Andal Aerotropolis is a state government initiative. The two governments have been formed by different political parties which may lead to the political-economic conflict of interests and affect the future prospects of the Andal Aerotropolis project.

Asansol–Durgapur is basically a coal-mining and heavy industrial area. Although the tertiarisation of the economy had started to take place in different forms, it was still not enough to generate a large number of customers for the airlines. The area lacked investments from big domestic as well as foreign entrepreneurs. After several years and many trials, the number of passengers still had not reached the minimum threshold level for the successful operation of airlines.

PRIVATE GOVERNANCE

From the analysis of news reports over the last few years and the vision and mission statements of BAPL on their website, it is very clear that both BAPL and the West Bengal government had high hopes for this aerotropolis project. Following the usual trend of overestimation of demand and benefits of mega infrastructure projects, as noted in the literature (Flyvbjerg 2007; Salet et al. 2013; Robbins 2015), the expectation was that like many other aerotropolises in the world, Andal would bring about a real estate as well as industrial boom, and would make the Asansol–Durgapur region the second metropolitan area of West Bengal after Kolkata. In that direction, the Government of West Bengal merged all the nearby small statutory cities with Asansol Municipal Corporation to make it a bigger city covering an area of 326.48 sq km and 11.6 million people as per the 2011 census.

The state government has granted 'industrial township' status to the aerotropolis. The 74th constitutional amendment under Article 243Q makes special provision for governance of industrial townships, and the state government has the right to confer this status to such townships (Basak 2015). It means that this city does not need a democratically elected government. This status empowers promoters of the township to act as a municipal authority in collecting taxes and delivering services. A newsletter of the BAPL, namely 'Giving Wing to Growth: Government of West Bengal's Initiatives to Take Development to the Skies' (BAPL 2017), stated that the Andal Aerotropolis has been adopted under the state's 'Smart City' initiatives with the appellation 'Golden City', to be administered by an autonomous urban local body namely 'Golden City Industrial Township Authority' (GCITA), which would autonomously take up all municipal approvals and clearances, thus ensuring prompt sanction of projects through a single-window clearance system. A promotional video (Big Bulls Realty 2013) promised a world-class city with all kinds of modern facilities and industries, including manufacturing.

New urban megaprojects in India are often granted exception to traditional rules and regulations applicable to statutory cities, so they can operate as enclaves with private governance and planning (Idiculla 2016: 102). Andal Aerotropolis has also been given the same status of private governance, and to facilitate this condition the West Bengal government declared this township as an 'industrial township'. These kinds of initiatives facilitating a new urban regime of private governance are defined as 'bypass urbanism' (Sawyer et al. 2021). Besides institutional bypasses, spatial bypasses develop the new townships at the peripheries of existing cities (Idiculla 2016: 103). The location of the Andal Aerotropolis can be seen as a case of spatial bypass between Durgapur and Asansol Municipal Corporation.

Governance in the hands of private promoters develops service provider and customer relationship between the city government and the residents, which contrasts with the democratic system of urban governance practised elsewhere in India. If there is no democratically elected city government, the citizens would not have any voice in the management of the city. This can create a crisis in future as the private city government will always be interested in profit maximisation rather than citizens' rights (Mukhopadhyay 2015).

CONCLUSION

Starting in 2007, the Andal Aerotropolis project was proposed to be developed under a private company called BAPL within a period of 13 years. The project showed little sign of finishing by the committed deadline of 2020. The progress of the entire project was abnormally slow and the functionality of the airport was under doubt, especially in terms of passenger traffic. The project suffered from overestimation of demand and underestimation of cost, which are endemic in megaprojects. The cost overrun was proved by the increase of the state government's share in the project. However, the real estate speculation in the surrounding areas of the project site has been set in motion by various categories of actors with the expectation of change in the entire area.

The benefits of urban megaprojects in India are still contested, either in the context of the development of local economy or from the point of view of profit-making by the government and private agencies. However, the development of such megaprojects results in nuanced impacts especially in terms of transformation, speculation and (re)organisation of land and economy in the local area. In the surrounding areas of the proposed Andal Aerotropolis, a shift from mining and heavy industries to service sector activities has been set in motion. The development of IT, educational institutions and health institutions is evident in the entire area surrounding the aerotropolis. Significant proportions of all these service institutions are developing under private ownership and targeting the middle class. The middle-class people during our conversations with them showed great interest and expectation in the development of both the airport and aerotropolis. Investment was expected to take place in the service sector activities in the region as lands were purchased by people for commercial establishments along the major transport arteries of the area.

Still, there were a number of hitches observed in the field, which resonated with the existing literature. Studies conducted in other parts of the world (Flyvbjerg 2007; Salet et al. 2013; Robbins 2015) have observed that megaprojects tend to underestimate costs and overestimate benefits. Therefore, overrun costs and delays are far more common than expected. These are all parts of complexities and uncertainties inherent to large infrastructure projects (Salet et al. 2013). Here too, as we have seen, although the aerotropolis was expected to develop under private enterprise, the state government had already started to pump money into the project with increased share from 11 per cent to 26 per cent. The construction work was stalled by the delay in payment of construction workers at places under residential allocation of the plan outlay. The overestimation of benefits was also partially proved by many trials and failures of making the KNI airport financially viable and sustainable for the long term.

However, the development of all other activities inside the aerotropolis depends on the successful operation of the airport. To make the airport viable, BAPL would need to undertake rigorous groundwork to understand what people want from the area and how to negotiate with the airlines. This is part of the learning which is often recommended in a megaproject because of its long formulation and realisation time, and associated changes of market, environment and technologies impacting the overall situation in a particular area. Such learning is a process in which the contracting parties mutually exchange knowledge such that the meaning of the project and the project contracts develop over time (Van Der Veen and Korthals Altes 2012). It is probably too early to predict the future of the Andal Aerotropolis project and claim it as a failing project. We hope that we do not reach Flyvbjerg's 2009 conclusion: 'why the worst infrastructure gets built'.

NOTES

1. http://www.esopb.gov.in/Static/PDF/GSDP/Statewise-Data/StateWiseData.pdf, published on 1 August 2018 (accessed on 23 October 2018).
2. https://kniairport.com/andal-back-on-aviation-map (accessed on 2 June 2022).
3. A *mouza* is a revenue village.
4. *Bargadar* is a Bengali term for registered sharecroppers, following land reforms in 1980s in West Bengal.
5. *Katha* is the lowest unit of land purchase in West Bengal. About 20 kathas of land make 1 *bigha* and 3 bighas make 1 acre.
6. The market price in 2015 for a bigha was Rs 60 lakh.

REFERENCES

ABP News. 2018. 'Resuming Direct Flights between Durgapur-Delhi by Air India'. 15 April. Available at http://abpananda.abplive.in/state/ai-resumes-delhi-durgapur-direct-flight-service-462278 (accessed on 6 April 2018).

Adhikar. n.d. 'Durgapur Biman Nagari ba Aerotropoliser Swarup (The Nature of Durgapur Airport City)'. Asansol: Adhikar NGO.

Asansol Durgapur Development Authority (ADDA). n.d. 'ADDA at a Glance'. Asansol Durgapur Development Authority. Available at http://addaonline.in/adda-at-a-glance/ (accessed on 24 March 2018).

Banerjee, Sumanta. 2006. 'Peasant Hares and Capitalist Hounds of Singur'. *Economic & Political Weekly* 41(52): 5296–98.

Basak, Prabal. 2015. 'Industrial Township Status for New Airport City in Bengal'. *Business Standard*, 9 January.

Bengal Aerotropolis Project Limited (BAPL). 2017. 'Bengal Government Accelerates the Aerotropolis Project'. *Giving Wing To Growth: Government of West Bengal's Initiatives to Take Development to the Skies.* Available at www.bengalaero.com/pdf/BGBS.pdf (accessed on 6 March 2018).

Big Bulls Realty. 2013. 'Sujalaam Airport City Durgapur (Andal-Durgapur).' Available at www.youtube.com/watch?v=kq5wrXAcqp0 (accessed on 15 April 2018).

Bose, Pratim Ranjan. 2017. 'Private Airport at Durgapur Zooms Back into Business'. *The Hindu BusinessLine*, 17 April. Available at https://www.thehindubusinessline.com/economy/logistics/private-airport-at-durgapur-zooms-back-into-business/article9644769.ece (accessed on 27 April 2018).

Chatterjee, A. 2011. 'Land Compensation Heat on Andal Airport Project'. *The Telegraph*, 5 May.

Flyvbjerg, Bent. 2007. 'Policy and Planning for Large-Infrastructure Projects: Problems, Causes, Cures'. *Environment and Planning B: Planning and Design* 34: 578–97.

———. 2009. 'Survival of the Unfittest: Why the Worst Infrastructure Gets Built—And What We Can Do About It'. *Oxford Review of Economic Policy* 25(3): 344–67.

Flyvbjerg, Bent, Massimo Garbuio and Dan Lovallo. 2009. 'Delusion and Deception in Large Infrastructure Projects: Two Models for Explaining and Preventing Executive Disorder'. *California Management Review* 51(2): 170–93.

Goldman, M. 2011. 'Speculative Urbanization and the Making of the Next World City'. *International Journal of Urban and Regional Research* 35(3): 555–81.

Government of India. 2016. Draft Report of Regional Connectivity Scheme, Government of India. Available at http://www.civilaviation.gov.in/sites/default/files/Draft_RCS_01July2016_7_0.pdf (accessed on 6 April 2018).

Idiculla, Mathew. 2016. 'New Regime of Private Governance: The Case of Electronic City in Peri-urban Bangaluru'. *Economic & Political Weekly* 51(17): 102–109.

Kennedy, Loraine. 2007. 'Regional Industrial Policies Driving Peri-urban Dynamics in Hyderabad'. *Cities* 24(2): 95–109.

Kennedy, Loraine and Ashima Sood. 2016. 'Greenfield Development as Tabula Rasa: Rescaling, Speculation and Governance on India's Urban Frontier'. *Economic & Political Weekly* 51(17): 41–49.

Majumdar, A. D. 2017. 'West Bengal to Infuse Rs 300 Crore in BAPL which Runs Durgapur Airport Near Kolkata'. *LiveMint*, 15 September. Available at https://www.livemint.com/Politics/Q1iUyhfTCeNPGspeRkr3YL/West-Bengal-to-infuse-Rs300-crore-in-BAPL-which-runs-Durgapu.html (accessed on 10 May 2018).

Mandal, Sanjay. 2017. 'State Shuts Door on Flight Subsidy—Failure Prompts Payout Policy Reversal'. *The Telegraph*, 13 January. Available at https://www.telegraphindia.com/1170113/jsp/calcutta/story_130068.jsp (accessed on 15 April 2018).

Mathew, George. 2018. 'Maharashtra's Outstanding Debt Highest in Country'. *The Indian Express*, 28 April.

Mukhopadhyay, Partha. 2015. 'The "Unsmart" City'. *Seminar* 665: 2–6.

Niyogi, Subhro, and D. Chakraborty. 2011. 'Take-off Town'. *The Times of India*, 25 March.

Ramachandraiah, C. 2016. 'Making of Amaravati: A Landscape of Speculation and Intimidation'. *Economic & Political Weekly* 51(17): 68–75.

Raman, Bhuvaneswari. 2016. 'Reading into the Politics of Land: Real Estate Markets in the South-west Peri-urban Area of Chennai'. *Economic & Political Weekly* 51(17): 76–84.

Robbins, Glen. 2015. 'The Dube Trade Port-King Shaka International Airport Mega-project: Exploring Impacts in the Context of Multi-scalar Governance Processes'. *Habitat International* 45: 196–204.

Salet, Willem, Luca Bertolini and Mendel Giezen. 2013. 'Complexity and Uncertainty: Problem or Asset in Decision Making of Mega Infrastructure Projects?' *International Journal of Urban and Regional Research* 37(6): 1984–2000.

Samanta, Gopa. 2015. 'Making an Indian Airport City'. *Economic & Political Weekly* (Web Exclusives) 50(16): 1–8.

Sawyer, Lindsay, Christian Schmid, Monika Streule and Pascal Kallenberger. 2021. 'Bypass Urbanism: Re-ordering Center–Periphery Relations in Kolkata, Lagos and Mexico City'. *Environment and Planning A: Economy and Space* 53(5): 1–29.

Shatkin, G. 2011. 'Planning Privatopolis: Representation and Contestation in the Development of Urban Integrated Mega-Projects'. In *Worlding Cities: Asian Experiments and the Art of Being Global*, eds A. Roy and A. Ong, 77–97. Chichester, West Sussex; Malden, MA: Wiley Blackwell.

The Hindu BusinessLine. 2013. 'Durgapur Airport Named After Poet Nazrul Islam'. 20 September.

——. 2016. 'Air India to Discontinue Flights on Kolkata–Durgapur–Delhi Route'. 15 June. Available at https://www.thehindubusinessline.com/economy/logistics/air-india-to-discontinue-flights-on-kolkatadurgapurdelhi-route/article8733329.ece (accessed on 6 April 2018).

The Indian Express. 2015a. 'Durgapur Airport Starts Operations with Flights to Kolkata'. 19 May.

——. 2015b. 'Mamata Takes Inaugural Air India Flight to Meet PM'. 8 December.

The Times of India. 2017a. 'Zoom Air Eyes Hub in Durgapur'. 13 February.

——. 2017b. 'More Zoom Flights for Durgapur by Month-end'. 18 March.

Van Der Veen, Menno, and Willem K. Korthals Altes. 2012. 'Contracts and Learning in Complex Urban Projects'. *International Journal of Urban and Regional Research* 36(5): 1053–75.

PART III

AFTERMATHS

POLITICAL, ECONOMIC AND SOCIAL

7

New Town Building in the Postcolonial Era

ANNA DEWAELE[1]

In 2015, the Indian federal government launched the Smart Cities Mission, an urban planning programme based on a competition between a 100 cities around the country.[2] Preselected by the state governments, each candidate city had to propose either a redevelopment project for certain areas of the city or a greenfield development project. The proposals were to employ smart solutions to transform urban infrastructures and services with the aim of improving quality of life in the city (Ministry of Urban Development 2015). Equally funded by the federal government and the states for a total of US$ 130 million, the Smart Cities Mission encouraged the use of public–private partnerships (PPPs) in the spheres of urban design, construction and management.

Based on the concept of the same name, the Smart Cities Mission is an excellent example of the international dissemination of models (Ong and Roy 2011), in particular within the framework of the New Urban Agenda (United Nations 2016). However, the Smart Cities Mission needs also to be understood in the Indian context as the most recent variant on the new town model, that is, the establishment of new urban hubs. The creation of new towns was an urban planning tool favoured first by the British Raj, for example, with the railway towns of the colonial era (Sivaramakrishnan 1978); then by independent India through the building of state capitals (Kalia 1987, 1994, 2004); and, more recently, would-be eco-cities (Datta 2012). Although initially intended to create new cities from scratch, the Smart Cities Mission revised its mandate to favour the development of new urban centres either within or around existing cities. Thus, it represents something new in the models of urban renewal in India. The introduction of the Smart Cities Mission is an opportunity to analyse the change in the cast of urban planning actors, with what appears to be the emergence of a new balance between public and private sectors, and between Central and state government levels (Datta 2015; Kennedy and Sood 2016; Hoelscher 2017).

Most research on India's new towns has taken the form of analytical monographs on certain emblematic examples (Evenson 1966; Sarin 1982; Kalia 1987, 1994, 2004; Jacquemin 1999; Shaw 2004; Papillault 2007, 2011) or on the emergence of new planning procedures (Datta 2012; Sami 2013; Dey et al. 2013). Several publications have approached new towns as a useful framework for thinking about new urban dynamics in India such as the creation of exclusive enclaves in Kolkata (Wang et al. 2010), the growing role of private property developers in Gurgaon (Searle 2014), the emergence of an entrepreneurial urbanism in Dholera (Datta 2015) or the impact of industrial development in Jamshedpur (Sood 2015). This chapter establishes a critical inventory of India's postcolonial new towns, that is, those that developed between Independence in 1947 and the liberalisation of the economy in the early 1990s. The hypothesis of this chapter is that this attempt at a typology will reveal the shift in the role of the Central government in the planning of new towns within a broader context of change in the methods and models of city-making.

The research for this chapter draws on 13 months of fieldwork conducted between 2010 and 2014 in Chandigarh, Gurgaon, Magarpatta City, Navi Mumbai and Salt Lake City.[3] It consisted of more than 200 semi-structured interviews with residents, mainly from the middle and upper classes, and local urban actors (municipal authorities, private sector operators, non-governmental organisations and local media), as well as the collection of secondary data and grey literature. In this chapter, the field data are weighed against the scientific literature in a critical analysis of the town projects, focusing on the founding of the new towns and not on their development or appropriation. By establishing a genealogy of India's new towns, the aim is to generate insights about the development projects currently underway in India.

The first part of the chapter will explore the topic of the new town within the framework of twentieth-century urban planning, more specifically in a postcolonial situation, and will explore the context of public urban planning in India as background to the use of the new town as an urban development tool. The second part will sketch out a critical typology of the new towns founded in the two decades following Independence after the launch of a national policy. The third section will draw on the detailed analysis of the founding of three new towns to shed light on the change in the forms of public urban planning that occurred in the 1970s and 1980s.

THE NEW TOWN AS A PLANNING TOOL

Urban scholarship differentiates two categories of city that structure the urban landscape in time and space (Lavedan 1926; Le Corbusier 2011). On the one hand, sedimentary cities, also called *villes de création* (Papillault 2011) or spontaneous cities (Roncayolo 2001; Devisme 2003), emerge over time through the contributions of a variety of actors. On the other hand are planned cities, also called artificial cities (Lavedan 1926) or foundation cities (Roncayolo 2001; Vidal 2002; Papillault 2011). These different terminologies focus on the process of city-making.

Dissemination of the New Town Concept in the Twentieth Century

The term 'new town' refers to projects for towns that are planned as single and unified entities (Merlin 1969). Two waves of new town creation can be observed in the twentieth century around the world.

In the first wave, between the 1940s and the 1970s in Europe and North America, new towns were a favoured planning tool used to foster economic development in particular regions and to meet the housing and infrastructure needs of local populations. Typical of this first wave are three examples: the new towns founded in the UK under the authority of a Development Corporation formed by the Department of Urban Planning through the provisions of the New Towns Act; the new towns built in the US by private real estate developers for the upper middle classes with a view to generate profit; the new towns developed in France following the *Schéma Directeur d'Aménagement et d'Urbanisme* (Urban Master Plan) for the Paris Region. In the 1970s, this new town model became a target of criticism in developed countries, where it failed to achieve the anticipated success (Merlin 1969; Chaline 1985).

In the second wave, there was a proliferation of new town development in countries of the global South, where they were perceived as an appropriate response to political, economic and social changes. Most of the new towns and cities created between the 1980s and 2010 are thus located in Asia and the Middle East, a fact that prompted Rachel Keeton to describe the founding of new cities as an 'everyday practice' in these rapidly growing regions (Provoost and Vanstiphout 2011). Three types of new town can be identified: political and administrative capitals, like Brasília in Brazil; regional growth hubs, for example, San Pédro in Ivory Coast; satellite towns designed to help control the growth of megacities, like Shenzhen in China. Although the new towns in the second wave were inspired by examples in the global North, they differ in that the majority of them were created for privileged social groups (Chaline 1985; Keeton 2011). In this respect, they perform a showcase role that can be misleading for new inhabitants. Moreover, like the new towns of the US, these urban projects were not always undertaken by public actors (Ong and Roy 2011). In this respect, their analysis provides a good perspective on the change in the cast of urban planning actors in the cities of the global South.

Urban Planning in Postcolonial India

Like a number of developing countries, such as Egypt or China, postcolonial India adopted the concept of the new town to tackle its urban challenges and promote development. The analysis of the successive variations reveals that the public authorities participated in varying degrees to the founding processes, which can be attributed to political choices.

At the time of Independence, Gandhi's public advocacy of the village as the fundamental unit of the Indian nation (Prakash 2002) contrasted with Nehru's emphasis on urbanisation as the vehicle of industrialisation and modernisation (Lang et al. 1997). Following Gandhi's assassination in 1948, the so-called Nehruvian doctrine prevailed within the context of a planned socialist economy (Prakash 2002). For the Indian Prime Minister, modernity entailed projects for agricultural, industrial and urban development. This meant government becoming a major player in urban planning, seen as one of the main components of the country's economic development (Shaw 1996). In this respect, the new town can therefore be understood as the postcolonial project par excellence.

From Independence until the end of the 1980s, the Indian Union restricted private sector participation and maintained a degree of protectionism in order to foster the country's autonomy (Racine 1989). The federal government took the lead as the main player in urban planning. However, despite the ambitions for urban development expressed by the Indian government at Independence, urban growth remained modest. Indeed, the Census of India 2011 estimated India's urbanisation rate at 31 per cent, as compared with 17 per cent in 1951. Moreover, the city seems not to have been the preferred sphere of intervention of government, but an ancillary domain occasionally occupied by the Central government in the context of big industrial hydroelectric projects dictated by the five year plans (Shaw 1996; Dupont and Heuzé 2007). As a result, the new town seems to have been just one tool of urban planning among others and was adopted as such by several states.

After 1991, economic liberalisation transformed urbanisation processes in the country. On the one hand, the breaking up of state monopolies, the lowering of customs barriers and the authorisation of foreign investment led to growth in residential, office and retail construction in the large cities (Shaw 2012). On the other hand, economic liberalisation gave more influence to the urban middle classes, whose needs guided the new urban projects (Auclair 1998). Little by little, the new town emerged as a favoured instrument for private sector intervention, in that it enabled the property developers to break away from the conditions of existing urban areas and the difficulties associated with them. At the same time, the concept of the new town once again came into favour with the Central government, this time as a counterweight to the rapid growth of the metropolitan cities. For example, a project for several satellite cities was discussed within the framework of the Jawaharlal Nehru National Urban Renewal Mission (JNNURM), a major urban infrastructure and service modernisation programme undertaken between 2005 and 2014. More recently, the debates around the Smart Cities Mission have reflected continuing interest in the new town model, as well as a renewal in the forms and modalities of new town development (Datta 2015; Hoelscher 2017). This context of promotion is an opportunity to return to the dissemination of the new town concept in the decades that followed Independence in order to better understand its contemporary variations and priorities.

THE POST-INDEPENDENCE NEW TOWNS (1940–50)

The building of new towns has a long history in India, with examples like Fatehpur Sikri in the sixteenth century, Jaipur in the eighteenth century, or the construction of New Delhi by the British in the 1910s and 1920s. Postcolonial India also proved fertile ground for new towns, which were developed on an unprecedented scale from 1947, becoming a major characteristic of Indian urban history in that period in a context of demographic and administrative change. During the two decades that followed Independence, a particularity of the new towns was that they were Central government initiatives undertaken within the framework of big projects guided on the one hand by territorial reorganisation and on the other hand by economic policies.

The New Town Programme in Independent India

It was because of the need for an overhaul of the methods of urban production (Kalia 1987; Shaw 1996) that the Indian government proposed founding new towns to generate growth and to promote more balanced urbanisation of the country (Kalia 2009). In 1948, the New Delhi Town Planning Institute announced the creation of some 50 new towns within the framework of an urbanisation programme. The justifications for these towns were both functional and symbolic.

First, they were part of a necessary reorganisation of territory and were intended to become central hubs that would both structure new inter-regional connections and be vehicles of economic growth. Although most of the borders of the colonial provinces were originally retained in the 1950 Constitution, the territories of Punjab and Bengal were cut in half by Partition, which also led to massive population movements.

Second, the Town Planning Institute's new town programme was a symbol of independence and modernity for the young Indian Union. In a postcolonial context, the Union's aim was to create urban spaces that had not previously been occupied by the colonial authorities, in order to highlight the status of business centres and living places that would be representative of a new united nation, a *tabula rasa* (Evenson 1966; Kalia 2009). In addition to leaving behind the legacy of colonialism, the development of new towns was a response to the saturation of infrastructure in the large cities. At the time, these cities were characterised by sharp segregation between the colonial city and the native city, and were also experiencing an urban crisis because of a 41 per cent growth in the urban population between 1941 and 1951 (Shaw 2012). The planning of new towns was thus advanced as an ambitious response to the country's urban challenges.

Despite the scale of the programme launched by the Town Planning Institute, it is worth observing that this institution was never mentioned by the different urban planning actors we met during our fieldwork in India's new towns. By contrast with the reputation of the British New Town Act or the Paris Region's *Schéma Directeur d'Aménagement et d'Urbanisme* (Development and Town Planning Master Plan for the Paris Region) (Merlin 1969), this omission reflects the absence of the perception of a unified project around the concept of the new town, but probably also the lack of discussions around various planning experiments.

Typology of Postcolonial New Towns

The impact of the Town Planning Institute programme is difficult to assess today insofar as the postcolonial new towns acquired a variety of statuses, making it problematic to review and evaluate them. For instance, whereas K. C. Sivaramakrishnan identified 100 new towns built after Independence (Sivaramakrishnan 1978), Annapurna Shaw counted 112 new towns developed between 1947 and 1971 (Shaw 2009). Given the heterogeneity of the conditions under which they were built and their diverse forms, it is useful to establish a typology of the new towns. They were characterised by master plans of modernist inspiration, in contrast with the towns inherited from the Buddhist, Mughal and British periods. Nevertheless, they differed in their functions. Four categories of new town can be identified: capital cities, relocation towns, industrial towns and satellite towns.[4]

First, three state capitals were founded in the immediate aftermath of Independence. Although small in number, these were the most emblematic projects in the Town Planning Institute programme in that their function was to represent government authority within the framework of the nation's new territorial organisation. These cities were Bhubaneswar in the state of Odisha, designed by German architect Otto Koenigsberger; Chandigarh, developed in Punjab under the supervision of Franco-Swiss architect Le Corbusier; and Gandhinagar founded in Gujarat by Indian architects H. K. Mewada and Prakash M. Apte (Kalia 1987, 1994, 2004).

Second, several new towns were developed near major cities to accommodate the populations displaced following Partition. Annapurna Shaw identifies 14 such relocation towns established between 1947 and 1951 (Shaw 2012). These include Faridabad in Punjab (currently in the state of Haryana) and Gandhidham in Gujarat. These towns represent one of independent India's first urban planning efforts (Sarin 1982). Built quickly, they initially resembled residential suburbs, before economic activities located there in the decades following their creation.

Third, several new towns were founded across the country in the framework of state-owned industrial projects. This category corresponds to the largest group of postcolonial new towns' developments (Shaw 2004). They formed part of the public investment process and should be seen in connection with the five year plans, in particular the first two which focused on heavy industry. The main emphasis of the First Five Year Plan (1951–56) was irrigation, energy and dam-building, which led to the creation of towns like Nangal Township in Punjab. For its part, the Second Plan (1956–61) was the origin of new towns linked with steel such as Durgapur in West Bengal.

Fourth, several new towns were founded on the periphery of large cities to manage metropolitan growth and the increase in urban population (Sivaramakrishnan 1978). The objective of these satellite towns was to become autonomous while still maintaining strong social and cultural bonds with the main city. This model led to the creation of towns such as Kalyani in West Bengal.

The Emblematic Example of Chandigarh

Among the new towns developed immediately after Independence, Chandigarh was one that may be understood as a showcase for the urbanisation programme, as well as a model for other new towns. While a study of the Town Planning Institute programme shows that the Central government provided the guidelines for numerous new towns, it was involved to a greater extent in the case of Chandigarh, to the point that it gradually made the town the emblematic flagship of its urban planning policy. Chandigarh was designed as the new capital of the state of Punjab following Partition, which divided the former province of Punjab and placed the old capital, Lahore, in Pakistani territory. For a while, the historic cities of Amritsar and Shimla were considered as alternatives, but New Delhi quickly decided to found a new city as the best way to compensate for the materially and psychologically difficult loss of Lahore, the region's ancient economic and cultural centre. The objective of the founding of Chandigarh thus became to assert the modernity and identity of a new nation.

The extensive literature on Chandigarh reveals the influence of the Central government in its creation. First, this was reflected in the highly symbolic choice of the Franco-Swiss architect Le Corbusier.[5] With this choice, the young nation was seeking to capitalise on Le Corbusier's reputation and the poetics of change associated with him in order to reinforce the new city's image of modernity (Prakash 2002). At the same time, Le Corbusier produced a series of texts to mark the founding of the city and thereby endowed the new town with numerous symbols that contributed to the establishment of what have been called urban mythologies around Chandigarh (Papillault 2011). These mythologies enhanced the reputation of the new town and helped to transform it into a national—and even international—showcase. Second, the Central government's involvement in the founding of Chandigarh was reflected in the fact that Nehru played an active part in the project and sought from the start to make Chandigarh a symbol of independent India, free of its Mughal and British past. Though Delhi was retained as the national capital, its architecture was a reminder of the colonial past and Nehru felt it necessary to establish a city that would represent the rebirth of the nation in one of the country's richest regions, an image of India's new-found freedom. In that respect, the choice of creating a new city symbolised a tabula rasa. Speaking of Chandigarh, the Prime Minister said: 'Let this be a new town symbolic of the freedom of India, unfettered by the traditions of the past, an expression of the nation's faith in the future' (Kalia 2009: 159). Nehru's words are repeated on many advertising hoardings in Chandigarh, as well as by scholars (Kalia 1987; Prakash 2002; Papillault 2007). It is, in a way, a motto for the new town.

The fieldwork conducted in Chandigarh between 2010 and 2014 confirmed the still important influence of the figures of Le Corbusier and Nehru for middle-class residents of the city. Almost all of them spontaneously mentioned the involvement either of a European architect or one of the leaders of India's independence movement in their description of the new town. In interviews, it was not so much the issue of the heritage value of the buildings that was highlighted, as the value of an ideal urban way of life. The new town was perceived as a public production implemented following Independence so that the future inhabitants could enjoy a modern urban environment then unique in India.

THE SATELLITE NEW TOWNS (1960–80)

Among the post-Independence developments, several new towns were constructed on the peripheries of India's large cities between 1960 and 1980. Once the period of reorganisation of national territory was completed, the new town ceased to be an iconic object and became just one of a number of planning tools at a time when the preference in Asian urban policies was to build new towns to reduce and control the growth of metropolitan cities (Phillips and Yeh 1987). At this time, it was the satellite town model that was mainly adopted in India and which became the principal legacy of the 1948 new towns programme. This third section analyses the modalities of the planning of satellite towns during this period through the prism of three case studies: Gurgaon next to Delhi, Navi Mumbai next to Mumbai, and Salt Lake City next to Kolkata.

Three Satellite Towns Initiated by State Governments

The satellite new towns of Gurgaon, Navi Mumbai and Salt Lake City were developed along similar functionalist lines. Located south of Delhi, near the international airport and the motorway linking the capital to Jaipur, Gurgaon was built around an old village and became a high-density urban space consisting of a grid of numbered sectors allocated to residential, commercial or industrial activities. Navi Mumbai is located opposite Mumbai, east of Thane Creek, like a mirror-image twin. The satellite town is structured around urban nodes conceived as small, mutually independent urban entities, named after the villages present on the original sites. Finally, Salt Lake City is situated north-east of the city of Kolkata, halfway between the city centre and the airport, and near major road arteries such as VIP Road or EM Bypass. It is organised into five specialised sectors, forming a grid of blocks separated from each other by a hierarchy of roads and streets.

Unlike the towns founded immediately following Independence as part of a national policy, Gurgaon, Navi Mumbai and Salt Lake City were initiatives of their individual states. They, therefore, reflect the shift of certain urban planning activities from the national level to the state level. The foundation of satellite new towns needs to be understood in the context of the Third Five Year Plan (1961–66) which placed particular emphasis on urban planning (Shaw 1996). In particular, it provided for the creation of a fund to help the growing cities to prepare new master plans, to support the introduction of urban legislation at individual state level and to provide assistance in establishing new towns. Nonetheless, this urban agenda was not an indication of a real decentralisation of urban planning (Ruet and Tawa

Lama-Rewal 2009; Kennedy and Zérah 2011). Apart from the impact value, the satellite new towns were more like isolated experiments in planning, conceived independently of each other by the urban authorities of the individual states. The fieldwork in Gurgaon, Navi Mumbai and Salt Lake City found no traces of discussion and coordination between the bodies responsible for establishing the new towns in Haryana, Maharashtra and West Bengal, respectively. In interviews, the representatives of the different public planning authorities in each case described them as isolated initiatives.

The following analysis of Gurgaon, Navi Mumbai and Salt Lake City reveals three different forms of public urban planning in the respective states. The satellite town model was not implemented in the same way, or with the same enthusiasm, in each case. In particular, the analysis based on the grey literature and perspectives gleaned from institutional interviews reveals differences in projects not only in terms of their level of preparation, but also of ambition. Moreover, the interviews with local actors, in particular middle-class residents, provided insight into the differences in representations regarding the processes involved in the founding of these satellite towns.

Salt Lake City

The analysis of the foundational project for Salt Lake City highlights one initial aspect of state-level urban planning. The new town can be understood here as a concept implemented by a state to embody its vision of the ideal city and in response to contemporary urban problems. While this new development was not part of a larger urbanisation programme, it clearly resonated with the new towns developed at the initiative of the national government in the aftermath of Independence. In this respect, the analysis of the foundation of Salt Lake City reveals the transposition of national-scale planning models to the state level.

Nonetheless the history of Salt Lake City as retraced from the grey literature is above all one of a planning project conducted from the start by the state government. Although there had been a succession of proposals to develop the edges of Kolkata dating back to the 1830s, none of them was implemented because of the cost and the technical difficulties. It was finally in the 1950s that the Government of West Bengal decided to drain part of the marshlands east of Kolkata in order to develop a new town (Figure 7.1). In 1953, a site development plan for an area of 12.5 sq km around a salt lake was proposed by an engineering company based in the Netherlands

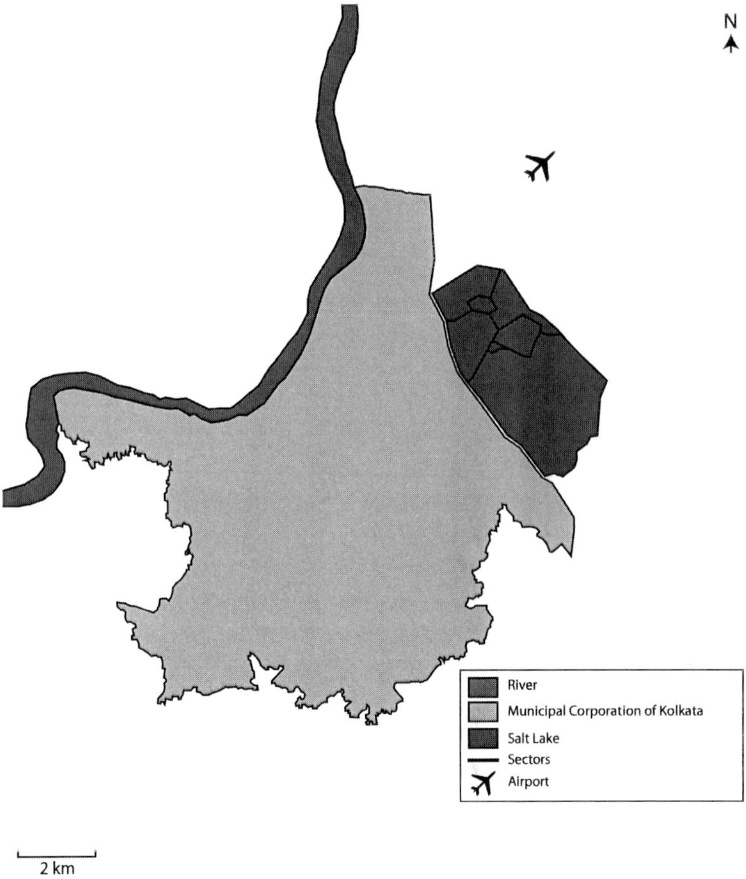

Figure 7.1 Location map of Salt Lake City in the Kolkata agglomeration

Source: Google Earth 2015; Census of India 2001; Bidhannagar Municipality Land Use 2012; Kolkata City Map Eicher 2010.

at the request of the state authorities. Following an international call for tenders, it was a Yugoslav firm that won the contract to implement the plan. Preliminary work began in 1961 and accelerated in 1962, when the chief minister of West Bengal, Bidhan Chandra Roy, officiated at a foundation ceremony for the new town.

The foundational ideals of the satellite town reproduced at state level those that had applied to the construction of the new towns of Independence at national level. Just as Nehru had presented Chandigarh as a symbol of independent India, the Salt Lake City project was backed by the chief minister of West Bengal, who declared a wish to make it a town for 'the man of the people' (Chattopadhyaya 1990); in other words, a town designed for lower-middle-class Bengalis who could not afford to buy homes in Kolkata.[6] This social ideal seems to have been familiar to the first residents we interviewed during fieldwork, who frequently mentioned Bidhan Chandra Roy as the founding father of the new town. One of them, at the time chairman of the residents' association, the Bidhannagar (Salt Lake) Welfare Association, explained: 'Dr Bidhan Chandra Roy, founder of this place, wanted Salt Lake to be a place for the middle-class, not for the well-off populations. That is why land prices were well below the market levels. The inhabitants could get interest-free loans in order to pay.'[7]

The founding of Salt Lake City also resembled the new towns of the post-Independence era in that it was overtly inspired by the same planning models. The choice of a foreign architect, Dobrivoje Toskovic, to design the master plan for Salt Lake City, reinforced the modern dimension of the new town project, in that the architect was strongly inspired by the principles of the International Congresses of Modern Architecture, as well as by Le Corbusier's proposals for Chandigarh or Oscar Niemeyer's and Lucio Costa's for Brasilia.[8] From the point of view of the architect and the Bengali public authorities, the importance of these connections was to link the new town with a set of internationally recognised models. In 1964, the first Master Plan for Salt Lake City proposed a functionalist layout and resembled a smaller scale variation of the acclaimed model of Chandigarh. Unlike these models, however, Salt Lake City was not imagined as a tabula rasa. It was designed as a new urban centre in counterpoint to the inconveniences of Kolkata: the noise, the congested streets, the bad air quality, the dirt. In an interview in March 2011, for example, the former director of the Kolkata Metropolitan Development Authority (KMDA) explained that Salt Lake City was designed by its builders to be a reverse mirror image of Kolkata. This observation was consistent with the accounts of the inhabitants we interviewed, who described Salt Lake City in terms of its contrasts with Kolkata.

Navi Mumbai

The case of Navi Mumbai reveals a second form of urban planning initiated by a state government (also see Shaw 2004). It reflects the shift in the concept of the new town from the emblematic to the ordinary. In contrast with those of the post-Independence period, the new town here is seen less as the embodiment of an ideal than as a necessary planning tool. More than anything else, it conveys the impression of pragmatic urban planning.

The first factor that distinguishes Navi Mumbai is that the idea for the project was not initiated by a public authority. Several proposals had been formulated since the beginning of the twentieth century to manage Mumbai's metropolitan growth, and the satellite town model had been raised as a possibility in the 1940s first by the architect Foster King, then in the discussions of the Bombay City and Suburbs Post-war Development Committee, in the *Brave Report*, and finally in the Development Plan Mumbai (Dwivedi and Mehrotra 1995). However, the origins of Navi Mumbai can actually be traced to 1965, with the publication of an article in the arts magazine *Marg* in which the architects Charles Correa and Pravina Mehta, together with the engineer Shirish Patel, called for the founding of a new satellite town east of Mumbai, on the other side of Thane Creek (Correa et al. 1965) (Figure 7.2). It was therefore an idea proposed by experts that prompted the state of Maharashtra to consider adopting the new town model. The *Marg* article aroused enthusiasm among the elites of Mumbai, resulting in 1966 in the establishment by the Maharashtra Economic Development Council (MEDC) of a working group consisting of 18 specialists, including Charles Correa, Pravina Mehta and Shirish Patel, tasked with looking into the possibilities of urban and industrial development east of Mumbai.

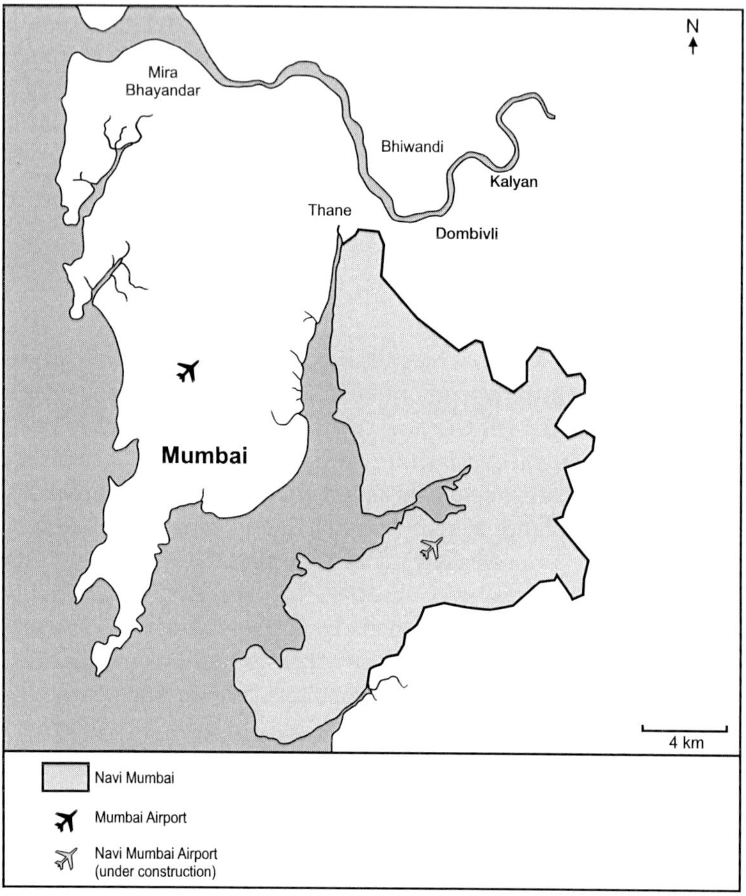

Figure 7.2 Location map of Navi Mumbai in the Mumbai agglomeration

Source: Google Earth 2015; Navi Mumbai CIDCO Development Plan 2008; Mumbai City Map Eicher 2009; Navi Mumbai City Map Eicher 2009.

The genesis of the Navi Mumbai project clearly illustrates the general trend towards a more moderate investment role by state authorities in the planning of new towns, in contrast with the earlier national programmes. From this perspective, it is interesting to note that the first residents we met during the fieldwork in Navi Mumbai only rarely mentioned the public planning authorities when speaking about the origins of their town, whereas the figures of Nehru and Le Corbusier in Chandigarh or even of Bidhan Chandra Roy in Salt Lake City were frequently mentioned during the fieldwork in those two places.

The second particularity of the Navi Mumbai new town project was the early abandonment of some of the foundational ideals that had characterised the post-Independence era, wherein the initial project remained an important reference for the development of the new towns. Following the creation in 1970 of the City and Industrial Development Corporation (CIDCO)—Maharashtra's state urban planning agency—the Draft Development Plan for Navi Mumbai was published in 1973. This document reveals the social ideal that presided over the founding project, specifying in its preface:

> The effort has been made to avoid the spectacular, to provide minimally for the affluent few and to promote the convenience of the greater number. New Bombay, then, will not be another Grand City; it will be a city where the common man would like to live (City and Industrial Development Corporation [CIDCO] 1973).

The strong response to the *Marg* article, and the ambitions set out in the preparatory document for Navi Mumbai, would seem to place the satellite town within the legacy of the urban projects of Independence. However, the implementation that quickly followed the initial proposals was minimal, especially in the view of the authors of the *Marg* article, who quit the project in 1973. In an interview, Shirish Patel explained that the increase in the cost of housing, the postponement of the construction of an adequate transport system as well as the refusal of the state government to move its administrative offices to Navi Mumbai were seen by the authors of the *Marg* article as compromising the successful operation of the satellite town, and in this respect as a negation of the foundational project.[9] On the occasion of the reproduction of the article, Charles Correa for his part explained that his chief mistake was to think that an ambitious urban project could be implemented in the absence of genuine public support: 'Cities do not change because of ideas—but because of political will. Something that, in the context of this city, has never been forthcoming' (Dwivedi and Mehrotra 1995: 314).

It should be noted that the early abandonment of the foundational ideals in no way hindered the development of the new town. From the perspective of a critical typology of postcolonial developments, however, this abandonment nevertheless reflects a shift in the concept of the new town at the state level into the realm of so-called everyday planning (Provoost and Vanstiphout 2011).

Gurgaon

The study of the genesis of the new town of Gurgaon points to a third form of state-level new town development. In the absence of a genuine vision for the town project and because of a lack of financial and political commitment by the authorities, the development of the satellite town was slow. Gurgaon should be understood here as an extreme case, which illustrates the limitations of public urban planning initiatives at the level of an individual state. This situation contributed to giving the private sector an unprecedented role in the new town project and in this respect was a preview of the 'new' new town models that gained ascendancy in the 1990s.

Unlike earlier new towns, the founding of Gurgaon should be understood less as the culmination of a public urban project than the outcome of a series of opportunities. From the fieldwork, in fact, it became clear that the territory of Gurgaon was seen above all as a strategic space for the Delhi metropolis as a whole. In 1962, the district of Gurgaon was identified in Delhi's first urban master plan as an area suitable for new urban spaces and new economic activities (Figure 7.3).[10] That is why the state of Punjab took the decision to establish a Controlled Area over part of the district, an area outside all municipal jurisdictions with potential for urban, industrial, commercial or institutional development. However, not much came of this change of status. In 1966, Punjab was divided along linguistic lines and the district of Gurgaon fell within the jurisdiction of the new state of Haryana. It was not until 1971 that the first timid signs of the development of the satellite town of Gurgaon emerged with the publication of the first Gurgaon Development Plan by the District Town and Country Planning Department (DTCPD). Urban development was more sustained from 1977 with the publication of the second Gurgaon Development Plan, and above all the creation of the Haryana Urban Development Authority (HUDA), a state planning agency. Finally, the foundation of the satellite town accelerated more markedly

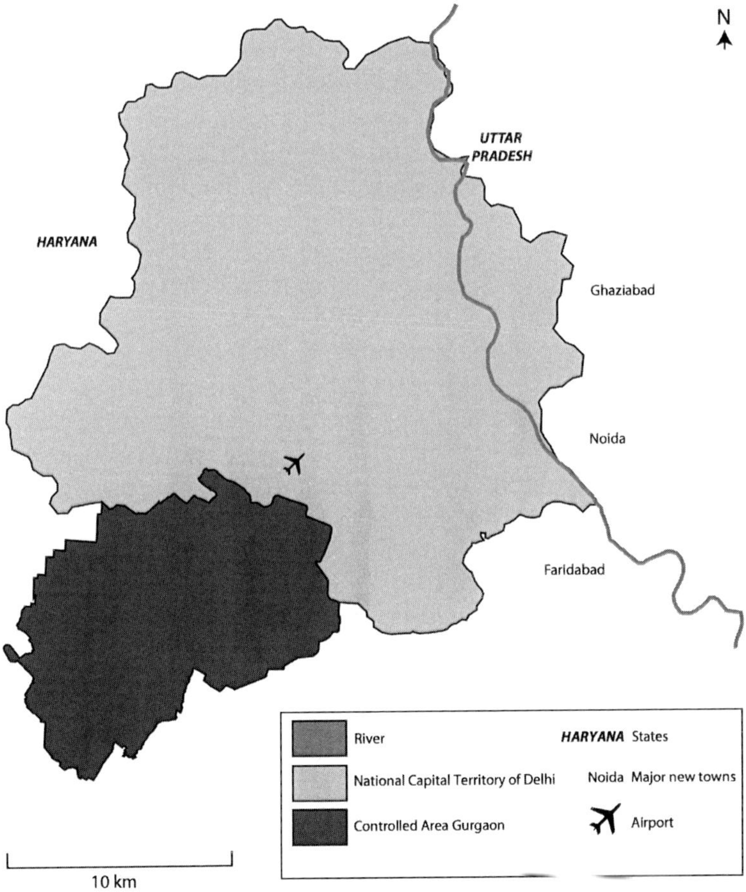

Figure 7.3 Location map of Gurgaon in the Delhi agglomeration

Source: Google Earth 2015; Gurgaon–Manesar Master Plan 2021; Delhi City Map Eicher 2010.

with the arrival of the first private real estate developers in the 1980s, following the Haryana Development and Regulation of Urban Areas Act (HDRUAA). Passed in 1975, this law included the private sector in the different stages of urban development and therefore enabled real estate developers to acquire, assemble and develop buildable land. It is important to note that it was only through the grey literature that we were able to establish the chronology of the successive development plans for Gurgaon. The narratives provided by the public authorities are both partial and punctuated with omissions, and the genesis of urban development planning was rarely mentioned by the first inhabitants in interviews. Conversely, most of the residents we spoke to recognised the impact of private property developers on the development of the satellite town. The result of this is that there are some surprising perceptions regarding the genesis of Gurgaon among newer residents. For example, a software company employee who has been living as a tenant in Gurgaon since 2007 asserted: 'The development of Gurgaon has nothing to do with the government. The government came in after the [private automobile] factory[11] and the private residential colonies[12] [...] Those companies developed everything.'[13]

Before the arrival of the private sector, it would appear that there was no real enthusiasm for the creation of Gurgaon from the state government. The first Gurgaon Development Plan in 1971 was limited to a map of the first 58 sectors and did not include any declaration of intent. In an interview in March 2014, the chief planner of the Haryana DTCPD admitted that he had never seen this map and that it was rarely mentioned in discussions on the planning of Gurgaon. The analysis of the grey literature shows moreover that there exists no founding document proposing a final town plan for Gurgaon, in contrast with the initial projects for Salt Lake City and Navi Mumbai. Urban development was envisaged in successive strata, with the addition of sectors and business zones based on residential and economic opportunities and needs. There was no global picture or overarching vision. In this respect, it is significant to note that the property developers were not required to follow the layout in numbered sectors set out in the different Gurgaon development plans when developing their colonies. Indeed, most did not use the existing numbering system, but preferred to name their colonies after their property companies or to give them a name with a strong evocative power. From this point of view, the attempt to transpose the model of the new town to the state level was synonymous with urban fragmentation and the proliferation of planning actors, in the absence of an explicitly defined urban project.

CONCLUSION

The different new towns developed in the decades following India's independence mark the consolidation of this model within the sphere of urban planning. Although the postcolonial new towns were built for diverse reasons and on the basis of urban projects that varied in ambition, what they had in common was that they appeared to be an appropriate territorial structuring solution for the states and the major metropolises. Nonetheless, they constitute two distinct groups insofar as the projects have not been sustained by the same public actors over the decades. Indeed, the new towns initiated by the Central government and those developed by the states demonstrate different principles and models of urban planning.

The new town continues to be a favoured tool of urban development. The contemporary examples echo the models and organisation tested in the past, while reflecting current urbanisation issues, such as the growing participation of the private sector or the slow progress of decentralisation (Leducq 2009; Marius-Gnanou 2010; Varrel 2010). Moreover, just as the postcolonial new towns revealed the ambitions of the young nation, the new towns currently developing could be described as post-postcolonial (Racine 2015) and can be seen as mirroring the changes in an 'emerging' India. New towns remain a relevant framework for understanding the transformations underway, not just urban but also social and economic, of the country. The attempt to establish a typology of postcolonial developments helps us better understand the procedures and principles applied in contemporary projects.

Experiments in new town development (Datta 2012, 2015 about Lavasa and Dholera; Sami 2013 about Magarpatta; Dey et al. 2013 about Rajarhat; Sood 2015 about Jamshedpur) point to a withdrawal of the Central government in favour of action by the states, and above all by the private sector, as prefigured in the Gurgaon experiment. Nevertheless, the Central government seems to be looking for new ways of promoting the new town concept in the current period. The Smart Cities Mission is interesting here insofar as the programme shows New Delhi in the role of a designer, like an orchestra conductor, and the states in the role of contractors, proposing their own vision of the smart city concept and relying on an ensemble of relevant public and private actors to realise it. In this respect, unprecedented new interplays and balances between the Centre, state governments and private actors may be observed in the years to come with the Smart Cities Mission.

NOTES

1. This essay was first published in French in *Annales de Géographie* in Number 720 in 2018. I am grateful for the helpful comments of the reviewers and the editors, and I want to thank the publisher Armand Colin for giving permission for the publication of the translated version. The translation was funded by Lab'Urba (Paris Est) and the Centre for South Asian Studies (CEIAS, CNRS-EHESS), and I want to express my gratitude for their support.

The fieldwork was done as part of graduate work at École des Hautes Etudes en Sciences Sociales (EHESS) and at the Centre d'Étude de l'Inde et de l'Asie du Sud (CEIAS), supervised by Jean-Luc Racine. The doctoral research was organised around the concept of urbanité among social elites residing in the new towns of Gurgaon, Navi Mumbai and Salt Lake City. The fieldwork was funded from three sources: the 'Aires culturelles' travel scholarship from the EHESS; the CEIAS fieldwork scholarship and the PRES héSamNExT Programme fieldwork scholarship in 'Asian dynamics: Exchanges, networks, mobilities'.

2. Information is available on the official website: http://smartcities.gov.in/content/ (accessed on 6 July 2018).

3. The new town of Salt Lake was renamed Bidhannagar in the 1990s in tribute to West Bengal's former chief minister Bidhan Chandra Roy. The name Salt Lake is nevertheless used in this article because it corresponds to the terminology employed by almost all the people interviewed during the fieldwork. The new town of Gurgaon was also renamed Gurugram in 2016 by the Haryana government with reference to Guru Dronacharya. The name of Gurgaon is nevertheless used in this chapter as it was the name of the town during the fieldwork.

4. Other typologies are described in the literature. K. C. Sivaramakrishnan proposed distinguishing between new towns on the basis of whether they were economically dependent or independent (Sivaramakrishnan 1978). For his part, N. S. Saini divided the new towns into nine categories based on their specialisation: administration, education, industry, port, transport, market, leisure, religion, military (Saini 1989).

5. While the American Albert Mayer was first put in charge of the project because of his experience as a civil engineer for the US Army in India in the 1930s, his abandonment of the project in 1950 forced the Indian leaders to look for a new team in Europe. Le Corbusier had just received several rejections within the framework of the post-War Reconstruction process, and was looking for a way to apply his modern urban theories. Despite some hesitations, he saw the design of Chandigarh as an opportunity to apply his principles at the scale of an entire town, and finally agreed to take over Albert Mayer's project with Jane Drew, Maxwell Fry and Pierre Jeanneret, as well as a team of junior architects and Indian engineers (Kalia 1987; Papillault 2011).

6. This social objective should be seen within the context of large-scale population displacement with the Partition of the old Indian Empire in 1947. The chief minister of West Bengal's project moreover took a singular turn with the new population displacements caused by the Bangladesh War of Independence in 1971. While the socio-economic profile of the first inhabitants reflects the success of the initial objective, it should nevertheless be specified that Salt Lake City today is a town that increasingly attracts the wealthier classes.

7. Interview conducted on 9 October 2012.

8. The references to other new town projects are documented in the book published by Dobrivoje Toskovic (Toskovic 2009), but also by several interviews conducted in 2011 and 2012 with three architects living in Salt Lake City.

9. Interview conducted on 17 February 2014.

10. The first urban master plan for Delhi proposed the creation of a National Capital Region (NCR) consisting of the territory of Delhi together with some of its periphery divided between the sub-region of Uttar Pradesh, the sub-region of Punjab (today Haryana) and the sub-region of Rajasthan.

11. The reference is to an Indian automaker. Although the parent private company was founded in the 1970s, the company was officially established in 1981 when it entered into a partnership with the Indian Union for the development of a car model suited to the needs of Indian citizens. Initially, the manufacturer imported cars from Japan before

opening its factory in Gurgaon and in 1983 launching one of the bestselling cars in India.

12. A colony is a planned area of housing generally made up of detached houses and resembling a housing estate. It is a generic term used to refer to certain districts in both sedimentary and planned cities in modern India. It was used in the colonial era to refer to 'a district or neighbourhood inhabited by a number of people having the same occupation, situated among others' as defined by Murray in 1888, quoted by A. D. King in 1976 in *Colonial Urban Development* (Auclair 1998).

13. Interview conducted on 16 January 2012.

REFERENCES

Auclair, C. 1998. *Villes à vendre: voie libérale et privatisation du secteur de l'habitat à Chennai (Inde)* [City for Sale: Liberalization and Privatization of the Housing Sector in Chennai (India)]. Pondicherry: Institut Français de Pondichéry.

Chaline, C. 1985. *Villes nouvelles dans le monde* [New Towns in the World]. Paris: Presses Universitaires de France.

Chattopadhyaya, H. 1990. *From Marsh to Township East of Calcutta: A Tale of Salt Water Lake and Salt Lake Township (Bidhannagar)*. Kolkata: University of Calcutta.

City and Industrial Development Corporation (CIDCO). 1973. *Draft Development Plan of Navi Mumbai*. Navi Mumbai.

Correa, C., P. Mehta and S. Patel. 1965. 'Planning for Bombay'. *Marg* 18(3): 30–46.

Datta, A. 2012. 'India's Eco-city? Urbanisation, Environment and Mobility in the Making of Lavasa'. *Environment and Planning C* 30(6): 982–96.

——. 2015. 'New Urban Utopias of Postcolonial India: "Entrepreneurial Urbanization" in Dholera Smart City, Gujarat'. *Dialogue in Human Geography* 5(1): 3–22.

Devisme, L. 2003. 'Ville nouvelle' [New Town]. In *Dictionnaire de la géographie et de l'espace des sociétés* [Dictionary of Geography and Societies' Space], J. Lévy and M. Lussault, 993–94. Paris: Belin.

Dey, I., R. Samaddar and S. Sen. 2013. *Beyond Kolkata: Rajarhat and the Dystopia of Urban Imagination*. New Delhi: Routledge.

Dupont, V., and D. G. Heuzé. 2007. 'Introduction'. In *La ville en Asie du Sud: Analyse et mise en perspective* [Cities in South Asia: Analyses and Prospects], eds V. Dupont and G. Heuzé, 13–39. Paris: Éditions de l'EHESS.

Dwivedi, S., and R. Mehrotra. 1995. *Bombay: The Cities Within*. Mumbai: India Book House.

Evenson, N. 1966. *Chandigarh*. Berkeley: University of California Press.

Hoelscher, K. 2017. 'The Evolution of the Smart Cities Agenda in India'. *International Area Studies Review* 19(1): 28–44.

Jacquemin, A. R. A. 1999. *Urban Development and New Towns in the Third World: Lessons from the New Bombay Experience*. London: Ashgate.

Kalia, R. 1987. *Chandigarh: The Making of an Indian City*. New Delhi: Oxford University Press.

———. 1994. *Bhubaneswar: From a Temple Town to a Capital City*. New Delhi: Oxford University Press.

———. 2004. *Gandhinagar: Building National Identity in Postcolonial India*. New Delhi: Oxford University Press.

———. 2009. 'Chandigarh and Urban India'. In *Le Corbusier: Chandigarh and the Modern City. Insights into the Iconic City Sixty Years Later*, ed. Khan Hasan-Uddin, 152–65. Ahmedabad: Mapin Publishing.

Keeton, R. 2011. *Rising in the East: Contemporary New Towns in Asia*. Amsterdam: Sun.

Kennedy, L., and M. H. Zérah. 2011. 'Villes Indiennes sous tutelle? Une reflexion sur les échelles de gouvernance à partir des cas de Mumbai et Hyderabad' [Indian Cities under Trusteeship? A Reflection on the Scales of Governance Based on the Cases of Mumbai and Hyderabad]. *Métropoles* 9. Available at https://journals.openedition.org/metropoles/4433 (accessed on 6 July 2018).

Kennedy L., and A. Sood. 2016. 'Greenfield Development as Tabula Rasa. Rescaling, Speculation and Governance on India's Urban Frontier'. *Economic & Political Weekly* 51(17): 41–49.

Lang, J., M. Desai and M. Desai. 1997. *Architecture and Independence: The Search for Identity. India 1880 to 1980*. New Delhi: Oxford University Press.

Lavedan, P. 1926. *Histoire de l'urbanisme. Antiquité-Moyen-âge* [History of Town Planning. Antiquity-Middle Age]. Paris: H. Laurens.

Le Corbusier. 2011. *Urbanisme* [Urbanism]. Paris: Flammarion.

Leducq, D. 2009. 'Secteur TIC et refonte de la gouvernance urbaine: Une reflexion sur les nouveaux acteurs de Pune' [Recasting of Urban Governance: Considerations from the Burgeoning ICT Sector in Pune]. *Netcom* 23(3/4): 221–44.

Marius-Gnanou, K. 2010. 'Nouvelles activités économiques et dynamique métropolitaine: le cas de la périphérie Sud de Chennai (Inde)' [New Economic Activities and Metropolitan Dynamics: The Case of the Southern Periphery of Chennai (India)]. *Annales de Géographie* 671–672: 28–51.

Merlin, P. 1969. *Les villes nouvelles: urbanisme regional et aménagement* [New Towns: Regional Town Planning and Development]. Paris: Presses Universitaires de France.

Ministry of Urban Development. 2015. 'Mission Statement and Guidelines Smart City Mission Transformation'. Government of India, June. Available at: http://smartcities.gov.in/upload/uploadfiles/files/SmartCityGuidelines(1).pdf (accessed on 4 August 2017).

Ong, A., and A. Roy, eds. 2011. *Worlding Cities: Asian Experiments and the Art of Being Global*. Malden: Blackwell.

Papillault, R. 2007. *Chandigarh*. Paris: Institut Français d'Architecture, Cité de l'Architecture et du Patrimoine.

———. 2011. *Chandigarh et Le Corbusier: Création d'une ville en Inde 1950–1965* [Chandigarh and Le Corbusier: Creation of a City in India 1950–1965]. Toulouse: Éditions Poïésis.

Phillips, D., and A. Yeh, eds. 1987. *New Towns in East and South-East Asia: Planning and Development*. Hong Kong: Oxford University Press.

Prakash, V. 2002. *Chandigarh's Le Corbusier: The Struggle for Modernity in Postcolonial India*. Seattle: University of Washington Press.

Provoost, M., and W. Vanstiphout. 2011. 'Introduction'. In *Rising in the East: Contemporary New Towns in Asia*, R. Keeton, 9–42. Amsterdam: Sun.

Racine, J. L. 1989. 'Développement et indépendance: jusqu'où compter sur ses propres forces?' [Development and Independence: How Far Can We Rely on Our Own Strengths?] *Tiers-Monde* 30(119): 491–512.

———. 2015. 'Penser l'Inde émergente: de l'altérité orientaliste aux temps post-postcoloniaux. En jeux locaux, en jeux globaux' [Thinking Emerging India: From Orientalist Alterity to Post-postcolonial Times. Local Issues, Global Issues]. In *Penser global: Internationalisation et globalisation des sciences sociales et humaines* [Think Globally: Internationalization and Globalization of the Social and Human Sciences], eds M. Wieviorka, L. Lévi-Strauss and G. Lieppe, 161–80. Paris: Éditions de la Maison des Sciences de l'Homme.

Roncayolo, M., ed. 2001. *Histoire de la France urbaine, 5e tome: La ville aujourd'hui—Mutations urbaines, decentralisation et crise du citadin* [History of Urban France, 5th Volume: The City Today—Urban Changes, Decentralization and the Crisis of the City Dweller]. Paris: Éditions du Seuil.

Ruet, J., and S. Tawa Lama-Rewal, eds. 2009. *Governing India's Metropolises*. New Delhi: Routledge.

Saini, N. S. 1989. 'Critical Experience of New Town Development India'. In *New Towns World-Wide 2*, eds A. K. Constandse and T. Ohba. Proceedings of the Symposium, 'Working Party New Towns', Amsterdam.

Sami, N. 2013. 'From Farming to Development: Urban Coalitions in Pune, India'. *International Journal of Urban and Regional Research* 37(1): 151–64.

Sarin, M. 1982. *Urban Planning in the Third World. The Chandigarh Experience.* London: Mansell Publishing Limited.

Searle, L. G. 2014. 'Conflict and Commensuration: Contested Market Making in India's Private Real Estate Development Sector'. *International Journal of Urban and Regional Research* 38(1): 60–78.

Shaw, A. 1996. 'Urban Policy in Post-independent India: An Appraisal'. *Economic & Political Weekly* 31(4): 224–28.

———. 2004. *The Making of Navi Mumbai.* New Delhi: Orient Longman.

———. 2009. 'Town Planning in Postcolonial India, 1947–1965: Chandigarh Re-examined'. *Urban Geography* 30(8): 857–78.

———. 2012. *Indian Cities.* New Delhi: Oxford University Press.

Sivaramakrishnan, K. C. 1978. *New Towns in India: A Report on a Study of Selected New Towns in the Eastern Region.* Kolkata: Indian Institute of Management.

Sood, A. 2015. 'Industrial Townships and the Policy Facilitation of Corporate Urbanisation in India'. *Urban Studies* 52(8): 1359–78.

Toskovic, D. 2009. *Salt Lake City: From an Idea to a Realization.* Belgrade: Grafomark.

United Nations. 2016. 'New Urban Agenda'. Resolution adopted by the United Nations General Assembly, 23 December. Available at https://www.un.org/en/development/desa/population/migration/generalassembly/docs/globalcompact/A_RES_71_256.pdf (accessed on 6 July 2018).

Varrel, A. 2010. 'La clôture des espaces résidentiels à Bangalore: Processus, pratiques et acteurs' [The Enclosure of Residential Spaces in Bangalore: Processes, Practices and Actors]. In *Circulation et territoire dans le monde Indien contemporain* [Circulation and Territory in the Contemporary Indian World], eds V. Dupont and F. Landy, 283–307. Paris: Editions de l'EHESS, Collection 'Purushartha'.

Vidal, L. 2002. *De Nova Lisboa à Brasilia: L'invention d'une capitale (XIXe–XXe siècles)* [From Nova Lisboa to Brasilia: The Invention of a Capital (19th–20th Centuries)]. Paris: IHEAL.

Wang, L., R. Kundu and X. Chen. 2010. 'Building for What and Whom? New Town Development as Planned Suburbanization in China and India'. *Research in Urban Sociology* 10: 319–45.

8

The Rise of Private Governance in Bengaluru's Electronics City

MATHEW IDICULLA

New modes of urban organisation are being unleashed across India by the designation of certain spaces as Special Economic Zones (SEZs), special investment regions, infrastructural corridors, industrial corridors, industrial townships, smart cities, among others. Many of these spaces have been granted exemption from many laws and regulations and operate as enclaves with private modes of governance and planning. Here, the very instrument of law is used to circumvent the operation of multiple laws, rules and regulations and create a 'zone of exception' (Ong 2006). This chapter presents a grounded understanding of these processes by examining the transformation of the governance systems in Electronics City in peri-urban Bengaluru with the creation of the Electronics City Industrial Township Authority (ELCITA).

How can we conceptualise these new urban regimes? What is the institutional character of these spaces? Why are they created and what are the implications? While there have been multiple studies on specific projects, especially with regard to SEZs, the changes in governance systems brought about by these new urban regimes have been inadequately conceptualised. This chapter explains the emergence of new privatised urban governance regimes conceptually and examines the creation and operation of one such space—the ELCITA. It employs a focused theoretical lens to make sense of the institutional and socio-spatial transformation effected.

The creation of Electronics City in the late 1970s played a major role in Bengaluru emerging as the 'Silicon Valley of India' (Idiculla 2017). Located on the outskirts of Bengaluru, it falls within the jurisdiction of gram panchayats and has lately become a site of contestation between various groups—the industries association, the local village panchayats and the city corporation, especially over material claims like land revenue. Despite opposition from gram panchayats as well as Bengaluru's Municipal Corporation, the state government declared Electronics City as an industrial township in

March 2013 after the Electronics City Industries' Association (ELCIA) lobbied for the same.

ELCITA now operates as a municipal body performing functions like urban planning, regulation of buildings, water supply and solid waste management. It hence operates as a private government with a parallel system of service delivery for a limited set of consumers. While ELCITA has been able to provide high levels of infrastructure and service within its boundaries, the 'external governance' (Sood 2015) implications of such a governance regime are more complicated. The sharp contrast in the levels of infrastructure and services in ELCITA with that of the surrounding areas reveals the operation of 'splintering urbanism' (Graham and Marvin 2001) in the region.

Even though ELCITA is not a democratically elected body, it is vested with the powers of a municipality including the power to levy property tax. While the 74th Amendment Act of the Constitution is hailed as a beacon of urban self-governance, on closer examination we understand that it allows for exceptions to spaces designated as 'industrial townships' to operate without elected local governments. This has allowed Karnataka to incorporate a provision for industrial townships in the Karnataka Municipalities Act, 1964, under which ELCITA was notified. Hence, though ELCITA operates at a level separate from the traditional bureaucratic state, the mechanism for its autonomy is constituted by the state itself through the formal enactment of laws.

This chapter argues that new regimes of private governance like ELCITA are created to bypass the social and political realities of Indian cities by geographically and legally locating them outside the cities' jurisdiction. New urban regimes bypass the chaotic order of the Indian city by physically migrating outside the city boundaries. They also have a privatised governance architecture that enables them to operate as enclaves which retain tax revenues within their boundaries. Hence, through a dual bypass—spatial and institutional—new urban regimes are able to locate themselves outside the jurisdiction of Indian cities.

This chapter provides a theoretical and empirical lens to examine the emergence of such private governance enclaves. It examines the institutional character of ELCITA by analysing the various laws, policies and case laws governing it. To understand the processes and politics behind institutional transformation, semi-structured interviews were conducted with members of ELCITA, village panchayats and residents of the area. Newspaper articles, reports and other secondary literature were also utilised to trace the genealogy and transformation of Electronics City. Hence, by a combination of qualitative primary research and an analysis of laws, policies and secondary sources, this chapter provides a granular account of the creation and operation of ELCITA.

The chapter is divided into five sections. The first section provides a conceptual frame for understanding Electronics City's governance transformation by explicating how new urban regimes bypass the informality of the Indian city. The second section traces the evolution of Electronics City and the contestations around the creation of ELCITA. The third section examines the institutional character of ELCITA by analysing the legal basis of its creation and the mechanics by which it governs its territories. The fourth section analyses how the creation of ELCITA has splintered the landscape of peri-urban Bengaluru with unequal provision of infrastructure and services. The fifth section examines the politics behind the transformation of Electronics City into an industrial township. The conclusion highlights the key arguments of the chapter.

BYPASS URBANISM AND NEW GOVERNANCE REGIMES

In the current global order, the state has been undergoing massive transformation with its scale shifting to multiple levels and its relationship with the market morphing into that of facilitation rather than regulation. Henri Lefebvre (1991) had explained how states provided the geographical scaffolding for the circulation of capital. However, with capital being restructured and re-territorialised, state spaces are reorganised to create new geographical scaffoldings necessary for the current mode of capitalist growth (Brenner 1998). Hence, the state does not wither away with globalisation but is reincarnated in a plethora of forms on different socio-spatial scales by constructing new territorial infrastructures and institutions that enable the expansion of capital accumulation (Keil 1998).

The attempt of global capital to transform new territories is, however, met with various forms of resistance from existing social systems of the global South. India's urban spaces are characterised by informality since a large portion of the population operates outside the planned vision of the city. This sphere has been conceptualised as a 'political society' where the daily life of the poor is marked by routine violations of the law and everyday negotiations with the state (Chatterjee 2004). In fact, the 'planned' Indian city can be seen as an actively deregulated space where the planning process is itself characterised by informality and where the application of law is also left open-ended (Roy 2009). Here capital is confronted by a form of urban localism which is embedded in the peculiarities of local municipal politics in which poor groups make claims on the state through various techniques (Benjamin 2008).

In such a complex urban political space, new urban regimes are created to bypass the Indian city in two different ways—spatially locating themselves in the peripheries of existing cities and legally locating themselves under exceptional governance regimes. New urban regimes like SEZs and industrial townships are mostly located outside the centres of existing cities and also have parallel legal and governance structures that are devoid of democratic representation. Since the institutional character of these spaces is different from that of traditional state institutions, their creation can be characterised as what Mariana Prado (2011) identifies as an 'institutional bypass'. To avoid resistance to 'reforms', an institutional bypass avoids fixing the traditional 'dysfunctional institutions' of developing countries and instead creates alternative institutional frameworks by changing certain parts of the system rather than transforming the entire system.[1]

Along with the 'institutional bypass', there is also a 'spatial bypass' by which such enclaves are built in the peripheries of cities. Rajesh Bhattacharya and Kalyan Sanyal (2011) argue that India follows such a 'bypass' approach to urbanisation to sidestep the peculiarities of a 'political society' which hampers planners' attempts to engage in Western-type gentrification. New urban regimes seek to bypass the 'street politics' (Bayat 1997) of existing cities by creating new townships in peri-urban areas where laws of public space and private property are enforced more strictly. They function as economic spaces that are more aligned with the global economy than the local economy (Bhattacharya and Sanyal 2011).

New urban regimes disassociate themselves from the immediate surroundings and operate as 'premium network spaces' (Graham and Marvin 2001) with a parallel private governance system in the form of an 'urban club' (Sood 2015). As Graham and Marvin (2001) argue, infrastructural development in the post-Fordist era often takes the form of 'splintering urbanism' in which public goods like power, water and transportation are provided unequally across different urban spaces. New technologies effect an 'infrastructural bypass' by creating customised spaces and services though parallel infrastructural networks to valued consumers, bypassing the majority of the population.

While the legal form might differ, what all these urban regimes do is alter the manner in which the state regulates certain territories. Such spaces, according to Ong (2006), are zones of variegated sovereignty where states make exceptions to their usual governing practices in order to align themselves with the market-centred logic of the global economy. Unlike the chaotic and disruptive nature of the Indian city, these spaces are highly ordered and disciplined and hence can be said to characterise a new regime of spatial governmentality, a form of ordering through the construction and management of governable spaces (Foucault 1991; Merry 2001). In this manner, new urban regimes operate by locating themselves spatially and legally outside the traditional 'dysfunctional institutions' of the global South.

THE CONTESTED CONSTRUCTION OF ELCITA

The city of Bengaluru has been a site at which new urban innovations reflecting the policy priorities of post-liberalised India have unfolded. Since 2005 the Central and state governments have provided various 'enabling' policies for the information technology (IT) industry like granting SEZ status and exempting the sector from key labour regulations.[2] In this period, the city has undergone transformations in its institutional and infrastructural architecture with the promotion of megaprojects, high-end infrastructures, parastatal agencies, elite civil society–government partnerships like Bangalore Agenda Task Force (BATF) and other forms of 'speculative urbanism' (Goldman 2011; Benjamin 2010). Electronics City hence emerged as an enclave of private governance in a context where the state and market have been devising measures to transform Bengaluru into a 'world class city' and a global hub of the IT industry (Idiculla 2017).

Though Electronics City was originally set up in 1978 by the state government to promote the electronics industry, it became an international IT hub only in the mid-1990s after India opened up its markets for foreign investment. The first phase of Electronics City was established on 332 acres of land in Konappana Agrahara and Dodda Thoguru villages by the state-controlled Karnataka State Electronics Development Corporation Limited (KEONICS) with the Karnataka Industrial Areas Development Board (KIADB) performing the task of land acquisition.[3] In 2003, Electronics City was expanded by creating two more phases under the aegis of KIADB, the third phase primarily catering to the biotechnology industry. The trigger that transformed Electronics City from an electronics industry centre to an IT hub was the establishment of the Software Technology Park of India, a Government of India undertaking, in Electronics City in 1991 (Heitzman 2004). Electronics City has hence progressively become the nucleus of Bengaluru's growing IT and biotechnology industries.

Before the establishment of the technology park, the areas constituting Electronics City were primarily used for agriculture.[4] However, with KIADB's land acquisition for Electronics City, the topography of the area changed and agricultural activities came to a virtual standstill. KIADB, a wholly owned infrastructure agency of Government of Karnataka, has been derisively called a 'real estate agent'[5] by the Karnataka High Court and has often been found to have acquired land in contravention of the prescribed land use patterns in Comprehensive Development Plans (CDPs). The report of the comptroller and auditor general of India (CAG) on the performance audit of KIADB found that in some cases, KIADB held no prior consultation with local planning authorities to ensure that land earmarked for non-industrial use was not notified for industrial acquisition.[6]

To promote the interests of the industries in Electronics City, the ELCIA consisting of the various units operating in the IT Park was formed in 1992.[7] ELCIA acted as a forum for addressing common problems faced by the industries, one of the chief concerns being the lack of infrastructure.[8] In 1997 the Government of Karnataka handed over the maintenance of basic facilities of Electronics City to ELCIA for which it collected annual maintenance charges from the various industrial units within the park.[9] ELCIA was in charge of providing basic maintenance work including roads, drains, street lights, waste management, water management, safety and security.

The Electronics City region has, since 2016, increasingly become a site of contestation. ELCIA had made a formal request to the state government for converting Electronics City into an industrial township way back in 2006.[10] Bengaluru's Municipal Corporation had also been trying to bring Electronics City within its jurisdiction. However, when the state government extended the boundaries of the Corporation in 2007 with the formation of Bruhat Bengaluru Mahanagara Palike (BBMP, or Greater Bangalore Municipal Corporation), it did not include Electronics City though areas next to it were included. In August 2012, the elected council of the BBMP passed a resolution to include the gram panchayats in which Electronics City was situated in to come under its jurisdiction, a move widely protested by ELCIA. The cash-strapped Corporation estimated that around Rs 300 crore could be raised as property tax from various IT companies that operate in Electronics City.[11]

The BBMP's resolution for including Electronics City within its boundaries was rejected by the state government and instead it decided to constitute the area as an industrial township. After issuing a draft notification inviting objections on 29 December 2012, the state government issued a notification on 18 March 2013 creating ELCITA.[12] The Jagdish Shettar-led Bharatiya Janata Party (BJP) government took this decision just two days before the model code of conduct for the 2013 Karnataka State Assembly election came into force. As per the notification, more than 903 acres, consisting of parts of Dodda Thoguru, Konappana Agrahara and Veerasandragram panchayats, came under its jurisdiction. However, the gram panchayats opposed the move to create the township and passed resolutions to stall the government's move (Ramani 2013a).

While the resolutions against the formation of ELCITA have not yielded any respite, the politics around its creation shows that Electronics City is a deeply contested space. The most important change the creation of ELCITA entailed is that the industrial units in Electronics City are no longer required to pay property taxes to any external government agency—either the panchayats or the BBMP. Instead, ELCITA itself collects taxes and spends it for civic functions and services for the tax-paying units within the 903 acres. Essentially, ELCITA's creation ensures that the taxes collected from the IT Park largely stay within its own boundaries, for its own use. The conventional theory of taxation that taxes, unlike fees, are payments to a public authority with no quid pro quo has hence been challenged. The creation of ELCITA may be seen as a form of urban secession in which high tax-paying areas secede from the region by forming urban clubs with privatised governance systems (Cashin 2000).

MECHANICS OF PRIVATE GOVERNANCE

With the creation of ELCITA, Electronics City now operates in a zone of relative autonomy, with no form of control from democratically elected bodies like village panchayats or city corporations. While its antecedents can be traced to industrial towns like Jamshedpur, the present promotion of industrial townships represents a shift to modes of private governance that bypass the requirement of an elected municipal government by invoking an exception provided under the 74th Constitutional Amendment. States have invoked the industrial township exception in varying degrees, with Karnataka, West Bengal, Maharashtra, Tamil Nadu and Jharkhand having separate legislative provisions for industrial townships (Sood 2015).

Industrial townships are possible because Article 243Q of the Constitution (introduced by the 74th Amendment) which mandates the creation of elected municipal governments (either a nagar panchayat, a municipal council or a municipal corporation) has a proviso which states: 'Provided that a Municipality under this clause may not be constituted in such urban area or part thereof as the Governor may, having regard to the size of the area and the municipal services being provided or proposed to be provided by an industrial establishment in that area and such other factors as he may deem fit, by public notification, specify to be an industrial township.'

This proviso lays down an exception to the constitutional requirement of the formation of elected municipal governments in all urban areas by allowing the state government to declare a specific area as an industrial township. Interestingly, as K. C. Sivaramakrishnan (2014), a senior bureaucrat who was one of the chief architects of the 74th Amendment, notes, the proviso was a last-minute introduction into the constitutional amendment. It was not present in the previous versions of the bill or in the parliamentary joint select committee's report but was introduced as an amendment when the constitutional amendment bill was taken up for clause-by-clause consideration (Sivaramakrishnan and Joshi 2015).

The proviso is present only in Part IXA of the Constitution which deals with municipalities and not in Part IX, which deals with panchayats. Whether the industrial township exception can be invoked in rural areas was a question that came up in the Supreme Court in *Saij Gram Panchayat* v. *The State of Gujarat & Ors.*[13] This is an important question since like Electronics City, Kalol Industrial Area in this specific case was also under the jurisdiction of panchayats. The contention of the panchayat in this case was that since the notified area forms a part of a panchayat under Part IX of the Constitution it cannot be treated as an industrial township under Part IXA of the Constitution. However, the industrial areas in question were developed by the Gujarat Industrial Development Corporation, which provided certain municipal services in the area. Hence, the court reasoned that even though the areas notified legally fell within the boundaries of the panchayats, 'they can hardly be looked upon as rural areas covered by Part IX of the Constitution'.[14] Essentially, the case upheld the state government's power to invoke the industrial township exception in rural areas though Part IX of the Constitution does not have any provision for the same.

The notification to create ELCITA was issued under the Karnataka Municipalities Act, 1964. In 1994, the Act was amended to bring it in conformity with the provisions of the 74th Amendment and provided for industrial townships as 'small urban areas'.[15] In 2003, the Act was further amended to insert a separate chapter for industrial townships providing for their composition, functions and duties.[16] The amendment also conferred on the Industrial Township Authority the powers of a municipal council specified in the Karnataka Municipalities Act. Karnataka could pass such an amendment because of the proviso to Article 243Q of the Constitution.

As per the Karnataka Municipalities Act, 1964, the governor may notify an area as an industrial township only after the concerned local authority (in this case, the panchayats affected) is consulted and a draft of the notification is published in the official gazette inviting objections and suggestions.[17] While a draft notification of creating the 'e-City Industrial Township Authority' was published in the gazette on 29 December 2012 as required, the panchayat officials contend that the state government did not formally consult the panchayats.[18] However, the final notification creating the township issued by the Urban Development Secretariat on 18 March 2013 states that 'consultation with the concerned Local Authorities' were held and 'suggestions received within the stipulated time have been considered by the Governor'.[19]

ELCITA is headed by a council which largely consists of nominated members representing the companies operating in Electronics City. As per Section 364(B) of the Karnataka Municipalities Act, an industrial township authority shall consist of a chairperson, five members representing the owners of industrial establishments, one representative each from the departments of commerce and industries, town planning and urban development, one resident with experience in urban management and one representative of the local authorities from the areas from which the industrial township was carved out. As per the Act, the quorum required for the meeting of the authority is five and the decisions regarding any business transacted at such a meeting is to be taken by a simple majority.[20]

The functions and duties that ELCITA is mandated to perform under the Karnataka Municipalities Act are regular municipal functions including regulation and construction of buildings;

planning for economic and social development; water supply; solid waste management, etc.[21] ELCITA is also responsible for granting approvals to building, registering *khata* and issuing trade licences and other certificates.[22] The executive authority of ELCITA is vested in the chief executive officer (CEO) who is responsible for the supervision and management of the day-to-day affairs of ELCITA.[23] Along with the CEO, ELCITA also has a chief operating officer (COO), a chief security officer (CSO) and expert committees on governance and finance; town planning; estate management; security and traffic management; and sustainability and environment.[24]

The Karnataka Municipalities Act empowers the industrial township authority to levy property tax on all buildings and lands, the same powers as a municipal council. It is empowered to collect levies, tolls, fees, rent, profits, costs and charges, and also receive money from the government by way of grants, loans and advances.[25] The Act prescribes that 30 per cent of the property tax collected by the authority must be remitted to the local authority from which its territory was carved out. Hence, ELCITA is required to provide Konappana Agrahara and Dodda Thoguru gram panchayats 30 per cent of its property tax revenue. Though there were delays in transferring these funds at the early stages of ELCITA's formation, it now promptly transfers the required share.[26]

Though ELCITA has been provided with substantive powers and autonomy in its functioning, the Karnataka Municipalities Act empowers the state government to issue directions to ELCITA with which it is bound to comply.[27] The government also has the power to appoint an administrator for the industrial township authority if, in the opinion of the government, ELCITA has failed to perform its duties or functions satisfactorily. In such situations, all powers and duties of the industrial township authority will be exercised and performed by the administrator.[28] However, these provisions are not unique to industrial townships and similar clauses allowing the state government to unilaterally dissolve democratically elected local bodies govern all municipal bodies in Karnataka.[29]

With its unique governance system, ELCITA is often regarded to be more effective in regulating its territories than Bengaluru's 'dysfunctional' municipal corporation. As a news report postulates, ELCITA's proposed Geographical Information System (GIS)-based survey of properties will allow it to 'keep a hawk-eye vigil to deter violations' and make it impossible for property owners to violate building norms or 'resort to any illegalities that so far have been rampant under the BBMP jurisdiction' (Kidiyoor 2015). ELCITA also has transparent e-governance processes that enable online transactions; it has also provided on its website voluntary disclosure of information under Section 4(1)(b) of the Right to Information Act.[30]

The territories under ELCITA are also under strict physical and technological surveillance. Along with the local police, ELCITA has been provided with Central Industrial Security Force (CISF) Quick Reaction Teams due to security threats determined by the intelligence bureau.[31] The 903-acre township is also manned by a battery of private security guards who also manage the traffic within its territories. ELCITA's partnership with a technology company for converting a 5 sq km area in Electronics City into a 'Living Lab' has also enabled the establishment of a 'Smart City' Command Centre in May 2015 which provides for the surveillance of its territories through measures such as safety cameras, smart lighting with sensors and licence plate recognition.[32] So while the Indian city is characterised by informalities and illegalities, ELCITA is able to construct a 'spatial governmentality' (Merry 2001) that enables the creation of a disciplined and ordered space through various technological tools.

SPLINTERING URBANISM IN THE ELECTRONICS CITY REGION

Though ELCITA provides necessary municipal facilities within its boundaries and has adopted transparent governance processes, an analysis of its creation also needs to examine the wider ecosystem in which it operates. Hence, it is not just the 'internal governance' mechanisms of ELCITA, but also the implications they have on 'external governance' (Sood 2015) of the region that are relevant. As the area of Electronics City was carved out of parts of three gram panchayats (primarily two panchayats—Konnapana Agrahara and Dodda Thoguru), there exist perceptible differences in the physical characteristics of the areas under ELCITA and those under the neighbouring panchayats. Modern high-tech corporate offices of IT companies lie next to informal houses, small residential buildings, paying guest accommodations, hotels, *dhabas*, *chai* shops and other *gram thana* areas. While areas under ELCITA have wide well-maintained roads and walkways with abundant tree cover, those under the panchayats mainly have narrow *kacchha* roads with minimal facilities.

The difference in basic services like drinking water is perhaps where the distinction is most evident. The areas under ELCITA have a well-connected piped water distribution network established by the Bangalore Water Supply and Sewerage Board (BWSSB). The BWSSB, the state-controlled parastatal agency responsible for water distribution in Bengaluru, provides water to ELCITA in bulk and ELCITA distributes it to the various units within its jurisdiction.[33] Interestingly, the Electronics City region is presently the only area outside the limits of BBMP where BWSSB supplies water.[34] While the units in ELCITA get assured water supply, for the areas lying just outside the boundaries of ELCITA, access to water is difficult due to the absence of a piped water distribution network. The residences and businesses in the region outside ELCITA use public taps provided by panchayats, private water distribution networks and water tanks installed by ELCIA, but there is still severe scarcity of water in the region.[35]

The varying levels of basic amenities like water supply between ELCITA and its surrounding region highlight the operation of 'splintering urbanism' in peri-urban Bengaluru. As Graham and Marvin (2001) argue, urban infrastructure can also foster spatial inequality and fragmentation of the city by creating 'premium networked spaces' for the affluent, bypassing the non-valued users. Splintering urbanism is also evident in the creation of high-end physical infrastructures like the elevated expressway connecting Electronics City with Bengaluru City. After the IT lobby pushed for its creation, a 9-km-long elevated tollway was created between the Silk Board Junction in the south-eastern part of the city and Electronics City in 2010 by a special purpose vehicle (SPV) called the Bangalore Elevated Tollway Private Limited (BETPL).[36]

The elevated tollway was created after ELCIA and the bosses of Bengaluru's IT industry publicly demanded the creation of such an infrastructure to make commute to Electronics City easier for IT professionals (Hariprakash 2010). Before the elevated road's construction, ELCIA undertook some novel forms of protest against the poor condition of the Hosur Road which connected Electronics City to Bengaluru city. In the late 1990s, ELCIA also pushed for the speedy completion of the Bangalore–Mysore Infrastructural Corridor (BMIC) since its road provided the people working in Electronics City an alternative route to commute. When the BMIC project came under a storm due to the controversies surrounding land acquisition, ELCIA mobilised IT professionals to go on a walk on the road to support its construction.[37]

The creation of infrastructure like the elevated expressway splinters the urban landscape by creating certain valued consumers who can use the expressway by paying toll and others—the majority of citizens—who cannot access these infrastructural facilities and hence rely on the regular, messy roads below the flyover. Creating such premium networked spaces which splinters citizens' access to infrastructure is actually flaunted by BETPL, which declares on the homepage of its website: 'You can virtually fly over the ground level traffic congestion between Silk Board Junction and the Electronics City Junction on the Elevated Toll Road in just under 10 minutes instead of over one hour on the congested ground level road during peak hour!'[38]

THE POLITICS OF GOVERNANCE TRANSFORMATION

How was the IT lobby able to get the government to convert Electronics City into an industrial township, a move that would potentially have been politically risky? To get the industrial township status, ELCIA had to engage with various levels of the government in a sustained manner. Interestingly, while it was not very difficult to convince the higher levels of the bureaucratic order about the need for setting up an industrial township, it was much more difficult to get the middle-level bureaucracy to act.[39] The fact that the top IT czars supported the creation of such a body also seems to have benefited ELCIA. In its annual report ELCITA declares, 'Once again, we salute the captains of industry, and the

Government of Karnataka for their vision and far-sightedness that have been instrumental in the creation of this township.'[40]

The Federation of Karnataka Chambers of Commerce and Industry (FKCCI) had also been pushing for industrial township status for many industrial areas including Electronics City (Ramani 2013b). Along with the strong initiative from the industry, the fact that members of the top levels of the state bureaucracy backed the project was instrumental in ELCITA getting its demands met.[41]According to ELCITA's CEO, the primary reason why the government provided ELCIA with the industrial township authority status was because they had a good track record in maintaining the industrial area since 1997. The other reason cited is that since the area for which township status was requested did not have any residential units within it, it was more politically feasible.

Interestingly, to get the industrial township status, ELCIA claims that it did not approach any politician and relied solely on the upper bureaucracy.[42] In fact, there was political opposition to the creation of ELCITA from the member of legislative assembly (MLA) representing the Electronics City area who supported the panchayats' opposition to ELCITA and wrote letters to the state government against giving industrial township status to Electronics City.[43] The loss of revenue is the chief reason behind the local political opposition to the formation of ELCITA. Officials of Konappana Agrahara and Dodda Thoguru gram panchayat estimate the loss of about Rs 1.5–2 crore each, which is about 75 per cent of their total revenue. Since this is a substantial amount, the village panchayats have much less money to spend on public works now.[44]

The village panchayats have an uneasy but largely non-confrontational relationship with ELCITA. To maintain good relations with the neighbourhood, ELCIA has been engaged in some corporate social responsibility (CSR) activities in the area.[45] It has been providing free drinking water facilities to parts of Konappana Agrahara and Dodda Thoguru panchayats, though the quantity of water provided is quite limited.[46] However, ELCIA has often been found to be responsive to grievances from residents regarding non availability of water.[47] ELCIA has also formed a trust which is engaged in various charitable activities in the nearby villages including providing mid-day meals to neighbouring schools, building toilets in schools, running various health check-ups and holding training programmes on using computers.[48] In addition to this, various companies located in Electronics City have also been doing many CSR activities in the villages. A leading IT company has built a popular school in Konappana Agrahara which is run by the government. The company has also been ready to build an office for the panchayat, though this has not materialised since finding land for the same has been difficult.[49]

The loss of revenue due to the formation of ELCITA remains the biggest issue the panchayats have with ELCITA. Another concern is that Electronics City has not been able to provide employment for the people living in the village, other than employing a few in unskilled labour. Although there are claims about an agreement with the government that 30 per cent of employment in Electronics City would be for locals, it has still not materialised.[50] Despite these issues, many of the members and officials of the panchayats do not see the creation of ELCITA as patently unjust, primarily because the panchayat even earlier had little role in the maintenance of Electronics City area beyond collection of revenue and issue of licences.[51] Some residents, however, feel that the panchayat itself is dominated by dominant caste groups; this does not allow the voice of the weaker sections to be heard.[52]

Ever since the KIADB acquired land, the panchayat lost control over the area and subsequent changes in the governance structure did not have a direct bearing on the lives of the residents. According to a gram panchayat member, one of the main reasons why there was no widespread opposition to ELCITA was because 'not one inch' of the residential land in the panchayat was included within its jurisdiction.[53] The notification creating ELCITA accurately demarcated the industrial areas from the residential areas of the panchayats and only those areas acquired by KIADB were included under ELCITA's jurisdiction.[54] And since Electronics City was never under the jurisdiction of BBMP, its resolution to bring it within its boundaries was merely seen as a way to fill up its empty coffers. In such a circumstance, ELCIA was able to negotiate with higher levels of the state government and get Electronics City declared as an industrial township.

Soon after the declaration of Electronics City as an industrial township, Peenya Industrial Association intensified its demand for the Peenya Industrial Area in west Bengaluru to also be given the status of an industrial township (Ramani 2013b). However, the Peenya Industrial Area is within the BBMP limits, covering multiple wards and includes many residents and hence faces tougher political opposition. The panchayats in Electronics City, on the other hand, felt helpless when the notification creating ELCITA was issued. While they passed resolutions against its creation, the panchayats did not have much influence over the urban development department which issued the notification since they functioned under the rural development and panchayati raj department.[55]

CONCLUSION

The ELCITA occupies an interesting space in Bengaluru's governance system. As the first industrial township authority in Karnataka, it is a unique experiment that represents a new institutional architecture that can be potentially replicated elsewhere. It displays good internal governance practices with transparent procedures and discharges municipal functions with minimum interference from the state. Though the state was an instrumental force in its creation, whether it was through land acquisition or through legalising ELCITA's authority, and government representatives in ELCITA's council can participate in the council meetings, it is not involved in ELCITA's daily operations.

ECLITA may be characterised as 'premium networked spaces' (Graham and Marvin 2001) and an 'urban club' (Sood 2015) where higher levels of infrastructural and service provision are made available to an affluent few in demarcated enclaves by a non-elected private government. While the formation of such a private regime of governance is possible due to an exception provided for 'industrial townships' under the 74th Amendment, this provision, according to K. C. Sivaramakrishnan (2014: 199) 'fly in the face of the 74th Constitutional Amendment, whose declared principal objective is for elected local bodies to emerge as institutions of self-governance'. The proviso to Article 243Q has allowed enclaves like SEZs and industrial townships to operate outside the requirement of local democratic accountability. Hence, while the 74th Amendment has done much to further the cause of local democracy, it leaves behind a contested legacy.

Beyond the concerns regarding its creation, it is important to note that ELCITA has been able to provide high levels of infrastructure and services within its territories. The roads and pavements within ELCITA are sprucely maintained, traffic is efficiently managed and there is high presence of security personnel. This is in sharp contrast to the character of most urban and peri-urban spaces in Bengaluru and other Indian cities characterised by ineffective and dysfunctional civic administration. ELCITA also has instituted appropriate e-governance practices with timely updates and user-friendly services on its website. Since it has been able to provide both physical and virtual infrastructure for its users, ELCITA may be said to be successful in achieving 'good governance' within its boundaries.

While a key motivation of creating such an autonomous institution would be its authority to retain tax revenues within its boundaries, the perceived inability of traditional local governance institutions to respond to the needs of high-end industrial units also needs to be considered. As one of the members of ELCITA's Council has argued, municipalities and village panchayats do not understand 'the specialised needs of industries' and this leads to 'disorganised management, and lack of development' (Narayan 2015). In contrast, a regime of private governance like ELCITA is able to respond to the specific demands of the industry and also produce governable spaces through techniques of spatial governmentality (Merry 2001) like 'smart' technologies and private security and management systems.

This chapter has argued that new urban governance regimes like ELCITA seek to operate in spaces removed from the daily pressures posed by the state and society by spatially and institutionally locating themselves outside the city's jurisdiction. As the creation of ELCITA shows, while there was some political opposition on the ground, the proponents of such a mechanism are able to enter into direct negotiations with the higher levels of the government and diffuse any serious contestation from below. By spatially locating itself outside the city boundaries and legally locating itself outside urban governance institutions, Electronics City is able to avoid the disruptive syndromes of 'vote bank politics' (Benjamin 2008) of 'dysfunctional institutions' (Prado 2011) like municipal corporations.

The fault lines in urban citizenship have been deepening in India in the post-liberalised era with the better-off citizens opting out of public goods and services in favour of private provision. The formation of new urban regimes like ELCITA represents the next stage of this trend as governance also becomes privatised as it gains autonomy from the legal, political and social power structures of the region. However, while ELCITA can be said to operate in a 'zone of exception' (Ong 2006), it is not completely divorced from the state government or immune from the pressures of local politics. The fact that ELCITA is required to pay 30 per cent of its property tax to the neighbouring panchayats and also engage in various CSR initiatives in the area shows how even new urban regimes cannot wholly secede from the state or society. Nevertheless, ELCITA represents a new regime of governance that questions some of the basic premises of state authority in a democracy.

NOTES

1. A more radical attempt at creating new cities by bypassing existing rules is the 'Charter Cities' initiative by Paul Romer under the 'Urbanization Project', housed in New York University's Stern School of Business (available at http://www.urbanizationproject.org/, accessed on 20 June 2022).

2. The information technology (IT) sector has been exempt from the Industrial Employment (Standing Orders) Act, 1946, in Karnataka since 2001. In Karnataka, most of the notified Special Economic Zones (SEZs) in operation are in the field of IT and biotechnology. The list of state-wise exporting SEZs (as on 31 March 2015) is available at http://sezindia.nic.in/upload/uploadfiles/files/ListofoperationalSEZs.pdf (accessed on 20 June 2022).

3. For details, see About Electronics City, https://www.electronic-city.in/about/ (accessed on 20 June 2022).

4. Interview with Jayaram Reddy, member and former vice-president, Konappana Agrahara Gram Panchayat, 23 July 2014.

5. See *The Hindu* (2012a).

6. See Comptroller and Auditor General of India (2010–11).

7. For details, see About ELCIA Business Portal, https://www.elcia.in/about-elcia-business-portal/ (accessed on 20 June 2022).

8. Interview with Rama N. S., CEO, ELCITA, and former CEO, ELCIA, 17 July 2014.

9. For details, see Electronics City Industrial Township Authority, https://www.elcita.in/welcome/ (accessed on 20 June 2022).

10. Interview with Rama N. S., 17 July 2014.

11. See *The New Indian Express* (2012); and *The Hindu* (2012b).

12. Notification No. UDD/69/MLR/2010, Government of Karnataka. Available at http://www.elcita.in/upload/GovtNote.pdf (accessed on 20 June 2022).

13. AIR 1999 SC 826; (1999) 2 SCC 366.

14. The operative part of the judgment by the division bench of the Supreme Court is as follows:

'The contention is based on a misconception about the relationship of the provisions of Parts IX and IXA of the Constitution with any legislation pertaining to industrial development.... The industrial areas which have been notified under Section 16 of the Gujarat Industrial Development Act on 7.9.1993 were notified as industrial areas under the Gujarat Industrial Development Act long back in the year 1972. These industrial areas have been developed by the Gujarat Industrial Development Corporation and they can hardly be looked upon as rural areas covered by Part IX of the Constitution.... Once such an area is a deemed notified area under the Gujarat Municipalities Act, 1964, it is equated with an industrial township under Part IXA of the Constitution, where municipal services may be provided by industries. We do not see any violation of a constitutional provision in this scheme' (*Saij Gram Panchayat* v. *The State of Gujarat & Ors*, AIR 1999 SC 826; (1999) 2 SCC 366).

15. Section 3 (3), inserted by the Amendment Act 36 of 1994.

16. Chapter XVI-A, inserted by the Amendment Act 24 of 2003.

17. Section 364(A).

18. Interviews with Jayaram Reddy, 23 July 2014 and Sunil L., Panchayat Development Officer, Konnapana Agrahara Gram Panchayat, 23 July 2014 and 28 January 2016.

19. Notification No. UDD/69/MLR/2010, Government of Karnataka.

20. Section 364(D).

21. Section 364(F).

22. Citizen's Charter ELCITA, available at http://www.elcita.in/upload/rti/citizencharterv04.pdf (accessed on 20 June 2022).

23. Disclosure under Section 4(1)(b), RTI Act 2005, available at http://www.elcita.in/upload/rti/ElcitaRTI41bv01a.pdf (accessed on 20 June 2022).

24. For details on ELCITA committees, see http://www.elcita.in/committee/ (accessed on 20 June 2022).

25. Section 364(J).

26. Interviews with Ms. Anusha, member and former president, Dodda Thoguru Gram Panchayat, 13 June 2014; and Sunil L., 23 July 2014 and 28 January 2016.

27. Section 364(M).

28. Section 364(N).

29. Karnataka Municipalities Act, 1964, and Karnataka Municipal Corporations Act, 1976.

30. Available at http://www.elcita.in/upload/rti/ElcitaRTI41bv01a.pdf (accessed on 20 June 2022).

31. ELCITA Notification/002/2014–15, available at http://www.elcita.in/upload/notification/deploymentcisfgeo1.pdf (accessed on 20 June 2022).

32. ELCIA Annual Report 2014–15, available at http://www.elcia.in/elcia-annual-report/annualreport.pdf (accessed on 20 June 2022).

33. Interview with Rama N. S., 17 July 2014.

34. BWSSB Jurisdiction: Subdivision, Expert Committee Report on BBMP Restructuring, Appendix IV, GIS Maps, Page A-63, available at http://www.bbmprestructuring.org/wp/the-final-bbmp-restructuring-report/ (accessed on 20 June 2022).

35. Interviews with Sunil L., 28 January 2016, and Vinod, Bill Collector, Konnapana Agrahara Gram Panchayat, 24 September 2015 and 25 January 2016.

36. Bangalore Elevated Tollway Private Limited (BETPL), a consortium of three infrastructure companies, built the tollway on a build, operate and transfer (BOT) model.

37. Interview with Rama N. S., 17 July 2014.

38. BETPL website, http://www.blrelevated.co.in/ (accessed on 20 June 2022).

39. Interview with Rama N. S., 17 July 2014.

40. ELCITA Annual Report 2014–2015, available at http://www.elcia.in/elcia-annual-report/ELCITA_update.pdf (accessed on 20 June 2022).

41. Interview with Rama N. S., 17 July 2014.

42. Ibid.

43. Interviews with Jayaram Reddy, 23 July 2014; Rama N.S., 17 July 2014; and Nagaraj, Panchayat Development Officer, Dodda Thoguru Gram Panchayat, 23 July 2014.

44. Interviews with Sunil L., 23 July 2014, and Jayaram Reddy, 23 July 2014.

45. Interview with Rama N. S., 17 July 2014.

46. Interview with Vinod, 25 January 2016, and Sunil L., 28 January 2016.

47. Interview with the priest of Sallapuriamma Devi Temple, Govinda Shetty Palya, Konappana Agrahara, 15 January 2016.

48. ELCIA Annual Report 2014–15, available at http://www.elcia.in/elcia-annual-report/annualreport.pdf (accessed on 20 June 2022).

49. Interview with Sunil L., 23 July 2014.

50. Interview with Jayaram Reddy, 23 July 2014.

51. Interviews with Jayaram Reddy, 23 July 2014; Sunil L., 23 July 2014; and Nagaraj, 23 July 2014.

52. Interviews with two residents, Govinda Shetty Palya, Konappana Agrahara, 15 January 2016.

53. Interview with Jayaram Reddy, 23 July 2014.

54. Interviews with Rama N. S., 17 July 2014, and Jayaram Reddy, 23 July 2014.

55. Interview with Sunil L., 23 July 2014 and 28 January 2016.

REFERENCES

Bayat, Asef. 1997. *Street Politics: Poor People's Movements in Iran*. New York: Columbia University Press.

Benjamin, Solomon. 2008. 'Occupancy Urbanism: Radicalizing Politics and Economy Beyond Policy and Programs'. *International Journal of Urban and Regional Research* 32(3): 719–29.

———. 2010. 'Manufacturing Neoliberalism: Lifestyling Indian Urbanity'. In *Accumulation by Dispossession: Transformative Cities in the New Global Order*, ed. Swapna Banerjee-Guha, 92–124. New Delhi: SAGE India.

Bhattacharya, Rajesh, and Kalyan Sanyal. 2011. 'Bypassing the Squalor: New Towns, Immaterial Labour and Exclusion in Post-colonial Urbanisation'. *Economic & Political Weekly* 46(31): 41–48.

Brenner, Neil. 1998. 'Global Cities, Glocal States: Global City Formation and State Territorial Restructuring in Contemporary Europe'. *Review of International Political Economy* 5(1): 1–37.

Cashin, Sheryll D. 2000. 'Privatized Communities and the Secession of the Successful: Democracy and Fairness beyond the Gate'. *Fordham Urban Law Journal* 28: 1675–92.

Chatterjee, Partha. 2004. *The Politics of the Governed: Reflections on Popular Politics in Most of the World*. New York: Columbia University Press.

Comptroller and Auditor General of India. 2010–11. 'Report of the Comptroller and Auditor General of India, No. 6 of 2010–11.

Performance Audit of Acquisition and Allotment of Land by Karnataka Industrial Areas Development Board'. Available at http://agkar.cag.gov.in/docs/AUDIT%20report/2011_KIADB%20-English.pdf (accessed on 20 June 2022).

Foucault, Michel. 1991. 'Governmentality'. In *The Foucault Effect: Studies in Governmentality*, eds Graham Burchell, Colin Gordon and Peter Miller, 87–104. Chicago: University of Chicago.

Goldman, Michael. 2011. 'Speculative Urbanism and the Making of the Next World City'. *International Journal of Urban and Regional Research* 35(3): 555–81.

Graham, Stephan, and Simon Marvin. 2001. *Splintering Urbanism: Networked Infrastructures, Technological Mobilities and the Urban Condition*. London: Routledge.

Hariprakash, Vasanthi. 2010. 'Bangalore's New Highway Spells Hope'. NDTV, 23 January. Available at: http://www.ndtv.com/cities/bangalores-new-highway-spells-hope-409398 (accessed on 20 June 2022).

Heitzman, James. 2004. *Network City: Planning the Information Society in Bangalore*. US: Oxford University Press.

Idiculla, Mathew. 2017. 'The Transformation of Governance in "India's Silicon Valley"'. *Seminar* 694: 17–21.

Keil, Roger. 1998. 'Globalization Makes States: Perspectives of Local Governance in the Age of the World City'. *Review of International Political Economy* 5(4): 616–46.

Kidiyoor, Suchith. 2015. 'ELCITA's Civic Blueprint Worthy of Emulating'. *Bangalore Mirror*, 18 May. Available at: http://www.bangaloremirror.com/bangalore/civic/Elcitas-civic-blueprint-worthy-of-emulating/articleshow/47321340.cms (accessed on 20 June 2022).

Lefebvre, Henri. 1991. *The Production of Space*, trans. Donald Nicholson-Smith. Cambridge, MA: Blackwell.

Merry, Sally Engle. 2001. 'Spatial Governmentality and the New Urban Social Order: Controlling Gender Violence Through Law'. *American Anthropologist* 103(1): 16–29.

Narayan, G. Raj. 2015. 'Unveiled! A Template for Self-Governing Townships'. *Deccan Herald*, 5 October. Available at: http://www.deccanherald.com/content/504491/unveiled-template-self-governing-townships.html (accessed on 20 June 2022).

Ong, Aihwa. 2006. *Neoliberalism as Exception: Mutations in Citizenship and Sovereignty*. Durham: Duke University Press.

Prado, Mariana Mota. 2011. 'Institutional Bypass: An Alternative for Development Reform'. SSRN. Available at: http://papers.ssrn.com/sol3/papers.cfm?abstract_id=1815442 (accessed on 20 June 2022).

Ramani, Chitra V. 2013a. 'Power Struggle Over an Authority'. *The Hindu*, 30 August. Available at: http://www.thehindu.com/todays-paper/tp-national/tp-karnataka/power-struggle-over-an-authority/article5073948.ece (accessed on 20 June 2022).

——. 2013b. 'Now, Peenya Industrial Area Seeks Township Authority Status'. *The Hindu*, 13 June. Available at: http://www.thehindu.com/news/cities/bangalore/now-peenya-industrial-area-seeks-township-authority-status/article4807895.ece (accessed on 20 June 2022).

Roy, Ananya. 2009. 'Why India Cannot Plan Its Cities: Informality, Insurgence and the Idiom of Urbanization'. *Planning Theory* 8(1): 76–87.

Sivaramakrishnan, K. C. 2014. *Governance of Megacities: Fractured Thinking, Fragmented Setup*. New Delhi: Oxford University Press.

Sivaramakrishnan, K. C., and Bhanu Joshi. 2015. 'Who Rules the City?' *Indian Express*, 10 February. Available at: http://indianexpress.com/article/opinion/columns/who-rules-the-city/ (accessed on 20 June 2022).

Sood, Ashima. 2015. 'Industrial Townships and the Policy Facilitation of Corporate Urbanisation in India'. *Urban Studies* 52(8): 1359–78.

The Hindu. 2012a. 'KIADB Worse Than a Real Estate Agent, Observes Court'. 28 June. Available at http://www.thehindu.com/todays-paper/tp-national/kiadb-worse-than-a-real-estate-agent-observes-court/article3579114.ece (accessed on 20 June 2022).

——. 2012b. 'ELCIA to Resist Move to Bring Electronics City Under BBMP'. 2 August. Available at http://www.thehindu.com/news/cities/bangalore/elcia-to-resist-move-to-bring-electronics-city-under-bbmp/article3713830.ece (accessed on 20 June 2022).

The New Indian Express. 2012. 'BBMP to Take Electronics City Under Its Fold'. 1 August. Available at http://www.newindianexpress.com/cities/bengaluru/article580664.ece (accessed on 20 June 2022).

9

The Politics of Urban Megaprojects in India

Income and Employment Linkages in Chennai's IT Corridor[1]

M. VIJAYABASKAR AND M. SURESH BABU

Following trends in global accumulation regimes, metropolitan regions have emerged as primary engines of growth in post-reform India (Kennedy 2007; Kennedy and Zérah 2008; Shaw and Satish 2007). The post-reform emphasis on attracting private investments through offer of a slew of incentives and efforts at 'worlding' cities has reconfigured urban spaces in India in ways that have been described variously as 'splintering urbanism' (Zérah 2008), 'enclave urbanism' (Sharma 2010) or 'exclusionary urbanisation' (Kundu and Saraswati 2012), suggesting a process of uneven spatial development. Crucial to recasting the urban as engines of growth is the emphasis on mega-infrastructure projects such as industrial or technology parks and corridors, special economic or manufacturing zones, satellite townships, metro rail, new airports and 'smart' cities (Kennedy et al. 2011; Kennedy et al. 2014). Meant to provide either competitive production platforms or specialised infrastructure, such initiatives are believed to help cities kick-start growth processes and move into higher order orbits of growth through generation of productive local linkages. Globally, such interventions are, however, seen to have overestimated benefits and underestimated costs leading to high risks and social losses (Flyvbjerg 2005, 2008). Further, though studies tend to posit a positive relationship between infrastructure and output, Misra's (2015) econometric study across Indian states points out that while investments in social infrastructure influence output positively, economic infrastructure's influence was statistically insignificant. At the micro-level, even as studies have noted the displacement and destruction of livelihoods by such ventures (Gellert and Lynch 2003; Robinson 2006; Coelho and Raman 2010), the implications of such projects for local employment linkages and consequently for pattern of urban development are less understood. This is particularly significant given the relative stagnation of incomes and economic status of the urban poor in post-reform India (Mitra 2010; Krishna 2013; Coelho et al. 2012).

The emphasis on metropolitan regions and megaprojects has only been matched by promotion of investments in information technology (IT) sectors by several state governments, particularly software services, since the onset of policy reforms (Saith and Vijayabaskar 2005). Incentivised by reforms to compete with one another to attract private investments, regional governments typically provide subsidised land, built-up office spaces, power and water supply to attract investments in the IT sector, among others (Jenkins et al. 2014). Among many such initiatives to transform Chennai city since the mid-1990s, of particular importance is the development of the Old Mahabalipuram Road (OMR, renamed as Rajiv Gandhi Salai) in south-east Chennai into an 'IT corridor' that is meant to be a world-class facility for IT and IT-enabled services (ITES) sectors.[2] An initiative of the state government, it was developed by the Tamil Nadu Road Development Company (TNRDC) which incorporated a special purpose organisation called 'IT Expressway Ltd' (ITEL) as a wholly owned subsidiary for this project.

Over the years, the corridor has become a hub of IT industry in Chennai, with most major IT/ITES companies having their development centres in the IT corridor. Covering a length of 20 km in the first phase, this corridor is now home to three large IT parks and smaller IT and business parks and firms. During our fieldwork, industry informants reported that more than a lakh employees worked in the IT companies on this corridor. Driven by these and other related developments, several high-rise housing complexes that promise 'world class' amenities for owners, like swimming pools and sports complexes, have also come up along the OMR.

This chapter, primarily based on a survey of employees working with software firms and in support services in two of the major IT parks, examines the quality of local employment and consumption linkages of IT parks located in the 'IT corridor'. In doing so, the chapter contributes to a closer understanding of the linkages between creation of new mega-infrastructures and additional employment creation in the area. It argues that the development of the IT corridor has been accompanied by rise of highly segmented labour markets marked by wide gaps in terms of wages and conditions of work, across gender and age. This segmentation also spatially manifests itself in terms of segmented housing markets leading to higher rental returns among property-owners in the neighbourhood and possible exclusions of other segments from accessing housing in this area. We also point out that substantial employment linkages are an outcome of poor provisioning of public services like water, transport and housing, and therefore cannot be read as positive multiplier effects of such projects.

METHOD

Economic linkages can be direct, indirect and/or due to spin-off effects. Direct linkages refer to immediate outcomes like employment and income effect arising from construction of infrastructure, and to employment and profits generated from firms moving to benefit from the infrastructure created. Indirect linkages include supplementary employment and income generated through new services that cater to demand emanating from direct effects. Transport services, food supply, security and gardening services, housing, banking and other commercial services are examples of such linkages. In the case of the IT sector, it is believed that for every direct job created, there are three to five such indirect jobs generated (Mukherjee 2011). Spin-offs refer to the possible productive linkages that are generated due to demand for new inputs. Rather than capture the exact quantum of linkages, we focus our attention on the spatial dimension of linkages forged. In the context of uneven development in post-reform India, it is important to understand the sources of unevenness by looking at how labour markets and spatial linkages are implicated in this process. Our scope is confined to linkages created by employment generated in these parks and important indirect employment generated within the two parks and in the neighbourhood. We emphasise the differences in quality of employment generated, sourcing of labour and extent of labour drawn from within the neighbourhood, and, importantly, on the nature of segmentation. Income linkages are analysed through an examination of their demands on urban infrastructure such as housing, food, water, sanitation and transport. We, however, do engage with assertions made by business associations and policymakers on the amount of indirect employment created by highlighting the quality of such employment and its drivers.

Information was collected from employees within two major IT parks located on two ends of the IT corridor in 2012. One is a public–private partnership (PPP) venture started in 2005 housing 56 IT and ITES firms, and the other is run by State Industries Promotion Corporation of Tamil Nadu Ltd (SIPCOT), a publicly owned institution. The latter houses 18 major IT firms, including multinational corporations (MNCs). Table 9.1 gives the break-up of the sample respondents by gender and their place of origin.

Table 9.1 Survey sample: Break-up by gender and place of origin

Gender	Place of origin					Total
	Rural	Small town	Metro	Adjoining Chennai	Chennai	
Male	12	49	5	13	20	99
Female	4	26	3	4	18	55

Source: Primary survey.

The choice of respondents was guided largely by access and hence done primarily through snowballing techniques. Through interviews with managers of two software firms housed in the IT parks, we mapped the nature of demand for indirect services generated. We focus on four sectors that have contributed most of the local employment linkages—transport services, food vending, security services and housekeeping. Detailed and semi-structured interviews were conducted in 2012 and 2013 with major service providers and their staff (Table 9.2).

In addition, we also interviewed real estate brokers in the neighbourhoods adjoining the IT corridor and relied on newspaper archives to understand real estate developments.

Table 9.2 Break-up of interviewees in support services

Category of indirect livelihoods	Number interviewed	Male	Female
Cab drivers	20	20	0
Bus drivers	15	15	0
Security personnel	30	30	0
Housekeeping staff	20	0	20
Restaurant owners	25	25	0
Hostel owners	10	10	0
Owners of small commercial establishments	10	9	1
Street vendors/hawkers	10	7	3
Total	140	116	24

Source: Primary survey.

ASPECTS OF DIRECT EMPLOYMENT AND CONSUMPTION LINKAGES

Software firms in the two parks employed about 60,000 to 70,000 people at the time of the fieldwork. The share of new employment generated is, however, much less as many large firms had earlier set up development centres in different parts of Chennai. One of the biggest firms in fact had its branches in at least three other different locations in the city and this move to the IT corridor was therefore meant to spatially consolidate its workforce and reduce overhead costs. Further, the software labour market has high barriers to entry as it is open almost exclusively to those with tertiary educational qualifications.[3] The sector also deploys, as Upadhya (2007) points out, a notion of 'merit' that excludes youth from rural and lower caste and class backgrounds. Though we do not have information on caste, 60 per cent of the respondents hailed from small towns or villages (Table 9.1). Given a history of positive discrimination policies through reservation of seats in higher education for lower castes in Tamil Nadu (Pandian 2011), the software labour market may be more caste-inclusive in the state compared to other states. The average salary levels of the respondents are higher than average salaries in other sectors, including the public sector (Table 9.3).[4]

Table 9.3 Age-wise break-up of monthly salary of respondents (Rs)

Age group (years)	Less than 20,000	20,000–30,000	31,000–40,000	41,000–50,000	Above 50,000
20–25	12	7	3	2	0
25–30	43	26	20	14	14
30–35	0	0	3	1	2
Above 35	0	0	1	3	2
Total	**55**	**33**	**27**	**20**	**18**

Source: Primary survey.

The movement of this labour into the city and to work in the IT corridor generates additional demand for various public services, demands on urban housing, transport, water and sanitation being the most important. As we demonstrate, linkages generated are largely driven by an absence of appropriate public provisioning of these services in the neighbourhood.

i. Housing

Most sample respondents (107 out of 154) lived on rented premises and preferred neighbourhoods like Thiruvanmiyur, Velachery, Taramani, Thuraipakkam and Navalur that are either on or close to the corridor. Table 9.4 provides a break-up of the rentals paid by the respondents.

Table 9.4 Amount spent on rent by respondents (Rs per month)

Rental band	No. of respondents
0–2,500	7
2,500–5,000	49
5,000–7,500	19
7,500–10,000	20
10,000–12,500	5
12,500–15,000	4
Above 15,000	3
Total	107

Source: Primary survey.

Ninety per cent of respondents in the first three rental categories share accommodation with their friends or colleagues. Importantly, this demand from relatively high-paid software employees has led to tremendous increase in housing rentals and land/apartment values in these neighbourhoods. According to real estate brokers, rentals in these areas have increased three-fold to four-fold since 2003–04. Since salary levels of other formal sector employees such as public sector employees have not increased by more than two times during this period, higher rentals are likely to have led to greater gentrification and exclusion of lower income groups from these areas. Srivatsan (2012) confirms this tendency, arguing that this inequity in access to housing is aggravated by the lack of public investments in affordable housing in the city. Contrasting rental returns in north Chennai and south Chennai, the latter being home to bulk of the IT sector firms, Swahilya and Srivatsan (2007) point out that while an apartment of about 1,000 sq feet would fetch a rental income of only around Rs 3,500 per month in north Chennai, a similar apartment in Adyar, Thiruvanmiyur or Besant Nagar, which are close to the IT corridor, is likely to fetch a rent of Rs 10,000 per month. An overview of Chennai's residential real estate sector by

Table 9.5 Average rentals across Chennai city

Area	Rentals for 2 bhk/month (Rs)
Thuraipakkam*	14,000–16,000
Sholinganallur*	14,000–16,000
Semmancherry*	10,000–14,000
Padur*	12,000–16,000
Adyar*	22,000–30,000
Porur	8,000–10,000
Ambattur	10,000–12,000
Sriperumbudur	4,000–6,000
Perambur	10,000–12,000
Madhavaram	6,000–8,000
Tondiarpet	8,000–10,000
Nolumbur	10,000–12,000

Source: Collated from ICICI Property Services (2013).
Note: *Areas that are either in close proximity to or on the IT corridor.

ICICI Property Services clearly brings out the higher rental values in areas on and near the IT corridor (Table 9.5).

Adyar, in fact, is reported to have the highest rental range in the city, next only to Nungambakkam, the most expensive neighbourhood within Chennai city. Real estate promoters repeatedly highlight Adyar for investment in property, given its relatively better rental returns.[5] The expansion of the IT sector has had an influence on real estate development, with a slew of residential projects amounting to Rs 550 crore coming up along the IT corridor even by 2010.[6] The income generated through employment in the IT parks therefore tends to be shared with property-owners in the vicinity of the corridor. It needs to be remembered, however, that the income accruing to property owners due to rental increases is therefore not an additional income but a share of the income of software employees appropriated through property ownership. Further, absence of investments in affordable housing and demand from the IT employees tend to generate an upmarket housing supply that reinforces such exclusionary tendencies.

ii. Transport

Even though a majority of respondents stay in proximity to the IT corridor, 112 respondents report travelling more than 10 km to reach their workplace, forging new transport networks and demands on transport infrastructure in the city (Table 9.6).

Table 9.6 Mode of transportation

Mode of transportation	1–5 km	5–10 km	More than 10 km
Walking	13	0	0
Bus	3	6	18
Train	0	0	2
Company bus	1	5	58
Own car	4	4	9
Two-wheeler	1	3	25
Others	0	0	1
Total	22	18	113

Source: Primary survey.

Since the SIPCOT park is located at the far end of the corridor, even living in neighbourhoods close to the beginning of the corridor like Adyar or Thiruvanmiyur implies a commute of more than 15 km. Respondents cited their ties to other parts of the city through social networks or absence of amenities, particularly schools, on the IT corridor as two major reasons for not moving closer to their workplaces. The absence of proper planning for transport infrastructure is all too evident as one travels along the OMR. Massive traffic jams are an everyday affair, particularly visible at two intersections with two arterial roads, and at the three toll booths meant for collecting tolls to access this road. Tankers transporting water, autorickshaws, shared autorickshaws and vans run by private operators, cars of middle and higher rung IT employees driven more often by paid drivers than owners themselves, public transport buses carrying passengers who are predominantly working in the many less-paying non-IT jobs along this area or long-term residents returning from work in other parts of the city, private air-conditioned buses carrying IT employees, cabs engaged by IT firms for senior staff, heavy vehicles carrying water and construction material for the various ongoing works on this road, in addition to the large number of two-wheelers divided between IT and non IT-employees, all vie for space on what has been increasingly recognised as a traffic hotspot in the city.

Although the parastatal Madras Metropolitan Transport Corporation (MMTC) runs 400 trips to the IT corridor daily, only a small number of respondents (27 out of 154) used public bus service. Poor frequencies, crowded buses and having to walk some distance from the bus stop in case of the SIPCOT park were cited as the reasons by the other respondents for not availing this facility. Rather than take up this issue with public authorities, firms in the park started providing company buses for their employees. Sixty-four of the respondents use company bus as their mode of transportation. A single large firm ran as many as 225 bus services per day for its employees. Others rely on private modes such as two-wheelers, cars, shared autos and a combination of private with public transport. With regard to expenditure on travel, 60 per cent of respondents report spending more than Rs 2,500 per month on travel. This accounts for more than 10–15 per cent of their monthly income, and taken together with expenditure on rentals is likely to account for nearly 40 per cent of the total income earned by the respondents on an average.

iii. Water and Sanitation

Almost 90 per cent of the respondents staying on rented premises buy branded water cans for drinking purpose and more than 55 per cent buy water from tanker lorries for other uses as well, creating another set of linkages (Table 9.7).

Table 9.7 Public provision of water facilities for those staying on rented premises

	Yes	No	Do not know	Monthly amount spent (Rs)	Total
Drinking water	9	98	0	500–750	107
General use	25	62	21	300–600	108

Source: Primary survey.

Some of the respondents actually did not know if their housing complex or hostel bought water from private actors. The issue of water provisioning once again reveals the pernicious nature of linkages generated. Most neighbourhoods in close vicinity to the IT corridor are either not serviced or under-serviced by the Chennai Metropolitan Water Supply and Sewerage Board (CMWSSB), the public water utility.[7] This has led to the rise of new private water providers and a thriving market for water (Venkatachalam 2014). These suppliers source water from wells or tanks in the peripheral regions bordering Chennai. Often, wells are dug on farmers' lands for supply of this water. To be sure, even the CMWSSB relies on a set of private tankers and suppliers to meet some of its supply requirements.

Once again, this linkage in terms of income accruing to water suppliers, including wages to those employed by them, is therefore not a productive linkage but one that essentially meets a demand for a public service that has not been met with by the state. Most apartment complexes that advertise 'world class amenities' rely on an ever-spiralling network of suppliers and water tankers that in turn rely on water from the peripheral farmlands and village tanks. Sewage facilities too are absent in the apartment complexes, spawning a set of local linkages with firms offering sewage clearance services. According to a news report, the failure of the CMWSSB to supply water and of the TNRDC to provide drainage facilities implies an annual expenditure of nearly Rs 100 crore by residents of the IT corridor to buy water from private suppliers and engage private sewage disposal firms (Stalin 2015). Apart from the residential demand for water, IT parks too require considerable amounts of water. While the CMWSSB supplies water to one of them, the SIPCOT park sourced water by sinking borewells on a piece of land owned by SIPCOT. However, the growing demand for water from wells and tanks in the peripheral villages has led to a series of conflicts,[8] including a strike by truck-owners that almost brought the firms in the IT parks to shut down for a day (Kandavel 2013).

Next we focus on local linkages generated through food consumption.

iv. Segmented Markets for Food

Given the preponderance of a young workforce and long hours kept in the software sector, there is considerable demand for food vending with both IT parks offering food court facilities. Most software industry respondents (75 per cent) said that they eat in food courts regularly since it saves time. A key feature of these food courts is the presence of global food retail outlets which co-exist with Indian and local food retail vending chains. In addition to restaurants within the food courts, there are also several other restaurants which have come up on the IT corridor to cater to this clientele. Importantly, most such restaurants are branches of existing chains of eateries with an established reputation, and not led by local entrepreneurship. Such restaurants through their presence in other parts of the city or country find it easier to step in to meet this demand.

Unlike in the previous phase of urban development that saw large private and public sector establishments offering basic subsidised food in canteens that could be accessed by all employees irrespective of hierarchy, here, the contract and indirect employees such as drivers, security staff, cleaning and other park staff are denied access to the food courts directly or indirectly by virtue of the higher prices charged in the restaurants there. Food markets are therefore segmented with the emergence of a large number of low-end, informal and mobile eateries along the corridor to cater to them. An average meal at lunch cost around Rs 40–70 in these places compared to a minimum of Rs 120–150 in the food court. Food vending services are therefore clearly segmented.

v. Other Consumption and Saving Linkages

In anticipation of demand from the IT firms and employees, a number of malls and high-end hotels are being built along the IT corridor. All these infrastructure investments are once again initiatives driven by pre-existing large firms in the respective sectors and are not an outcome of local entrepreneurship. This is also true of housing complexes that are being promoted in the area with large pan-Indian property developers entering the housing segment. The demand linkages through the incomes of the IT professionals appear to therefore favour non-local, pan-Indian or even global service providers except in the case of dubious linkages such as demand for water or sewage infrastructure. While it is possible that the entry of new players may bring in better services, the fact such high-end services tend to exclude low-income clientele needs to be taken into account.

Investment of employees' savings too has implications for the city. Nearly 50 per cent of respondents invested in real estate, of which 50 per cent invested in land on the outskirts of Chennai or in apartments in different parts of Chennai, including the IT corridor. Seventy per cent of all those who invested in real estate saw it as an investment for future appreciation of property value rather than for final use. The impact of this investment in real estate on supply and cost of housing for those outside this sector is unclear. It is, however, possible that such circuits are partly responsible for the city witnessing one of the highest increases in property prices during the period 2007–14 among major cities in the country (Jain 2015). Following this, we focus next on the indirect employment opportunities generated, particularly on the quality of supplementary employment generated through three major support services.

INDIRECT EMPLOYMENT LINKAGES

i. Transport: Cab Drivers and Bus Drivers

The inadequacy of public transport has spawned a spurt in demand for different kinds of vehicle drivers. To begin with, a segment is employed directly by higher end IT employees. Salary levels for this segment have increased three times, from Rs 5,000 in 2006 to Rs 15,000 in 2013, suggestive of a tight labour market. Since housing is not provided, the entrants into this segment tend to be those who have access to housing in close proximity to the employer's residence. In areas like Thiruvanmiyur, Adyar and Velachery, many employees draw their drivers largely from nearby poorer neighbourhoods/slums. While working for a household allows them some flexibility in terms of time, they are not entitled to formal social security benefits like provident fund or gratuity. Interestingly, though no aspect of this labour market is formally regulated, be it wage fixation or terms and conditions of work and employment, work is supposed to be less strenuous and more attractive compared to working formally for a private cab company.

The other labour segment which has grown along with the IT sector in the city is that of drivers employed with private cab firms working exclusively or largely for IT companies. According to the manager of a private cab firm, nearly 500 cabs are provided to one IT park on a daily basis. All the drivers we interviewed were below 45 years of age and more than 50 per cent of them had migrated from different parts of Tamil Nadu. Salary levels are lower by Rs 3,000 to Rs 5,000 per month compared to personal drivers. Though some of the firms provide them with social security, respondents preferred to work as personal drivers and not with private cab companies due to the long and erratic hours they need to put in the latter segment. In the absence of housing, migrant employees find employment with private cab companies viable as they also provide accommodation. Smaller firms allow them to stay on the premises of their office, and at times also offer a possibility of cooking their own food in a small kitchen inside the premises. Some of the larger firms, in fact, take a building on rent on the outskirts of the city and far end of the corridor to house some of the migrant workers. While this definitely enables the migrant workers with no housing access to work in the IT corridor, this arrangement also allows for greater control by the employees over their time. Importantly, many of them are of the opinion that once they are married and have children, it will be difficult to keep such work hours.

Social networks are crucial to enter into both the segments, beginning with learning to drive and acquiring a licence. Given their low-income backgrounds, it is not easy to get properly trained to drive cars. To offer themselves as full-fledged drivers in the market, they need to manoeuvre through heavy traffic, drive through narrow lanes and be able to drive different kinds of cars. This is made possible through access to owner-drivers who give out their second-hand cars for a fee to those who want to practise driving. Else, some of them work as mechanics in automobile repair shops who allow them to use the cars that come for repair to gain experience.

In the case of migrant workers, the move to Chennai too is therefore premised on access to family/kinship networks or networks of friends who have already entered into the drivers' job market in Chennai. A brother, a cousin, an uncle or a neighbour who is already a driver or a mechanic or working as a manager in a private cab company are possible routes for gaining access to this job market. Such networks also enable access to housing among migrant workers. In addition to the migrant segment, there is also a small local segment of drivers who come from the neighbourhoods/villages close to or off the IT corridor. However, many of the cab service firms are run by entrepreneurs from areas not adjoining the IT corridor and tend to source labour more through their own and their past employees' networks rather than from spatially proximate areas.

The other major segment is that of the drivers employed by private bus operators engaged by IT firms to transport employees from different parts of the city. There are a few large bus operators on the IT corridor. One of them runs more than 200 buses in one park out of which 110 buses run only for one large firm. While some firms provide social security benefits like employees' state insurance or provident fund, all the bus drivers we interviewed were employed by different travel service firms and not directly by the IT firms despite the fact that all of them drove exclusively for the latter. Though they make only two trips in a day, they start work early by 6 a.m. and end by around 9 p.m. The basic monthly salary they earned in 2012 was Rs 7,500 with a compulsory annual increment of Rs 250, which is lower than that of cab drivers or personal drivers. As a result of such long hours, most drivers stay within the buses.

Despite working for the same firm and even performing similar functions, bus drivers inhabit spaces quite distinct from that of the cab drivers. Many of the employees have been earlier driving heavy vehicles like lorries for transporting goods long distance across cities. And because lorry driving is again learnt on the job, joining as cleaners/helpers and then slowly getting to learn driving, many of them dropped out of school earlier and hence have low educational qualifications. An important aspect of their work is the need to take care of the buses overnight. Operators often expect the drivers to park the buses close to the place from where the morning trip starts. The buses are therefore parked in unauthorised spaces in different parts of the city and drivers often stay and sleep within the buses they are responsible for. As they do not have access to bathing or toilet facilities, they rely on public spaces and nearby ponds or other water bodies for this purpose. While this practice provides drivers 'free housing' in a new city, this also reveals the new demands on spaces that IT parks make on the city and its non-recognition by urban planners.

In addition to cab and bus services, IT parks have also spawned the growth of share-autos and mini-vans. Seven-to-eight-seater share-autos are visible all along the IT corridor, with 25 share-autos in front of one IT park alone to take employees from the bus stops to the entry to the IT park. This is one segment that is drawn mostly from the neighbourhoods of the IT corridor. This indirect employment linkage, just as the others in the transport services segment, is largely unregulated with hardly any security of employment or scope for vertical mobility. Drivers continue to be drivers with little scope for economic mobility except by attempting to buy a second-hand vehicle and become owner-drivers. Importantly, once again bulk of this linkage is generated by lack of adequate investments in public transport infrastructure.

ii. Security Personnel

Security service has come to be one of the fastest-growing segments of low-end service sector employment in big cities in the country (Nagaraj 2012). India is home to one of the largest private security industry in the world, employing anywhere between 5 million and 6 million guards (ibid.: 10). From being a small-scale informal sector, it has come to witness the rise of large domestic firms and the entry of foreign firms.[9] The formalisation and entry of large-scale firms into this segment has been accompanied by a growing share of inter-state migrant labour in this sector. Out of the 30 guards interviewed, only six were from the neighbouring districts. The SIPCOT park employed around 800–1,000 security guards according to middle-level staff in the security firms. As is to be expected, security at the IT parks is almost exclusively dominated by young male workers. Access to this employment is once again largely through social networks.

It is interesting to note that despite being paid a monthly salary of anywhere between Rs 7,500 and Rs 13,500, a salary comparable to that of cab drivers, there are not too many security guards from within the state. Security service managers cite two reasons for the relatively lower presence of local labour in this sector. One, compared to a driver's job, working as a security guard has lower social status. Importantly, work as a guard is tougher than working as a driver. All security guards work a 12-hour shift and alternate between day and night shifts. With the requirement to stand for most part of the shift, work in this segment poses tremendous hardships, especially during night duty given the menace of mosquitoes. Most workers are young and unmarried. Normally, migrant youth undertake this job for about five years, after which they get married and do not return. In other words, few of the workers perceive a career in this sector despite the possibility of vertical growth, albeit limited, such as becoming section heads, unit heads and eventually field officers.

It is interesting to note that among the various categories of support staff in the IT parks, the security team received relatively better social security benefits like gratuity/provident fund from their employers. The fact that this does not attract local labour reveals the poor quality of such employment, provisioning of social security notwithstanding. Firms provide migrant workers with what is referred to as guesthouse accommodation by renting a largish room with a kitchen to house them in return for a monthly rent of Rs 400. The respondents, however, feel that the quality of this accommodation is quite bad as often 20 people have to stay in a single room. Cramped and often short of water, many move into rented premises of their own, as soon as possible, paying a higher rent.

iii. Housekeeping and Maintenance, and Food Vending

With accent on production for global clients, exterior facades, landscaping, interior design and cleanliness have come to constitute important markers of the firms' credentials, generating demand for gardeners, sweepers and cleaners. This is the only segment of indirect employment that is open to women workers. Recruited through a set of separate contractors who also at times provide transport facilities, the sourcing areas for maintenance staff tend to vary across two ends of the IT corridor. The IT park located closer to the city drew labour from nearby slums or low-income neighbourhoods. Kannagi Nagar, a resettlement colony off the IT corridor, for instance, is a source area for such labour (Coelho et al. 2012). Housekeeping staff employed in the other IT park came from villages located about 15 km away as the contractor in charge hails from that village. They commute to work in mini-vans provided by the contractor, revealing both the role of social networks in accessing employment and the disjuncture between physical proximity and access to employment. Receiving an average salary of Rs 4,000–5,000 per month, often without any social security benefits, many of them worked as domestic helpers before moving to this job.

The food courts and restaurants are once again dominated by male employees and feature waiters, cashiers and chefs from Tamil Nadu, Andhra Pradesh, Maharashtra and Bihar. However, some of the cleaners in these restaurants are women workers staying in nearby areas. Due to limited access to the employees' food court, staff from only one park was interviewed. Salary levels ranged from Rs 5,000 to Rs 7,000 per month and many of them lived in low-income neighbourhoods off the IT corridor in rented or own houses. Importantly, once again, all of them are young and unmarried, staying with their parents or larger families, contributing to the domestic expenses of the household. In some of the restaurants located outside the IT parks but along the IT corridor, waiters and cleaners largely consist of migrant labour. In most cases, housing is provided by the employer, either within the restaurant premises or in rented premises housing large number of employees, as in the case of security guards. The absence of low-cost housing once again allows for firms to exercise greater control over worker's time through control over their spaces of reproduction.

INTERPRETATIONS

The chapter has sought to establish how the phenomenon of 'uneven spatial development' in Indian metropolitan cities can partly be linked to developments in the labour market that have emerged in response to a policy emphasis on mega-infrastructure projects meant for promotion of the IT sector. Employment linkages are clearly segmented between those who are directly employed in the IT firms and those who work in the significant support segments of the IT parks. While the former enjoy premium salaries that are often tied to a career path, the latter segment consists of jobs that are much lower paid with little scope for vertical mobility, a long-term career path or any degree of employment security. A related aspect of indirect employment linkages is the masculine and relatively younger age profile of workers in most segments of support services, generating another source of segmentation and exclusion by gender and age. Though this requires more scrutiny, our fieldwork indicates that the quantum of indirect employment generated at the local level is lower than that anticipated by the industry bodies. Importantly, even when jobs are created at the local scale, not all of them are accessed by local populations. This brings us to the other important dimension of linkages, that is, the role of social networks in accessing employment.

Access to employment in the support services is primarily through kinship, neighbourhood or other social networks. Despite physical proximity, we find that not too many of the youth from the villages or neighbourhoods off the IT corridor have been able to enter such labour markets. Entrepreneurs offering various consumption services to software employees often tend to rely on their ethnic and kinship ties to source labour for their ventures. Given that a significant share of demand for support services is met by non-local, pre-existing firms, spatial proximity appears to matter less for employment access. We have also therefore drawn attention to the importance of recognising the spatial dimension of linkage effects of such projects. Since such projects have been found to destroy pre-existing economic linkages, the importance of ensuring a set of higher order linkages for the local population cannot be over-emphasised. Observations made in the chapter are likely to resonate with developments in other metropolitan locations in the country given the strong overlaps in policy direction.

Developments along the IT corridor also lend support to the nexus between accumulation through real estate investments and current urban development trajectories with substantial linkages generated through property development. While this contributes to increases in incomes of the propertied sections in the city and real estate investors, clearly rising rentals marginalise the non-propertied and those with incomes that are incommensurate with such rising rents. Further, the housing supply generated tends to belong to a 'premium' segment. Segmentation in housing has been accompanied by segmentation in markets for food as well. In terms of savings and investment too, we find a preference among IT employee respondents for land and housing in addition to gold. Apart from the limited productive linkages that such investments can generate, the increased demand for land and housing is likely to have an inflationary impact on their prices, reinforcing the exclusionary tendencies we drew attention to earlier. Lack of adequate public investments in housing, transport, water and sanitation tends to only aggravate such disequalising urban development. Lack of adequate low-cost housing, while generating barriers to access employment in the city, also works to capital's advantage as it is able to exercise greater control over labour through control over housing access. The demand for water, a public good, has spawned a market catered to by private suppliers and distributors. The uncertainty in quantity and quality of publicly provided water is the reason for a growing demand for 'quality' brands in drinking water supply. While this has generated some linkage effects with small local suppliers and distributors, the role of state failure in public provisioning of drinking water is quite evident. In fact, employment linkages in the domain of transport too have emerged on account of inadequate state provisioning. The emergence of private actors and markets for such public services to fill in 'institutional voids' and the labour market linkages thus created have to be therefore re-evaluated.

NOTES

1. This chapter is based on a study supported by the EU-funded Chance2Sustain Programme through the French Institute of Pondicherry. We gratefully acknowledge the field assistance provided by Sumirtha Gandhi, Supriya Gandhi, Aditi Samant Singhar, Rosmi Jose, Manjari Shankar and Pradyot Bharadwaj in the course of this study. We thank Ashima Sood, Aurelie Varrel, Eric Denis and Loraine Kennedy for useful discussions that helped shape this essay. The chapter also benefitted from comments in the course of a presentation made at the International Conference on Sustainable and Inclusive Urban Development in India, organised by the Institute for Human Development, New Delhi, and the University of Florida, 1–3 August 2015, New Delhi.
2. See http://itel.tnrdc.com/project-description/ (accessed on 24 January 2016).
3. Only 25 per cent are enrolled in tertiary education of any kind in India by 2013; see http://data.worldbank.org/indicator/SE.TER.ENRR/countries (accessed on 1 July 2022).

4. http://www.payscale.com/research/IN/Job=Office_Clerk%2c_General/Salary (accessed on 31 January 2016) shows that the median monthly salary for a clerk in the public sector is Rs 14,500 approximately whereas that of a software programmer is Rs 24,300 approximately. According to data provided by the Department of Economics and Statistics, Government of Tamil Nadu, the per capita annual income of Kancheepuram district, where bulk of the IT corridor is located, and Chennai is Rs 92,713 and Rs 66,240 respectively for the year 2011–12. Even assuming the Kancheepuram figure to be more accurate, we have an average salary of Rs 7,750 per month, which is much lower than the average salary levels of the respondents in the software sector. The entry-level monthly salary for a software programmer, on the other hand, in 2012–13 was about Rs 18,000–Rs 25,000, depending on the firm that one worked with.

5. See https://www.linkedin.com/pulse/20140707062652-199566679-chennai-properties-along-omr-promise-good-rental-returns (accessed on 24 January 2016).

6. This information is based on discussions with real estate developers.

7. While some schemes are underway to address this lack, it needs to be noted that there is an overall mismatch between supply by the public utility and demand from Chennai's residents. Per capita water supply in Chennai at 76 litres per capita per day (lpcd; as against a norm of 140 lpcd) is the lowest among all the metropolitan cities in India (Janakarajan 2013), leaving a large section of residents to rely on private wells and informal private water markets.

8. S. Ramamirtham vs The State of Tamil Nadu on 1 April, 2005, available at http://indiankanoon.org/doc/1133587/?type=print (accessed on 20 October 2015).

9. However, the presence of large firms is confined to only one end of the market. The patterns of employment vary from large firms to small firms, from large residential complexes to smaller apartment blocks.

REFERENCES

Coelho, K., and N. Raman. 2010. 'Salvaging and Scapegoating: Slum Evictions on Chennai's Waterways'. *Economic & Political Weekly* 45(21): 19–23.

Coelho, K., T. Venkat and R. Chandrika. 2012. 'The Spatial Reproduction of Urban Poverty'. *Economic & Political Weekly* 47(47 & 48): 53–63.

Flyvbjerg, B. 2005. *Policy and Planning for Large Infrastructure Projects: Problems, Causes, Cures*, Vol. 3781. Washington, DC: World Bank Publications.

——. 2008. 'Public Planning of Mega-projects: Overestimation of Demand and Underestimation of Costs'. In *Decision-Making on Mega-Projects: Cost–Benefit Analysis, Planning and Innovation*, eds Hugo Priemus, Bent Flyvbjerg and Bert van Wee, 120–44. Cheltenham: Edward Elgar.

Gellert, Paul K., and Barbara D. Lynch. 2003. 'Mega-projects as Displacements'. *International Social Science Journal* 175: 15–25. Available at http://citeseerx.ist.psu.edu/viewdoc/download?doi=10.1.1.519.8922&rep=rep1&type=pdf (accessed on 20 October 2015).

ICICI Property Services. 2013. 'Chennai Residential Real Estate Overview'. April. Available at http://www.icicihfc.com/property_pdfs/Chennai-Real-Estate-2013.pdf (accessed on 31 January 2016).

Jain, D. 2015. 'Housing Prices Hit the Roof in Indian Cities'. 17 July. Available at http://www.livemint.com/Opinion/xBhkeLlTHsC9OHAqTxRZvK/House-prices-touch-the-roof-in-Indian-cities.html (accessed on 2 July 2022).

Janakarajan, S. 2013. 'Optimising Local Water Resources and Availability in Urban and Peri-urban Chennai'. Presentation at the workshop 'Anil Agarwal Dialogue: Excreta Does Matter', organised by the Centre for Science and Environment, New Delhi, 4–5 March. Available at http://cseindia.org/userfiles/Janakarajan.pdf (accessed on 31 January 2016).

Jenkins, R., L. Kennedy and P. Mukhopadhyay. 2014. *Power, Policy and Protest: The Politics of India's Special Economic Zones*. New Delhi: Oxford University Press.

Kandavel, Sangeetha. 2013. 'Chennai's IT Corridor, Home to TCS, Cognizant & Infosys, Faces Shutdown due to Water Shortage'. *The Economic Times*, 6 July, available at https://economictimes.indiatimes.com/tech/ites/chennais-it-corridor-home-to-tcs-cognizant-infosys-faces-shutdown-due-to-water-shortage/articleshow/20885597.cms (accessed on 3 July 2022).

Kennedy, L. 2007. 'Regional Industrial Policies Driving Peri-urban Dynamics in Hyderabad, India'. *Cities* 24(2): 95–109.

Kennedy, L., and M. Helene Zérah. 2008. 'The Shift to City-Centric Growth Strategies: Perspectives from Hyderabad and Mumbai'. *Economic & Political Weekly* 43(39): 110–17.

Kennedy, L., G. Robbins, D. Scott, C. Sutherland, E. Denis, J. Andrade, L. Miranda, A. Varrel, V. Dupont and B. Bon. 2011. 'The Politics of Large-scale Economic and Infrastructure Projects in Fast-growing Cities of the South'. Work Package 2 Literature Review Paper. Chance2Sustain, 7e PCRD, European Association of Development Research and Training Institutes, Bonn. Available at http://www.chance2sustain.eu/26.0.html (accessed on 2 July 2022).

Kennedy, L., G. Robbins, B. Bon, G. Takano, A. Varrel and J. Andrade. 2014. 'Megaprojects and Urban Development in Cities of the South'. Thematic Report, Chance2Sustain Work Package 2, September. Available at http://chance2sustain.eu/fileadmin/Website/Dokumente/Dokumente/Publications/publications_2014/C2S_TR_No05_WP2_-_Megaprojects_and_Urban_Development_in_Cities_of_the_South_V2-3.pdf (accessed on 2 July 2022).

Krishna, A. 2013. 'Stuck in Place: Investigating Social Mobility in 14 Bangalore Slums'. *The Journal of Development Studies* 49(7): 1010–28.

Kundu, Amitabh, and Lopamudra Ray Saraswati. 2012. 'Migration and Exclusionary Urbanisation in India'. *Economic & Political Weekly* 47(26 & 27): 219–27.

Misra, B. S. 2015. 'Which Infrastructure Matters More for Growth: Economic or Social? Evidence from Indian States during 2001–2010'. *Review of Urban & Regional Development Studies* 27(3): 177–96.

Mitra, A. 2010. 'Migration, Livelihood and Well-being: Evidence from Indian City Slums'. *Urban Studies* 47(7): 1371–90.

Mukherjee, Writankar. 2011. 'Infotech, BPO are the Top Job Creators; Created 15 Lakh Jobs since Oct 2008'. *The Economic Times*, 2 August, available at https://economictimes.indiatimes.com/jobs/infotech-bpo-are-the-top-job-creators-created-15-lakh-jobs-since-oct-2008/articleshow/9450472.cms?from=mdr (accessed on 3 July 2022).

Nagaraj, Vijay K. 2012. 'Mapping the Political Economy of India's Private Security Industry'. *Economic & Political Weekly* 47(33): 10–14.

Pandian, M. S. S. 2011. 'New Times in Tamil Nadu'. *Seminar 620*, April, available at https://www.india-seminar.com/2011/620/620_m_s_s_pandian.htm (accessed on 30 June 2022).

Robinson, J. 2006. *Ordinary Cities: Between Modernity and Development*. London, New York: Routledge.

Saith, A., and M. Vijayabaskar, eds. 2005. *ICTs and Indian Economic Development: Economy, Work, Regulation*. London, New Delhi: Sage.

Sharma, R. N. 2010. 'Mega Transformation of Mumbai: Deepening Enclave Urbanism'. *Sociological Bulletin* 59(1): 69–91.

Shaw, A., and M. K. Satish. 2007. 'Metropolitan Restructuring in Post-liberalised India: Separating the Global and the Local'. *Cities* 24(2): 148–63.

Srivatsan, A. 2012. 'Urban Jungle: Will I Ever Own a House?' *The Hindu*, 12 March, Chennai. Available at http://www.thehindu.com/news/cities/chennai/chen-columns/will-i-ever-own-a-house/article2985658.ece (accessed on 31 January 2016).

Stalin, J. Sam Daniel. 2015. 'For Basic Amenities, Chennai IT Corridor Residents Nominate Shadow Councilors'. NDTV, 4 November. Available at http://www.ndtv.com/chennai-news/for-basic-amenities-chennai-it-corridor-residents-nominate-shadow-councilors-1239267 (accessed on 25 January 2016).

Swahilya, and A. Srivatsan. 2007. 'Of Cinderellas and Ugly Sisters: A Searching Look at Chennai's North–South Divide'. *Madras Musings* 17(6): 4, 1–15 July. Available at http://madrasmusings.com/older-archives/Vol%2017/Vol%20XVII%20-%20No%2006.pdf (accessed on 2 February 2016).

Upadhya, C. 2007. 'Employment, Exclusion and "Merit" in the Indian IT Industry'. *Economic & Political Weekly* 42(20): 1863–68.

Venkatachalam, L. 2014. 'Informal Water Markets and Willingness to Pay for Water: A Case Study of the Urban Poor in Chennai City, India'. *International Journal of Water Resources Development* 31(1): 134–45.

Zérah, Marie-Hélène. 2008. 'Splintering Urbanism in Mumbai: Contrasting Trends in a Multilayered Society'. *Geoforum* 39(6): 1922–32.

10

Making Sense of Place in Rajarhat New Town

The Village in the Urban and the Urban in the Village

RATOOLA KUNDU

Since India's economic liberalisation in the 1990s, there has been a deliberate, systematic and large-scale socio-spatial transformation of peripheral lands around large cities from rural to urban uses—a process that is still incomplete and fraught with multiple claims and counter-claims over land, livelihoods, resources and identities. With land prices in most central urban areas spiralling upwards, there has been a movement of urban middle and upper classes into more affordable yet spacious layouts in the peripheries. In some cases, private developers are constructing gated residential communities while in others, as in the case of Rajarhat New Town, the state is building large and planned new townships on erstwhile agricultural lands. Given that the violent erasures, dispossessions and displacements that underwrite the production of the periphery as spaces of urban consumption, living and working are shot through with exclusions, antagonisms and impoverishment (Roy 2011), what kind of relationships and mediations emerge between different groups that live here? How are inhabitants making sense and attaching meaning to these spaces and in turn being influenced by the dynamic shifts in the landscape? What can the study of these relationships, everyday practices, contestation and negotiations reveal about the future of peripheries as viable and liveable places?

This chapter seeks to understand the multiple ways in which different sets of actors struggle to consolidate their access and claims to the emerging urban periphery by examining social, spatial, cultural as well as discursive forms of place-making strategies (Lombard 2014). The particular emphasis of this chapter is on the lived life of existing and new inhabitants of Rajarhat New Town, inhabiting, respectively, urban villages and gated communities. It examines routine activities that go into the material and social construction of place as well as how the place itself and the meanings it carries can influence social interactions, livelihoods and aspirations. Common to both groups is the loss of longstanding, meticulously cultivated social contacts and changes in power and authority structures. The chapter argues that the urban villages and the gated communities represent a continuum of new urban living which is marked by a constant need to reclaim and remake one's identity and make sense of the changed reality through varied strategies of place-making. These spatial practices are in response to the multiple ways in which inhabitants of these very distinct settlement types have been unsettled by urbanisation.

A qualitative methodology was followed which included around 40 in-depth interviews, mapping, photo-documentation and observations over a period of five months in 2015.[1] Respondents included renters, committee members and owners of apartments from a selection of three residential complexes. In the village settlements, interviews were carried out with residents and the panchayat president. These findings were then contrasted with the discursive and material production of spaces through interviews with activists, real estate developers, officials and planners of West Bengal Housing Infrastructure Development Corporation (WBHIDCO). While the ethnographic methodology allowed the researcher to understand the complex connections that emerge between agency, social structures and the built and lived environment, the discursive analysis helped to situate these spatial practices of meaningfully defining and inhabiting spaces within the larger historical forces and the political economy of Rajarhat's urban transformations.

In particular, this study examines the modes through which different groups of inhabitants: (i) consolidate their claims to property (especially through housing and infrastructure), (ii) relate themselves to the ever-changing spatial contours of the New Town, and (iii) make incremental and experimental investments in a collective associational life geared towards enhancing their visibility and legibility in the shifting terrains of the periphery. This research highlights how routine and daily activities of inhabitants challenge abstract ideas of space conceived from above, thus producing perforations in the imagined master planned spaces. Thus, villages and gated communities are not bounded spatial entities, but rather, as this essay argues, fluid and dynamic places, imbued with heterogeneity and inherent conflicts.

The next section discusses the theoretical framework that is central to understanding place simultaneously as a process and a product. The chapter moves to the making of Rajarhat New Town, particularly the logic of abstract cartographic planning that drives it and the ways in which it annihilates and erases places while producing new spaces. This is followed by an examination of interactions, negotiations, contestations that emerge through active processes of place-making that tie together and yet set these settlements apart. The conclusion underscores how inhabitants of Rajarhat are actively engaged in simultaneous processes of de-territorialisation and re-territorialisation to produce multiple meanings of place. These processes at times reinforce and at other times challenge and destabilise a narrow and unitary formulation of space produced by the logic of capital accumulation. Thus, it opens up possibilities for a range of socio-spatial encounters and forms of place-making that are messier and open-ended.

THEORETICAL FRAMEWORKS OF PLACE-MAKING AS A PROCESS

Given the large-scale and multiple trajectories through which the peripheries of cities are undergoing socio-spatial transformation, it is important to understand how places are lost and recovered, made and unmade, valorised and devalorised in the process. Place-making is thus central to this enquiry; it is produced through the interaction of individual practices, beliefs, rituals and daily rhythms and institutions as well as structuration processes that provide the framework for such actions.

Existing scholarship on peri-urbanisation processes has tended to focus on actors such as the state and the market and their role in the large-scale displacement and dispossession of farmers, peasants and fishermen as central to the process of new modes of capital accumulation through urbanisation in the context of a neoliberal urban development regime. These studies have highlighted the process of economic liberalisation, the entry of private players and hybrid forms of urban governance in the provisioning of urban infrastructure and housing (Roy 2003; Shatkin 2011). A few studies have argued that the mode of primitive accumulation of capital produces a politics of resistance, which is necessarily contingent, tactical and coalitional in its approach (Dey et al. 2013: 239–40). Studies of peri-urbanisation processes have also highlighted how the squalor, chaos and infrastructural crisis of existing megacities are being bypassed in favour of the peripheries where land is commodified, where new forms of globalised, knowledge-based economy exerts hegemony over the transformed landscape and informalised labour (Bhattacharya and Sanyal 2011). It has been argued that these forms of peri-urban development are pandering to a new aesthetic order championed by the emerging urban middle class (Bose 2013). A number of these new urban development projects are actively produced by the routine bending and stretching of existing planning norms and regulatory frameworks (Kundu 2010; Roy 2011), which implicates a range of actors, including intermediary agents at the local level and a mode of territorial flexibility in the transformation of peripheral urban areas (Gururani 2013).

Another line of enquiry has consistently studied the transformation of villages or rural settlements due to the onslaught of urbanisation. Empirical research on urban villages (Shaw 2004; Shah 2012; Kumar 2015) has largely focused on the acts of expropriation of agricultural land, the conversion of land uses and built-up spaces within the settlements, and the ways in which these spaces remain disparate from the formal and planned city surrounding the villages. These studies have not explored what has happened to the existing social practices, structures and hierarchies that have influenced access to land, livelihood, social status and identity within these settlements and the ways in which villagers make sense of the changing contours of where they live and work.

Thus, in all of these critical discussions about peri-urbanisation, there is little deliberation over how people moving into these new places are coping with their built and lived environments. Neither is there much discussion on what residual agrarian settlements caught in the urbanising landscapes do to overcome the challenges created by the erasure of places. There is scant attention paid to the ways in which the new residents of these urban spaces interact with their surroundings and the politics that emerges from their quotidian practices and animates these spaces with new meanings and contestations. These are important queries in view of the rapidity with which the urban peripheries are being reimagined, planned and developed.

Notable exceptions are the works of Goldstein (2016), Cowan (2015) and Srivastava (2014). Goldstein's work on the politics of place-making as a mode of planning examines the ways in which the residents of Gurgaon's new apartment complexes have gone beyond the mandate of their resident welfare associations to influence the state-level planning agencies to provide infrastructure and services and better public transport networks. Srivastava (2014) on the other hand explores the dynamics of the gated communities in Gurgaon, how these built spaces influence behaviour patterns, choice of collectivisation and identities—particularly how these spaces are aspirational and at the same time act as the key site for the development of a new middle class identity and therefore pave the way for a new politics of engaging with the urban. The overwhelming concern with order, cleanliness, security, safety and wanting to create and maintain a distance with the 'unruly villagers' is common to these discussions around gated communities which results in the spatialised practices of excessive gating and surveillance (ibid.). Interestingly, there is a fluidity and heterogeneity in the spatial practices within these settlements although social structures of gender, caste and class intersect to infuse these spaces with the power to demarcate and fix particular identities and behaviours to particular spaces.

Srivastava's work is particularly important here as it strives to demonstrate how the slums and gated communities, and the new malls on the outskirts of Delhi are inextricably entangled through the social uses, activities, occupations of the users of these spaces (ibid.: xli). In this study, place-making plays a central role in understanding what kind of new social order and spatial codes are being written into the landscape and how these are being contested, challenged and negotiated through the everyday spatial practices of its inhabitants. Cowan (2015) on the other hand traces the linkages between residual urban villages and gated communities as being coproduced through the circuits of capital accumulation that fragment the periphery into spaces of inclusion and exclusion, planned and unauthorised, representing multiple and conflicting powers of governance.

Adopting an analytical approach that views place as a process helps to foreground the role and agency of people in the making and unmaking of places (Lombard 2014) through the routines and rituals that give shape to everyday life. When people form attachments and assign values to spaces, places are created (Cresswell 2004: 12). Place is therefore not an arbitrarily bounded geographic unit but something that is constantly being made and unmade through a complex network of flows and processes of spatial interactions (Pred 1984). Places impose certain restrictions on the everyday activities of people. Thus, place is shot through with power and constructed through hierarchies that influence the way people interact (Cresswell 2004). Given that actors interpret place in different ways or attach different values to place, it can lead to potential build-up of conflict over multiple interpretations and meanings.

This chapter explores the multiple and often contradictory place-making strategies of the inhabitants of Rajarhat New Town, arguing that places are formed within a particular political economic context of urbanisation. The chapter lays emphasis on the individual and collective actions in responding to the erasure of place and the simultaneous making of place (Pred 1984). In particular, it will focus upon the incremental modes of place-making (Simone 2004), by analysing the day-to-day efforts of inhabitants to invest in places, collaborate to secure claims, collectivise to consolidate access to better infrastructure. The next section illustrates the continuous processes of erasure of place by space and the material, social, political and economic dimensions of the loss of the sense of place.

OF ERASURES AND A LOSS OF SENSE OF PLACE

Rajarhat New Town is located to the northeast of the existing city of Kolkata, outside the Kolkata Metropolitan Area boundary. The township is spread over 37 sq km of village and agricultural lands, ponds and wetlands; the township was initiated in 1993 by the erstwhile Left Front government of West Bengal and has been projected as West Bengal's first 'green, eco-friendly, self-sufficient, and smart city' (West Bengal Housing Infrastructure Development Corporation [WBHIDCO] 1999). The township is divided into four action areas and a central business district (CBD) as per the master plan. The predominant land use category is residential, while the rest is dedicated to information technology (IT), public institutions, open spaces, commercial uses and circulation. A number of global and regional IT firms, real estate development companies, higher educational institutes, hotel chains and several big malls have been built. The bulk of housing in the township is in the form of gated high-rise apartment complexes (Sengupta 2013). Very few public amenities have been provided so far, and the dearth of facilities—particularly public transport—has deterred many people from living in New Town. A majority of the new inhabitants work in the IT sector and related service industries.

Within the notified Rajarhat New Town planning area, there are 16 village pockets where villagers continue to live. These are original homestead lands that were not acquired by the state in order to mitigate the effects of displacement of farmers. Agricultural lands surrounding the homestead lands were acquired by WBHIDCO, a special purpose vehicle, for the purpose of planning and developing the New Town.[2] Spatially, Rajarhat appears to be a patchwork of concrete, glass and steel high-rises, set amidst fallow lands which have been acquired but not built upon. The metalled roads sometimes end up in a dirt track that leads to village clusters with mud and thatch huts, clumps of banana and coconut trees and occasionally a water body. There are large IT multinationals clustered in the CBD. Many of the white-collar workers will be visible at the informal road-side eateries enjoying a cup of tea, shooing off the cows that graze on the empty fields and wander into the shacks. There is something unsettled and unsettling about the place as the landscape belies the strict categorisation of either a planned township or a pastoral village.

Prior to 1995, Rajarhat used to be a fertile agricultural area dotted with dense villages with long histories of settlement, ponds, orchards, flower nurseries and substantial water bodies. Inhabited by farmers and fishermen, two-thirds of who were from either the Muslim community or Dalit community, the locality was connected to the city through the exchange of fresh produce, goods and services (Dey et al. 2013). Landholdings were typically small and there were multiple tenure structures that enabled some to work as share-croppers, as tenants and even as farm labourers. Many inhabitants were engaged in fishing and in the trade and transport of fresh produce and fish. The villages in Rajarhat area had electricity, good primary schools, access to water (though filled with impurities), irrigation facilities and roads. An estimated 130,000 people lost their land and livelihood due to the large-scale project (Sengupta 2013). The following paragraphs analyse how the violent expropriation of land and the disruption in the daily spatial practices of the inhabitants of Rajarhat led to a deep and irreversible loss of place. New arrivals to the gated communities too are dealing with a sense of loss of place as they encounter a city in the making, and have no memories to guide them in their interactions.

The official records blatantly erased this pastoral past of Rajarhat by claiming that the area was specifically chosen for urban development because it was low-lying, marshy, low-yielding and sparsely populated (WBHIDCO 1999). It is not an accident if maps of the area (prior to the New Town development) are either unavailable or else these maps simply persuade one into thinking that the land was *tabula rasa*—devoid of forms of human settlements and meanings. This is one form of calculated informality through the act of 'unmapping' that Roy contends has enabled planners to plan exceptions through a logic of territorial flexibility (Roy 2003). Planning officials within WBHIDCO are not only aware of this but also perpetuate this myth of a vacant land waiting to be urbanised. In the words of the chief town planner, WBHIDCO '...majority of the area was marshy and barren land vacant in nature. Vegetation was less and if a township is made it would not affect agriculture or settlement. Under these considerations we have selected this place for new town development.'[3] These tactics of bureaucratic erasure of existing forms of living as well as the creation of formal records that establish false claims are typical discursive logics employed in the formation of newly planned territories (Benjamin 2015). These new records also helped to decontextualise existing places by expunging the history of its people and their settlement stories, and by reducing the rich narratives of life in these settings to mere statistics.

According to the chief town planner, 'The aim was how the displacement should be minimised. Therefore we have kept some settlements untouched and planned the development surrounding those areas. Thus the people were kept undisturbed and not displaced from their forefathers' land'.[4] One of the ways in which the production of Rajarhat New Town destroyed existing ways of living was by an intensely political and negotiated form of land acquisition. Although initially a buffer strip of land around the village was planned to enable villagers to grow vegetables or allow for their cattle to graze, this was reneged upon as land prices began to soar (Basak 2013). A high-powered land procurement committee was set up comprising of senior bureaucrats, local leaders and politicians, as well as WBHIDCO officials wherein land acquisitions boundaries went through intense negotiations and were redrawn to mitigate any resistance (Kundu 2010).

One of the farmers from a village pocket called Chhapna in Action Area II said, '...we did not agree with the land acquisition process. Some of the villagers from our village have not taken the money from the government as compensation for their land. We want our land back.[5] The reluctance to part with their land stems not only from a sense of unfair compensation, but also from a deep attachment with the land itself and the range of livelihoods that derive from it. A villager from Chapkachuria said, 'I have taken birth in this land, my son was born here. It is my grandfather's land. I am very much emotionally attached with this land'.[6] The residents of these villages fear that they will not fit into the emerging urban landscape or will be pushed out by developers and moneyed new migrants, thus losing their very meaning in life. One villager from Chhapna said:

> We have been here since our forefathers came here and made the land habitable. The government took away our lands and gave us meagre compensation. It is true we improved our houses with that money, but where do we go now? What do we do? Where will our cows graze? The big buildings will soon stifle us.[7]

The farmlands, ponds, water bodies, village roads and hamlets were all integrally linked together and now with the loss of land, the inhabitants have lost a part of their belongingness, leading to a loss of sense of place.

The residual village pockets and thereby the villagers are being discursively re-inscribed into the new urban landscape by the planners through the trope of integration. WBHIDCO had issues with villages in the midst of the township as these settlements did not fit in with the idea of a planned and 'modern' built environment. Thus, WBHIDCO decided that these areas would be integrated as 'service villages' in the master plan. Villages would function to provide cheap accommodations for the service class that would be required by those living in the apartment complexes. Planners assumed that villagers would turn to the informal service sector as the new developments would lead to an enormous demand for servants, housekeepers, drivers, cleaners, cooks, etc. (Roy 2005). Debaditya Kumar, an engineer associated with the planning of New Town, comments, 'All contractors and developers must include the unskilled workforce of the village. ... This is how the local inhabitants can be consumed in the upcoming urban economy' (quoted in Basak 2013: 46). Though villagers agreed that some job opportunities had opened up, these were few and far between and gave them little dignity. In fact, villagers were renting out their residences to migrants from other parts of West Bengal and the country who were working in the informal economy. A migrant from Medinipur residing in Chhapna village says:

> There are several people who have migrated from nearby states like Bihar, Jharkhand, Orissa to these villages for their livelihood. Some people are engaged with syndicates, some are running shops near the office buildings and some are working as security guards in residential buildings or offices. There are many people who just come as construction labour and are residing in these villages.[8]

The social fabric of these villages, thus far from being insulated, is now the site of emerging conflicts over resources between original residents and new migrants, further disembodying the experience of place.

FRAGMENTATION AND SPLINTERING OF SPACE

In order to prevent these villages from becoming unplanned 'eyesores', WBHIDCO proposed a set of separate land use controls to guide building activity therein (WBHIDCO 2008). Since the rest of New Town was on higher ground than the villages due to earth filling, WBHIDCO sought to alleviate the issue of drainage by building culverts along the edge of the villages to drain out excess rain water. In effect, WBHIDCO created islands that were excluded from the rest of the New Town. These new spatial codes, regulations as well as actual physical interventions have tried to expedite the process of spatial transformation and 'integrate' villages into the new township. Villagers have both welcomed as well as resisted the changes, leading to a fragmented and contested notion of the village and what it is morphing into.

Villagers complain of being directionless. Ajay Mandal, a villager from Jatragachi, says, 'We don't know where we are actually heading. We do not talk openly with each other these days. The ambience of the village has been intruded by the making of this megacity which is benefitting us in some ways' (quoted in Basak 2013: 63). Villagers also spoke of the ways in which their physical surroundings had changed, leading to the loss of well-established mental maps of their places. One villager from Chhapna said:

> We no longer feel as if we belong here. Metalled roads have been built, bringing in speeding motor cars. These are dangerous though the city is closer to us now. Buildings have come up on our fields. We have no direction sense now. Moreover, some of our neighbours have left the village. New people are coming in and we do not know them. The village community is changing. We have lost our social contacts.[9]

The area is perceived as chaotic, disorderly and split into islands of prosperity and poverty.

For the residents in the gated apartment complex, New Town Rajarhat is an unknown and unfamiliar territory, an untamed frontier, generating hope as well as fear. New residents arriving into New Town have little or no attachment to the new place. The dynamic and incomplete nature of New Town, particularly with respect to unfinished roads, lack of public transport, markets and water supply, thus appears as confusing, challenging and fragmented. A resident of Greenfield Heights, I. Poddar, commented, 'For the longest time, I did not know the postal code for my building. Neither did I know which police jurisdiction applies to our building. This made me anxious'.[10] In order to counter this feeling of helplessness, some apartment-dwellers reconstruct the 'arrival' narrative to highlight their agency in taming their surroundings. For instance, a resident of Akankha residential complex says, 'Initially this area had nothing. The apartment or complexes emerged as islands between vast, vacant land. Roads were not developed. And yet, the residents persevered in making the place liveable through their private initiatives and paying a lot of money for back-up electricity generators in the absence of such provision from the state'.[11]

To most residents, the gated communities they live in are safe havens and familiar places where 'people of the same mentality live'.[12] The preponderance of apartments that remain vacant throughout the year, however, makes it hard to foster meaningful social relations or form emotional attachments. The alienation that the new space produces is highlighted by a resident, Shantanu Ghosh. He says, 'I haven't sensed the neighbourhood feeling. There is no settlement around our complex. But even if more settlements, buildings come up there may not be neighbourhood feeling' (quoted in Basak 2013: 87). Distances within New Town seem amplified to the residents of gated communities because of the lack of any activities, unlike the 'crowded' and 'congested' Kolkata city. Debolina Poddar, from Akankha housing estate, says, 'I like most the open spaces and the clean roads here. But I think if more trees are planted on the roadside, it would minimise the bareness. We residents feel the lack of public transportation, markets and medical facilities. This actually needs improvement'.[13]

The simultaneous processes of erasure, displacement and dispossession, of fragmentation and splintering and integration imbue spaces with multiple and contradictory meanings that make it difficult to build stable and coherent attachment to place. Thus, the processes through which places are unmade have an immense influence on the kinds of social interactions inhabitants engage in. The systematic unmaking of places by the imposition of a cartographic spatial order that fragments places leads to a loss of identity that one develops with attachment to place. This is particularly true in the case of villagers whose lands and livelihoods have been expropriated and they are thrust into negotiating an entirely new spatial order.

These processes of erasure of place are contingent upon the larger political economic shifts of urban development in which the state and market are deeply implicated. The making of Rajarhat New Town has to be understood within the context of the structural transformations taking place since India's liberalisation in 1991 and the concomitant political economic shifts taking place within the state of West Bengal. In the mid- to late 1990s, the ruling Leftist political regime recast Kolkata and its peripheries as the site for major urban transformations. The focus was on the creation of the millennial city (Roy 2003). Housing became the stratagem to achieve this goal. Thus, the state government pushed ahead with several large-scale integrated township projects in the 1990s while simultaneously facilitating reforms and privatisation in the housing sector. Large swathes of farmlands and villages were brought into the folds of urbanisation.

Roy (2003) argues that the reconfiguration of the urban periphery of Kolkata was closely aligned to the ways in which the upper and middle class elite of Kolkata wanted to assert their '*bhodrolok*' identity by demanding a world-class township that would be integrated into the circuits of global capital and yet would bypass the poverty and squalor in the existing core city. Private developers were also central to the transformation and used discursive devices to attract investors to Rajarhat New Town. These forms of marketing devices compound the processes of erasure of places by creating a dominant discourse around the desirability of a planned, 'world-class' township. The next section highlights the multiple scales at and ways in which inhabitants across the periphery reassert their agency and engage in consolidating their attachments to place in the face of the violent erasure of place.

OF MAKING PLACE THROUGH INCREMENTAL EVERYDAY ACTION

Places are produced through the interaction of individual practices, beliefs, rituals and daily rhythms and institutions as well as structuration processes that provide the frameworks for such actions. In turn, identity and actions of the inhabitants are shaped by these places and the implicit social and cultural codes they embody. Place is thus treated as 'relational, historical and concerned with identity' (Auge 1995: 76).

Across the villages, long-time residents are engaged in making small but noticeable improvements in their properties. With the money they received as compensation for giving up their farmlands, inhabitants have changed their dwelling spaces, revealing new aspirations as well as strategies of renting. A villager from Chapkachuria explains: 'The villagers got money from the HIDCO for acquiring their land and majority of them has built their own houses or has remodelled it using that money. As a result kachha has become pacca, one storied buildings have become two storied'.[14] These additions and extensions of buildings within villages happen without any regulatory control and thus affect the overall layout and relationship of the built environment to the existing street patterns. While some villagers have rented out the extra space to new migrants, others have opened up small grocery shops, cable TV shops, mobile repair shops, tea shops, etc., revealing a changing village economy. Many of these products and services sold in the villages are extended to the residents of the adjacent gated communities. In Baligori village, due to its proximity to the newly opened cancer hospital, a number of residents are renting out their rooms to the patients' families. These new livelihood practices, entrepreneurial spirit, an emerging sense of private wealth and competition, and constant efforts to improve one's property permeate the village atmosphere. A villager from Chapkachuria hints at the ways in which the land market is now buoyant, 'Our village has seen development of new residential complexes. These are not the villagers' own houses. Builders or developers from outside have bought the land in our villages and several new constructions you can find out within our village boundary.'[15]

However, not all residents are able to seize these new opportunities, leading to a deepening of social and spatial inequalities in the villages. Some village residents have received paltry compensation packages because they had very small landholdings. The new urban economy has been absorbing non-skilled informal workers as security guards, maids, drivers, construction labourers but many villagers are sceptical about these kinds of jobs, which they consider undignified and underpaid (Basak 2013). Thus, investing in rental property has become a strategy for villagers to enter the informal land market in Rajarhat. Some of the younger men have joined the market intermediaries as land scouts and agents of builders (Kundu 2010; Basak 2013). Ajay Mandal, a resident of Jatragachi opines:

> The unity of the village has suffered. Earlier we lived as a community. We did everything as a community. There were rich, middle class as well as poor people in the village. With the transformation, rich have become richer, poor, poorer and in such a fashion that there are cultural alienation between them [...] money is spent in alcohol, in parties where drink is mandatory. Some people are participating in those gatherings. People are buying bikes, even cars with the accumulated money. Cigarette smoking, taking alcohol, all kind of urban culture is penetrating the village. We are on the edge of losing our village identities. (as quoted in Basak 2013: 63)

Apartment-dwellers in the gated complexes displayed a clear knowledge of how much their properties had appreciated in price since they had bought them. Anindita Guha Roy, resident in Akankha says, 'This apartment is actually a good investment. We got it at an appreciated price and moreover with the future development this complex and Rajarhat will become a nice place to live in. So I hope this investment will profit us in future'.[16] Some of them astutely observed that the development of the larger township, including that of the villages in the middle, was necessary for real estate prices to keep on appreciating. 'Gradually the situation is changing and we can say previously we were feeling left out or cut off but not now. Now the area is becoming highly developed and there are also more plans of development. With upcoming projects I guess this area will become a second Singapore in the long run.'[17]

However, interviews with residents of gated complexes revealed subtle yet powerful divisive forces within the seemingly homogeneous mass. One of the clear fractures among the residents was along the differential status of tenants versus owners, which becomes pronounced in the ways the residents' welfare associations are structured and function. Owners have decision-making powers about the day-to-day aspects of living—maintenance of buildings, common areas, amenities and facilities, and in framing rules and regulations with respect to entry of visitors' vehicles, parking, surveillance, etc. This brings out the paradox of urban living in these places because for many Rajarhat is an investment and not a place to live. The joint secretary points out ruefully, 'These investors do not live here, and neither do they have any attachment to the place. Tenants, no matter how active they are in the social and cultural life of the community, are excluded from these decision-making processes regarding the material improvement of the complex.'[18] The idea of ownership of property is thus pivotal to the attachment to place.

BUILDING BRIDGES

New Town is still in the process of becoming. Several infrastructure projects are incomplete. In the residual villages, the power of the panchayat has been effectively curtailed with respect to building permissions. This state of administrative limbo has led to a splintering of the geography and has impeded how inhabitants make sense of their surroundings and access basic infrastructure such as transport, water, electricity and garbage collection. In the villages, inhabitants openly challenged their physical exclusion from the New Town by building bridges over the peripheral canals, by realigning the village roads to connect to the grid of streets imposed by the master plan.

Bridges are being built in other ways too. The erstwhile farmers have become bridges for the apartment-dwellers by providing services that are absent in the New Town. There is a vibrant network of autorickshaws that ply in New Town area responding to the needs of residents to access markets, schools, offices in the absence of public transport. Apartment-dwellers highlighted their dependency on the villagers for a number of their daily requirements. Debolina sums up the uneven and complicated nature of this dependence:

> The surrounding area of the village is basically dominated by Muslims. We have never heard of any communal issues in this region. They are very helpful in nature; in fact all the service providers like drinking water, paper *wala*, milk provider, flower wala, maids, etc., are from their community. Somehow we are dependent on them. As it was their land they keep on reminding us about the matter that we are living on their land.[19]

The dependence is simultaneously built on an economic transaction and an act of social 'othering', which distinguishes apartment-dwellers from the villagers.

Some residential complexes in the New Town area such as Pinnacle Residency do not have access to waste collection in their neighbourhood. Thus, they pay to hire a person to collect the waste and deposit it at a nearby vat. On the other hand, several marginalised groups in the villages, particularly Muslims and Dalits, as well as some Adivasi populations, have turned to rag picking and recycling of waste with the loss of agricultural farmlands (Basak 2013; Dey et al. 2013). In this sense, it is the everyday occupations and work that forms the basis of forming social infrastructure, or as Simone (2004: 408) would have argued, 'This infrastructure is capable of facilitating the intersection of socialities so that expanded spaces of economic and cultural operation become available to residents of limited means.' In the absence of adequate infrastructure, people across the rural–urban divide have become part of the interconnecting infrastructure, filling in the gaps, through uneasy, temporary collaborations with unlikely partners born out of need in an unfamiliar territory.

Within the villages it seems that the associational life is slowly disintegrating, partly fuelled by disputes over property and an increasing wealth gap and partly because of the multiple voices that now assert their political weight in the village—starting from the politically motivated syndicates or cooperatives of land losers, to the fading voice of the village pradhan and the increasing intervention by WBHIDCO in the physical development of the villages. Thus, villagers argue that while WBHIDCO has built better roads and enhanced their connectivity with the city, they also complain that unlike the other residential areas in New Town, they have been excluded from better water schemes. They can no longer also apply for the rural work schemes as technically they are in an urban area.

On the other hand, members of housing welfare associations clearly stated how they were building bridges with the parastatals in order to have infrastructural issues taken care of. As long as they were being invited to participate and voice their views on infrastructure and service delivery, they were not disturbed by the lack of an elected urban local body. A committee member of Alaka Abasan articulates this as a deliberate middle-class strategy to steer clear of the messy and volatile politics in the periphery: 'Villages are controlled by political goons masquerading as syndicates. It is they who stand for elections. How will they know about our issues and problems? No. We cannot get involved in that.'[20] Clearly, the different constructions of citizenship identity and spatial jurisdictional tags convey that a hierarchy of rights to the city is being consolidated and negotiated through shifting configurations which will shape access to infrastructure in the future. Thus, place-making engenders particular ways in which new relationships between the state and the citizen are carved out and in turn influence the way in which inhabitants of different spaces are 'othered'.

SPACES OF ENCOUNTER

This section highlights some of those spatial practices which are fleeting encounters and more meaningful engagements structured through collaboration and sometimes through outright conflict. These spatial encounters offer us a way of understanding place as open-ended, porous and open to multiple interpretations. In spite of the attempts to draw clear boundaries around settlements and regulate entry, villagers and new inhabitants of gated complexes often find themselves in the same social spaces in their daily lives. Places as diverse as shopping malls, local fish markets, temples, village fairs, bus stops, parks, auto stands and tea shacks are frequented by the original villagers as well as the new middle class residents and migrant labourers from other parts of the state and country. If the spaces of residence depicted territorial forms of exclusion, these spaces of casual encounters offer the opportunity for interactions that may become more meaningful engagements.

Outside the residential enclaves of Greenfield Heights and Jal Vayu Vihar, a fresh vegetable, fish and meat market has sprung up as a row of well-organised shacks. This is locally known as 'Atharotola market'. B. Poddar, a long-time resident of Greenfield Heights, says:

> [T]he market continues to exist because we [meaning the residents] protected it from being evicted by HIDCO. They are illegally occupying land and they charge us more for fresh vegetables and fish. But without the market, we would have had to go to Salt Lake which is 5 or 6 km away. In the absence of transport, how do you expect a retiree like me to go that far?[21]

The road leading to Greenfield Heights is thus a lively social place with lots of people across classes and settlements intermingling. While most of the shopkeepers are from the villages within Rajarhat New Town and surrounding areas, the residents of gated communities and villages of New Town are the buyers. Unlike a mall, this market has evolved into a community space where shopkeepers keep a monthly account for regular customers, sellers and buyers engage in a daily ritual of haggling over prices, and residents gather around on the wooden benches to enjoy a fresh cup of tea and discuss politics every evening. Given that this market has no existence in the master plan, it can be ventured that the users have appropriated, reclaimed and suffused abstract spaces with lived reality. These practices therefore bring out a sense of stability: 'For many inhabitants, the rituals of daily life are a source of comfort to people, offering a sense of security and stability, as neighbours encounter each other, exchange greetings, strike up friendships, pass along gossip or deal with emergencies. They are a source of their attachment to place' (Friedmann 2007: 269).

Several places within Rajarhat New Town are thus repurposed through the activities and rhythms that have been established by the people. The lived reality of Rajarhat New Town belies master plan categorisations and overrides the unidimensional rational logic of spatial zoning. While the logic of the master plan seeks to fix a certain meaning to a certain space, people interpret the spaces through multiple lenses and through their use of these spaces, these become places. Thus, a traffic roundabout near Utsa housing estate in Action Area I has become a lively place for people of different walks of life to hang out in the evenings based on an unspoken and shared understanding amongst its users. Pavements designated for pedestrians have been partly occupied by the villagers to construct temporary tea stalls while some roads have deliberately made space for existing religious structures such as temples and mosques hinting at the everyday negotiations that take place between different claimants and counter-claimants to the emergent places of Rajarhat New Town.

Moreover, there are other spatial tactics that challenge the powers of the state. In Rajarhat, there has been a growing organised resistance to land acquisition from a few of the villages. Thus, in Balighori, some villagers have staged a unique protest by inundating their lands to stop further acquisition. In Chapna and Chapkachuria villages, some villagers have started to cultivate on lands which had been acquired by WBHIDCO. The re-appropriation is a deliberate challenge to the state's desire to carve a modern new town in Rajarhat. Not only villagers, but upper middle class residents also engage in spatial practices that lead to 'encroachment'. In the case of the peripheral canal along a water theme park, residents of the high-end gated colony of Sanjeeva Town have appropriated the canal banks for gardening and plantation purposes under the guise of beautification. However, erstwhile villagers have also set up informal shacks in these areas—tea shops, ironing shops, lunch shops, etc., that cater to the maids and private security guards working in the gated estates. Thus, there is constant friction between the residents groups and the shopkeepers with each claiming their right to use the canal banks. These tactics to reclaim land are intrinsically related to the politics of place-making through questions of identity, legibility and location.

CONCLUSION

This chapter reveals the messy, dynamic and historically contingent place-making processes. The erasure of places and resurgent place-making processes highlight the relationality that constitutes these places as marked simultaneously by tension, exclusion and porosity. People, through their individual actions and collective practices, are central to the processes of place-making as they constantly reconfigure landscapes, things and possibilities while at the same time attempting to establish a pattern. The processes of place-making and unmaking show that there are diverse logics that produce spaces that embody contradictory meanings. Sometimes meanings are shared and at other times contested. It may be argued that exclusion is at the heart of such place-making practices that fragment and divide. Ironically, however, these spatial practices force groups across the socio-economic divide to foster relationships of cooperation. Although often these bonds are temporary and reinforce existing power differences and social hierarchies along caste, class, ethnic or gender identities, they nonetheless help to redefine places, the meanings they carry and the possibilities they open up. Mapping these spatial practices reveals tensions and fragmentation even among the inhabitants of the original settlements.

This chapter also highlights the ways in which some of the urban imageries have leaked and soaked into the villages and are being reproduced by the villagers, evident through the furious pace of building construction activity in these village pockets and the growing demand for urban services and goods. The growing tensions between residents, the implicit modes of socio-spatial exclusion, the history of antagonism and the reinforcement of identities such as 'us' versus 'them' through the uneven distribution of resources across emergent territory, however, raise critical questions about the ability of the different groups of inhabitants to sustain these tenuous forms of socio-spatial navigation. Will the unsettled feeling continue to fester and coalesce into discontent and conflict or will more stable and predictable patterns of collaboration be produced through the place-making strategies of the residents?

NOTES

1. The author conducted fieldwork in Rajarhat area in 2008–10 as part of her Ph.D. dissertation work. In 2012, Poushali Basak carried out her MA dissertation on Rajarhat from Tata Institute of Social Sciences (TISS) under the author's partial guidance. In 2014, Angana Mukherjee, M.Phil. student at TISS, carried out ethnographic research in the region guided by the author. Three villages of Chapkachuria, Balighori and Chapna were chosen for the study along with three gated apartment complexes: Pinnacle Residency, Akankha and Alaka Abasan.
2. For a detailed understanding of the land acquisition and town planning process, please refer to Kundu (2010).
3. Interview with Prashanta Bhattacharya, WBHIDCO, 2015.
4. Ibid.
5. Interview with villager 1, Chhapna, 2015.
6. Interview with villager 3, Chapkachuria, 2015.
7. Interview with villager 2 from Chhapna, 2015.
8. Interview with villager 5 from Chhapna, 2015.
9. Interview with villager 4, Chhapna, 2015.
10. Interview, Greenfield Heights, 2008.
11. Interview with resident 1, Akankha Housing, 2015.
12. Interview with resident 3, Pinnacle Residency, 2015.
13. Interview, Akankha, 2015.
14. Interview with villager 2, Chapkachuria, 2015.
15. Interview with villager 3, Chapkachuria, 2015.
16. Interview, Akankha, 2015.
17. Interview with residents' welfare association member, Akankha, 2015.
18. Interview, Akankha, 2015.
19. Interview, Akankha, 2015.
20. Interview, Alaka Abasan, 2015.
21. Interview, Greenfield Heights, 2008.

REFERENCES

Auge, M. 1995. *Non-places: Introduction to an Anthropology of Supermodernity*. London, New York: Verso.

Basak, P. 2013. 'Place-making in New Town, Rajarhat: A Study of Place and Identity Creation in New Town in Its Transformation from Rural Landscape to Urban Township'. Unpublished M.A. dissertation thesis. Tata Institute of Social Sciences (TISS), Mumbai.

Benjamin, S. 2015. 'Cities Within and Beyond the Plan'. In *City in South Asia*, eds C. Bates and M. Minoru, 114–38. New York and Abingdon: Routledge.

Bhattacharya, R., and K. Sanyal. 2011. 'Bypassing the Squalor: New Towns, Immaterial Labour and Exclusion in Post-colonial Urbanization'. *Economic & Political Weekly* 46(31): 41–48.

Bose, P. S. 2013. 'Bourgeois Environmentalism, Leftist Development, and Neoliberal Urbanism in the City of Joy'. In *Locating Right to the City in the Global South*, eds Tony Roshan Samara, Shenjing He and Guo Chen, 139–63. London: Routledge.

Cowan, T. 2015. 'Fragmented Citizenships in Gurgaon'. *Economic & Political Weekly* 50(26–27): 63–73.

Cresswell, T. 2004. *Place: A Short Introduction*. Malden, MA: Blackwell Ltd.

Dey, I., R. Samaddar and S. K. Sen. 2013. *Beyond Kolkata: Rajarhat and the Dystopia of the Urban Imagination*. New Delhi: Routledge.

Friedmann, J. 2007. 'Reflections on Place and Place-making in the Cities of China'. *International Journal of Urban and Regional Research* 31(2): 257–79.

Goldstein, S. R. 2016. 'Planning the Millennium City: The Politics of Place-making in Gurgaon, India'. *International Area Studies Review* 19(1): 12–27.

Gururani, S. 2013. 'Flexible Planning: The Making of India's "Millennium City," Gurgaon'. In *Ecologies of Urbanism in India: Metropolitan Civility and Sustainability*, eds Anne Rademacher and K. Sivaramakrishnan, Vol. 1, 119–44. Hong Kong University Press.

Kumar, M. 2015. 'Erstwhile Villages in Urban India'. *Development in Practice* 25(1): 124–32.

Kundu, R. 2010. 'Examining the Role of Formal–Informal Nexuses in the Contested Production of Periurban Kolkata'. Unpublished Ph.D. diss., University of Illinois, Chicago.

Lombard, M. 2014. 'Constructing Ordinary Places: Place-making in Urban Informal Settlements in Mexico'. *Progress in Planning* 94: 1–53.

Pred, A. 1984. 'Place as Historically Contingent Process: Structuration and Time Geography of Becoming Places'. *Annals of the Association of American Geographers* 74(2): 279–97.

Roy, A. 2003. *City Requiem, Calcutta: Gender and the Politics of Poverty*. Minneapolis: University of Minnesota Press.

———. 2011. 'The Blockade of the World Class Cities: Dialectical Images of Indian Urbanism'. In *Worlding Cities: Asian Experiments and the Art of Being Global*, eds A. Roy and A. Ong, 259–78. London: Wiley-Blackwell Publishers.

Roy, U. K. 2005. 'Development of New Townships: A Catalyst in the Growth of Rural Fringes of Kolkata Metropolitan Area (KMA)'. Paper for the Annual Conference of Housing and Urban Development Corporation (HUDCO) Chair Institutes on 'Cities: Engines of Rural Development', 8–9 September, New Delhi.

Sengupta, U. 2013. 'Inclusive Development? A State-led Land Development Model in New Town, Kolkata'. *Environment and Planning C: Government and Policy* 31(2): 357–76.

Shah, A. M. 2012. 'The Village in the City, the City in the Village'. *Economic & Political Weekly* 47(52): 17–19.

Shatkin, G. 2011. 'Planning Privatopolis: Representation and Contestation in the Development of Urban Integrated Mega-projects'. In *Worlding Cities: Asian Experiments and the Art of Being Global*, eds A. Roy and A. Ong, 77–97. London: Wiley-Blackwell Publishers.

Shaw, A. 2004. *The Making of Navi Mumbai*. New Delhi: Orient Longman.

Simone, A. 2004. 'People as Infrastructure: Intersecting Fragments in Johannesburg'. *Public Culture* 16(3): 407–29.

Srivastava, S. 2014. *Entangled Urbanism: Slum, Gated Community, and Shopping Mall in Delhi and Gurgaon*. Oxford: Oxford University Press.

West Bengal Housing Infrastructure Development Corporation (WBHIDCO). 1999. 'New Town Kolkata: Project Report'. West Bengal Housing Infrastructure Development Corporation, Kolkata.

———. 2008. 'Strategy for Regulating Growth in the Existing Settlement Clusters Surrounded by New Town'. Government of West Bengal, unpublished report, Kolkata.

Notes on the Contributors

SHRIYA ANAND is Lead–Academics and Research, Indian Institute for Human Settlements, Bengaluru.

M. SURESH BABU is Professor, Indian Institute of Technology Madras.

SAI BALAKRISHNAN is Assistant Professor of Global Urban Inequalities, University of California, Berkeley.

AKASH BANERJEE is an independent researcher.

ANNA DEWAELE is Consultant Researcher at Agence Phare, Paris.

MATHEW IDICULLA is an independent legal consultant and Visiting Faculty, Azim Premji University, Bengaluru.

LORAINE KENNEDY is CNRS Research Director, Centre for South Asian Studies (Centre d'Etudes de l'Inde et de l'Asie du Sud, CNRS-EHESS), Paris.

RATOOLA KUNDU is Assistant Professor, Tata Institute of Social Sciences, Mumbai.

SUDESHNA MITRA is Senior Lead–Academics and Research, Indian Institute for Human Settlements, Bengaluru.

GOPA SAMANTA is Professor, University of Burdwan, Bardhaman.

NEHA SAMI is Associate Dean–School of Environment and Sustainability, and Senior Lead–Academics and Research, Indian Institute for Human Settlements, Bengaluru.

PREETI SAMPAT is Assistant Professor of Sociology, School of Liberal Studies, Ambedkar University Delhi.

ASHIMA SOOD is Associate Professor, Anant National University, Ahmedabad.

M. VIJAYABASKAR is Professor, Madras Institute of Development Studies, Chennai.

Index